Marco Mezzadri

Essential Italian Grammar in Practice

A reference and practice book for students from elementary to intermediate

English edition by Anila Scott-Monkhouse and Patricia Taylor

Guerra Edizioni

ISBN 88-7715-434-9

17. 16. 15.

2016. 2015. 2014.

Disegni: *Andrea Bruni*

Ha collaborato:
Linuccio Pederzani

Si ringrazia:

Scuola di Lingue Teletra, Parma
Centro Linguistico, Università di Parma
Escuela de Idiomas Modernos, Facultad de Humanidades y Educación, Universidad
Central de Venezuela
Facultad de Lenguas, Universidad de La Habana
Scuola Cocconi, Parma
Scuola Carducci, Reggio Emilia
Universität Erlangen-Nürnberg

Writing a book is very difficult and it is necessary to read through it over and over again.
It is almost impossible to produce an error - free publication. We can improve the future editions will the help of the readers.
Please send comments and/or queries to:
E-mail: geinfo@guerra-edizioni.com
E-mail: mezzadri@tin.it

Questo libro fa parte del progetto **Rete*!***

Essential Italian Grammar in Practice is a grammar book with exercises intended to accompany learners through their course of study from an elementary to intermediate level. The book follows a traditional progressive grammar syllabus using graded vocabulary suitable for each stage of development.
There are 96 units. Each unit covers a particular grammar point. On the left-hand page there are the explanations and examples, on the right-hand side there are the corresponding exercises to help consolidate and check the specific structures.
The textbook also has three appendixes, which have been created to make the text more user-friendly. The first two appendixes deal with problematic areas related to phonetics and written Italian. The third appendix contains brief, simplified explanations regarding the metalanguage used in the theoretical part of the book and can be used as a study aid for the student in an attempt to minimise any problems arising from such specific terminology. In some of the units follow-up references are made to the appendixes.
At the beginning of the book there is a list of units (Contents) and an Index at the end of the book for quick and easy reference.

Essential Italian Grammar in Practice should not be considered as a prescriptive or exhaustive grammar book but as a tool for the practical and immediate use of the language. It presents the grammar areas in simple and clear language, eliminating terms no longer relevant to everyday Italian. It can be used in class or at home alongside the language textbook as a way of offering immediate practice and consolidation of the structures presented in class or as a tool for extension or revision work on grammar. The book is also suitable for individual work as a source of reference for both self-study students and learners on a language course thanks to the answer key, which completes the edition.

contents

contents

Essere (to be) is the *infinitive form* of the verb.

Present indicative

Affirmative form

io	**sono**
tu	**sei**
(lui, lei)	**è**
(noi)	**siamo**
(voi)	**siete**
(loro)	**sono**

(Lui) **è** *giapponese.* (He's Japanese)

(Loro) ***sono*** *a scuola.* (They're at school)

For more information about the *present indicative*, see vedi Unità 3.

Note: it is often unnecessary to use the subject pronoun *(io, tu, ecc.) (I, you, etc.)*
See Unità 38 - *subject pronouns.*
Do you know what is meant by *affirmative, negative, interrogative* and *interrogative-negative form?* See Appendix 3.

Study the pictures below.

(Lui) ***non è*** *francese.* (He isn't French)

(Loro) ***non sono*** *in Germania.* (They aren't in Germany)

The *negative form* in Italian is made by putting the word **non** before the verb..

Study the pictures below..

"Sei stanco?" (Are you tired?)

"È una sedia?" (Is it a chair?)

The *interrogative form* in Italian is expressed by the **intonation** of the sentence.
What does *intonation* mean? See Appendix 3.

The *interrogative-negative form* in Italian is expressed by the **intonation** of the sentence and the word **non** before the verb.

"Non è un fiore?" (Isn't it a flower?)

"Non è un cane?" (Isn't it a dog?)

1. Complete with the correct form of *essere*.

1. Il libro ....è........ sul tavolo.
2. Claudio e Teresa .... a Roma.
3. (Noi) .... amici.
4. (Voi) .... simpatici.
5. (Tu) .... carina.
6. (Io) .... spagnolo.

2. Rewrite the sentences from exercise 1 in the negative form.

1. Il libro non è sul tavolo
2. ....
3. ....
4. ....
5. ....
6. ....

3. Write sentences about yourself and someone you know.

	Io	*Lui/Lei*
1. Oggi / triste.	Oggi non sono triste	....
2. Intelligente.	....	....
3. In Italia.	....	....
4. A scuola.	....	....

4. Write the questions.

1. Perché / (tu) / felice? Perché sei felice?
2. Dove / Roma e Firenze? ....
3. Di che colore / la tua macchina? ....
4. Tu / sposato? ....
5. Di dove / Klaus e Hans? ....
6. Chi / questa persona? ....
7. Di chi / questo libro? ....

5. Match the answers with the correct questions from exercise 4.

1. Sono in Italia. (2)
2. È di Luca. (   )
3. È mia madre. (   )
4. No, sono divorziato. (   )
5. Rossa. (   )
6. Perché sono innamorato. (   )
7. Sono tedeschi. (   )

Avere *(to have)* is the *infinitive form* of the verb.

Present indicative

Affirmative form

io	**ho**
tu	**hai**
(lui, lei)	**ha**
(noi)	**abbiamo**
(voi)	**avete**
(loro)	**hanno**

Carlo **ha** un gatto.
(Carlo has (got) a cat)

Lucia e Antonio **hanno** un figlio.
(Lucia and Antonio have (got) a son)

For more information about *presente indicative*, see Unità 3.

Note: it is often unnecessaryto use the subject pronoun (*io, tu, ecc.*).
See Unità 38 - *subject pronouns.*

Do you know what is meant by *affirmative, negative, interrogative*, and *interrogative-negative?* See Appendix 3.

Study the sentences.

- (Io) **non ho** la macchina. *(I haven't got a car)*
- (Noi) **non abbiamo** amici in Germania. *(We haven't got any friends in Germany)*

The *negative form* in Italian is made by putting the word **non** before the verb.

Study the following sentences.

"Hai una sigaretta?" (Have you got a cigarette?)

The *interrogative form* in Italian is expressed by the **intonation** of the sentence.

What does *intonation* mean? See Appendix 3.

The *interrogative-negative form* in Italian is expressed by the **intonation** of the sentence and the word **non** before the veb.

"Non avete il giornale di oggi?" (Haven't you got today's newspaper?)

Look at the pictures.

Some Italian expressions use the verb **avere**. Here are some common examples.

Avere fame	*(to be hungry)*	*Avere sonno*	*(to be sleepy)*
Avere sete	*(to be thirsty)*	*Avere caldo*	*(to be hot)*
Avere freddo	*(to be cold)*	*Avere 20/30/40 anni*	*(to be 20/30/40 years old).*
Avere paura	*(to be afraid)*		

The letter **h** in the words *ho, hai, ha, hanno* is not pronounced. This is because in Italian the letter **h** is not an autonomous sound and is only used to write some words or sounds.

1. Complete with the correct form of *avere*.

1. Luca ...*ha*... un cane.
2. Lara .... una macchina nuova.
3. Io .... una piccola casa a Venezia.
4. Tu .... un lavoro interessante.

2. Rewrite the sentences from exercise 1 in the plural form.

1. Luca e Stefania ...*hanno*... un cane.
2. Lara e suo marito .... una macchina nuova.
3. La mia famiglia e io .... una piccola casa a Venezia.
4. Tu e tuo fratello .... un lavoro interessante.

3. Rewrite the sentences from exercises 1 and 2 in the negative form.

1. *Luca non ha un cane*
2. ....
3. ....
4. ....
5. ....
6. ....
7. ....
8. ....

4. Complete the sentences with the negative or affirmative form of *avere*.

1. Mi piace molto leggere; ...*ho*... molti libri.
2. Luigi non può andare al lavoro. Oggi .... la macchina.
3. La Francia è bellissima e .... città molto interessanti.
4. .... una sigaretta? Grazie! Siete sempre così gentili!
5. Quello è tuo fratello? Ma .... solamente una sorella?
6. Dobbiamo andare al supermercato; .... il frigorifero vuoto.

5. Complete the sentences using one of the given words.

1. Vado al bar a comprare una birra; fa molto caldo e ho ...*sete*...	fame	sonno	sete	paura.
2. Loro tornano sempre a casa presto. Hanno.............. per strada di sera.	20 anni	freddo	fame	paura.
3. Se hai ...., prendi il mio maglione.	freddo	caldo	sonno	sete.
4. Abbiamo solo .... Dobbiamo ancora lavorare per molti anni.	sonno	paura	30 anni	fame.
5. Stefano va sempre a letto tardi, perché non ha mai..................	fame	sonno	caldo	sete.
6. A casa tua le finestre sono sempre chiuse. Non hai mai....................?	sonno	paura	freddo	caldo.

6. Read the answers and write the questions.

1. *Hai la macchina*? Sì, ho una Fiat Punto di due anni.
2. ....? No, solo una gatta e le vuole molto bene.
3. ....? No, carne no. In frigorifero abbiamo solo verdura.
4. ....? Sì, ha un fratello di 28 anni.
5. ....? Sì e hanno anche molta sete.
6. ....? Compio 32 anni, in ottobre.

Italian verbs can be divided into three groups: **I -are; (cantare); II -ere; (vedere) III-ire. (sentire - finire)**

Verbs belonging to group III-ire are divided into two further groups **III a (sentire)** e **III b (finire)**, due to some variations in endings; for example: tu sent**i**, tu fin**isci**.

I - ARE: cantare *(sing)*		II - ERE: vedere *(see)*		III a - IRE: sentire *(hear)*		III b - IRE: finire *(finish)*	
io	cant - **o**	io	ved **- o**	io	sent **- o**	io	fin - **isc- o**
tu	cant - **i**	tu	ved **- i**	tu	sent **- i**	tu	fin - **isc- i**
(lui, lei)	cant - **a**	(lui, lei)	ved - **e**	(lui, lei)	sent - **e**	(lui, lei)	fin - **isc-e**
(noi)	cant - **iamo**	(noi)	ved - **iamo**	(noi)	sent - **iamo**	(noi)	fin - **iamo**
(voi)	cant - **ate**	(voi)	ved - **ete**	(voi)	sent - **ite**	(voi)	fin - **ite**
(loro)	cant - **ano**	(loro)	ved **- ono**	(loro)	sent **- ono**	(loro)	fin - **isc -ono**

Note: It is often unnecessary to use the subject pronoun (*io, tu, ecc.*).
See Unità 38 - *subject pronouns.*

What is meant by regular or irregular verbs? See Appendix 3.

Here is a list of the most common verbs belonging to group III.

III a aprire, coprire, divertirsi, dormire, offrire, partire, seguire, servire, soffrire, vestire.
(open, cover, enjoy oneself, sleep, offer, leave, follow, serve, suffer, dress.)

III b capire, colpire, costruire, fornire, guarire, preferire, pulire, sostituire, spedire, unire.
(understand, hit, build, supply, get better, prefer, clean, substitute, send, join.)

For the *negative form* (- Io non canto mai) *(I never sing)*, *question form* (- Giochiamo a carte?) *(Shall we play cards?)* and *negative-question form* (- Non parli inglese?) *(Don't you speak English?)*, see Unità 1 and 2.

Study the following examples:

A) - La segretaria **comincia** a lavorare alle 9.
(The secretary starts work at 9 o'clock)

B) - Sandro **ascolta** la musica.
(Sandro is listening to music)

C) - Domani il Sig. Di Stefano **parte** per le vacanze.
(Mr Di Stefano is leaving on holiday tomorrow)

The **present indicative** is used to describe an action

A) that takes place habitually;
B) that takes place at the moment of speaking;
C) with future meaning.

Look at the position of the **word stress** in the present indicative:

	verbs with two syllables	verbs with more than two syllables
singular	p**a**rlo p**a**rli p**a**rla	risp**o**ndo risp**o**ndi risp**o**nde
plural	parli**a**mo parl**a**te p**a**rlano	rispondi**a**mo rispond**e**te risp**o**ndono

For the third person plural (loro) the word stress goes as far back as possible, towards the beginning of the word, sometimes even on the fourth syllable from the end, for example: ant***i***cipano, or on the third from the end: p**a**rlano.

What is meant by the words *syllable* and *word stress?* See Appendix 3.

3

esercizi

1. **Write the verbs in the correct form of the present indicative.**

1. Ascoltare:
io *ascolto*......; tu................; lui...............; noi................; voi...............; loro.............. .

2. Credere:
io ....; tu................; lui...............; noi................; voi...............; loro.............. .

3. Dormire:
io ....; tu................; lui...............; noi................; voi...............; loro.............. .

4. Capire:
io ....; tu................; lui...............; noi................; voi...............; loro.............. .

2. **Write the verbs in the correct form of the present indicative using the subject *io*.**

1. aprire ....*io apro*..........
2. capire ....
3. dormire ....
4. partire ....
5. spedire ....
6. unire ....
7. offrire ....
8. preferire ....

3. **Mark the correct position of the stress in the verbs.**

1. Oggi studio un po' di storia. ....*studio*....
2. Sandra e Nicola bevono spesso birra a cena. ....
3. Mia mamma e io partiamo domani per il mare. ....
4. Francesco e Monica cantano in un coro di musica polifonica. ....
5. Alida racconta spesso storie interessanti. ....

4. **Put the words into the right order and rewrite the sentences using the correct form of the verb.**

1. Avere/io/non/un/gatto/cane/ma. ......*Io non ho un gatto, ma un cane*......
2. Sentire/Claudia/al mattino/radio/la. ....
3. Quando/lavorare/Italiani/spesso/gli/cantare. ....
4. L'inglese/non/loro capire. ....
5. Treno/fra/partire/mezz'ora/il. ....

5. **Answer the questions.**

1. Come ti chiami?
....
2. Quanti anni hai?
....
3. Da dove vieni?
....
4. Che lavoro fai?
....
5. Perché studi l'italiano?
....

The most common irregular verbs in the present indicative:

potere *(can)*	**volere** *(want)*	**dovere** *(must)*	**sapere** *(know)*	**piacere** *(like)*	**bere** *(drink)*
posso	voglio	devo	so	piaccio	bevo
puoi	vuoi	devi	sai	piaci	bevi
può	vuole	deve	sa	piace	beve
possiamo	vogliamo	dobbiamo	sappiamo	piacciamo	beviamo
potete	volete	dovete	sapete	piacete	bevete
possono	vogliono	devono	sanno	piacciono	bevono
andare *(go)*	**stare** *(be, stay)*	**fare** *(do, make)*	**dare** *(give)*	**dire** *(say)*	**uscire** *(go out)*
vado	sto	faccio	do	dico	esco
vai	stai	fai	dai	dici	esci
va	sta	fa	dà	dice	esce
andiamo	stiamo	facciamo	diamo	diciamo	usciamo
andate	state	fate	date	dite	uscite
vanno	stanno	fanno	danno	dicono	escono

Numerous verbs such as contenere *(contain)*, comporre *(make up)*, ritrarre *(withdraw)* and intervenire *(intervene)* are formed from the following verbs:

tenere *(keep)*	**porre** *(put, set)*	**trarre** *(draw)*	**venire** *(come)*
ten**g**o *	pon**g**o *	traggo	ven**g**o *
tieni	poni	trai	vieni
tiene	pone	trae	viene
teniamo	poniamo	traiamo	veniamo
tenete	ponete	traete	venite
ten**g**ono *	pon**g**ono *	traggono	ven**g**ono *

* Some common verbs add a **g** to the stem only with io and loro. See **tenere, porre** and **venire**. The most common of such verbs are: rimanere *(stay)*, salire *(go up)* and valere *(be worth)*.

Verbs that end in **-cere** and **-gere**.
Before **-o** and **-ono** they change from [*tʃ*] to [*k*] and from [*dʒ*] to [*g*].

vincere *(win)*		**leggere** *(read)*	
vin**co**	[*vinko*]	le**ggo**	[' lɛggo]
vinci	[*vintʃi*]	leggi	['*lɛddʒi*]
vince		legge	
vinciamo		leggiamo	
vincete		leggete	
vin**cono**		le**ggono**	

Do you know the phonetic symbols? See Appendix 1.

1. Put the verbs in the correct from.

1. Dovere: tu ....devi........
2. Potere: lei ....
3. Volere: io ....
4. Andare: lui ....
5. Sapere: io ....
6. Uscire: tu ....
7. Dare: io ....
8. Fare: tu ....
9. Stare: lei ....
10. Dire: io ....
11. Mancare: tu ....
12. Leggere: io ....

2. Rewrite exercise 1 in the plural form.

1. Dovere: ......voi dovete......
2. Potere: ....
3. Volere: ......noi......
4. Andare: ....
5. Sapere: ....
6. Uscire: ....
7. Dare: ....
8. Fare: ....
9. Stare: ....
10. Dire: ....
11. Mancare: ....
12. Leggere: ....

3. Complete the sentences with the correct form of the verbs in brackets.

1. Luca non ...sa........ il tedesco. (Sapere)
2. Loro .... spesso al mare. (Andare)
3. Mia moglie .... lavorare anche la domenica. (Dovere)
4. Noi .... quasi tutte le sere. (Uscire)
5. A Giovanni .... molto giocare a calcio. (Piacere)
6. Voi .... spesso ai vostri amici di andare in discoteca? (Proporre)
7. Gli Italiani .... molto vino. (Bere)
8. (Io) non .... mangiare molti dolci. (Potere)

4. Look at the pictures and complete the sentences.

1. Lara ..fa colazione.... alle sette.

2. Lara .... alle otto meno dieci.

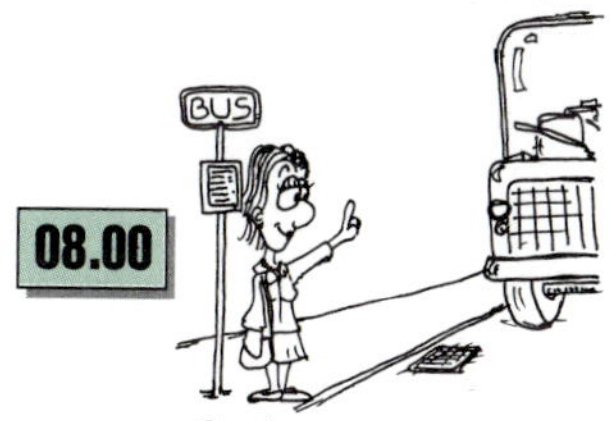

3. Lara .... alle otto.

4. Lara .... fino alle sei.

5. Lara .... alle sette.

5. Read the answers and write the questions.

1. ....Quanti libri leggi in un anno....? Più o meno un libro al mese.
2. ....? Sto a casa con la mia famiglia oppure andiamo al cinema.
3. ....? Comincio alle 8.
4. ....? Sì, ho un'ora di tempo per il pranzo alle 12.
5. ....? Sì, sono sposato da due anni.
6. ....? No, non abbiamo figli.
7. ....? Quest'anno vogliamo andare un po' al mare.
8. ....? No, preferisco visitare città d'arte; ma voglio riposarmi.
9. ....? Viviamo in un appartamento in città, in una zona molto verde.

- Do you know what is meant by vowels and consonants? See Appendix 3.

	SINGULAR		PLURAL	
MASCULINE				
BEFORE A CONSONANT	**IL**	Il cane	**I**	I cani
BEFORE S + CONSONANT, Z, PS, GN, X	**LO**	Lo studente lo zio lo psicologo lo gnomo lo xenofobo	**GLI**	Gli studenti gli zii gli psicologi gli gnomi gli xenofobi
BEFORE A VOWEL	**L'**	L'albero l'indiano	**GLI**	Gli alberi gli indiani
FEMININE				
BEFORE A CONSONANT	**LA**	La casa	**LE**	Le case
BEFORE A VOWEL	**L'**	L'acqua	**LE**	Le acque

- The definite article changes according to whether the noun is feminine, masculine, singular or plural..
- The definite article always comes *before* the noun.
- The definite article is used:

- when a noun is defined, in other words described or already referred to and known about.

Ecco **la** ragazza che mi piace.
(There's the girl I like)

- with abstract nouns.

– **L'**amore è un sentimento bellissimo.
(Love is a beautiful feeling)

- with nouns that indicate a category or species.
  – **Il** vino si fa con **l'**uva. *(Wine is made from grapes)*
- with continents, countries (almost all), regions, seas, rivers and lakes, but rarely with the names of towns or cities.
  – **L'**Europa è un continente. *(Europe is a continent)* – Bologna è vicino a Ferrara. *(Bologna is near Ferrara)*
- with names and titles: Signore, Signora, Professore, Dottore, etc., but never when you speak directly to a person.

- See Unità 11 for the use of the definite article with possessive adjectives and pronouns. See Unità 23 for the use of combined prepositions with the definite article.

▶ The definite article is not used in common expressions with the verb **avere**:
avere caldo/freddo, avere fame/sete, avere sonno, avere paura, etc.

1. Put in the correct form of the definite article.

1. L'............ albero.
2. .... cane.
3. .... finestra.
4. .... ragazza.
5. .... anno.
6. .... studente.
7. .... psicologo.
8. .... professore.
9. .... uomo.
10. .... donna.
11. .... area.
12. .... mare.
13. .... zio.
14. .... astronomo.
15. .... indiano.
16. .... libro.

2. Put in the correct form of the definite article.

1. ...Gli...... alberi.
2. .... cani.
3. .... finestre.
4. .... ragazze.
5. .... anni.
6. .... studenti.
7. .... psicologi.
8. .... professori.
9. .... uomini.
10. .... donne.
11. .... aree.
12. .... mari.
13. .... zii.
14. .... astronomi.
15. .... indiani.
16. .... libri.

3. Complete the sentences with the definite article where necessary.

1. ...La...... Torre di Pisa è un monumento conosciuto in tutto .....il......... mondo.
2. .... casa di Stefano è in periferia.
3. Ho .... fame, ma non ho niente da mangiare.
4. .... nonna di Silvia ha .... 80 anni.
5. .... libertà è un bene prezioso.
6. .... birra si beve fredda.
7. Non conosco .... Signora Turci.
8. .... Dottor De Santis è molto bravo.
9. .... calcio è uno sport violento.
10. .... poesia è un genere letterario.

4. Cross out the definite article where it is not necessary.

1. La Sicilia è una regione italiana.
2. Il Milano è un'importante città del Nord Italia.
3. L'Europa è detta il "vecchio continente".
4. Il Perù è un paese di lingua spagnola.
5. La mia città è la Parma e la mia regione l'Emilia Romagna.
6. Il Po è il fiume più lungo d'Italia.

	SINGULAR		PLURAL	
MASCULINE				
BEFORE A CONSONANT	**UN**	Un cane	**DEI**	Dei cani
BEFORE S + CONSONANT, Z, PS, GN, X	**UNO**	Uno studente uno zio uno psicologo uno gnomo uno xenofobo	**DEGLI**	Degli studenti degli zii degli psicologi degli gnomi degli xenofobi
BEFORE A VOWEL	**UN**	Un albero un indiano	**DEGLI**	Degli alberi degli indiani
FEMININE				
BEFORE A CONSONANT	**UNA**	Una casa	**DELLE**	Delle case
BEFORE A VOWEL	**UN'**	Un'italiana	**DELLE**	Delle italiane

Study the picture.

Vorrei **un** libro di poesie in inglese, per favore!
(I'd like a poetry book in English, please!)

The indefinite article is used when the noun has not been defined or specified.

Compare with the use of the definite article: Unità 5.

The indefinite article always comes *before* the noun.

The indefinite article changes according to whether the noun is feminine or masculine.

Un, uno, una, un' are only used before singular nouns.

The forms **dei/degli/delle** are often used with the plural forms of nouns.

– Ho **degli** amici francesi che non vedo da anni.
(I've got some French friends that I haven't seen for years)

See Unità 23 for the use of combined prepositions with the definite article.

1. Put in the correct form of the definite in article.

1. ...Un... albero.
2. .... cane.
3. .... finestra.
4. .... ragazza.
5. .... anno.
6. .... studente.
7. .... psicologo.
8. .... professore.
9. .... uomo.
10. .... donna.
11. .... area.
12. .... mare.
13. .... zio.
14. .... astronomo.
15. .... indiano.
16. .... libro.

2. Put in the correct form of *dei*/*degli*/*delle*.

1. ...Degli... alberi.
2. .... cani.
3. .... finestre.
4. .... ragazze.
5. .... anni.
6. .... studenti.
7. .... psicologi.
8. .... professori.
9. .... uomini.
10. .... donne.
11. .... aree.
12. .... mari.
13. .... zii.
14. .... astronomi.
15. .... indiani.
16. .... libri.

3. Complete the sentences with the definite or indefinite article.

1. ...La... Svizzera non fa parte dell'Unione Europea.
2. .... francese è .... lingua europea.
3. .... Signora Rozzi vive in .... appartamento molto grande.
4. Dov'è .... stazione?
5. C'è .... ristorante vicino a casa tua?
6. .... amicizia è importante nella vita.
7. Stasera esco con .... amici di Laura.
8. Come si chiama .... direttore della tua società?
9. C'è .... cane in giardino.
10. È .... cane di tua nonna?
11. .... figli di Maria sono al mare.
12. Ti racconto .... storia molto divertente.

4. Complete the sentences with the definite or indefinite article where necessary.

1. ...La... Gran Bretagna è .... paese del Nord Europa.
2. .... tennis è .... sport di moda oggi.
3. .... Lago di Garda è .... località turistica famosa.
4. .... studenti italiani hanno .... vacanze molto lunghe in estate.
5. Carlo è .... elettricista.
6. Giuliana è ancora in .... viaggio con suo marito.
7. .... Budapest è .... capitale dell'Ungheria.
8. C'è .... scuola molto buona a Roma per studiare .... italiano.

- Nouns ending in **-O** are usually *masculine:* **il** bambin**o**.
- Nouns ending in **-A** are usually *feminine:* **la** bambin**a**.
- Nouns ending in **-E** can be either *masculine* or *feminine:*

masculine	*feminine*
il professor**e**, **il** padr**e**, **il** can**e**, **il** pan**e**, **il** dottore	**la** chiav**e**, **la** madr**e**, **la** pac**e**, **la** class**e**.

- Some nouns ending in **-A** are *masculine:*
  - some of these end in **-MA**: **il** proble**ma**, **il** te**ma**, **il** cine**ma**, **il** siste**ma**, **il** programm**a**, **il** cli**ma,**
  - a few end in **-ista**: **l'**art**ista**, **il** dent**ista**, **il** giornal**ista,**
  - others indicate a male figure: **il** poet**a**, **il** pilot**a**.
- Nouns with the following endings are usually *masculine:*

-ORE **il** fi**ore**
-ONE **il** sap**one**
-ALE **il** giorn**ale**
-ILE **il** fuc**ile**

- Nouns that end with a consonant are usually *masculine*. These mostly derive from foreign words: **il** ba**r, lo** spor**t**.
- Some nouns ending in **-O** are *feminine.* These are often words that have been shortened: **la** radi**o**, **la** mot**o**, **l'**aut**o**, **la** man**o** i.e. **la** fot**o** = **la** fotografi**a**.
- Nouns ending in **-TÀ** and in **-TÙ** are *feminine:* **la** libert**à**, **la** gioven**tù**.
- Nouns ending in **-I** are usually *feminine:* **la** cris**i**, **l'**analis**i**, **la** sintes**i**.
- Nouns with the following endings are usually *feminine:*

-IONE **la** lez**ione**
-IE **la** ser**ie**
-ICE **la** lavatr**ice**

- Names of **continents**, **countries**, **regions**, **islands, towns** and **cities** are usually *feminine.*
- Names of **mountains**, **lakes**, **rivers**, and **seas** are usually *masculine.*
- **The months of the year** and **days of the week are always** *masculine.*

▶ Exception to the rule: **la** domenica.

1. Complete the words with the correct endings: *a/o/e/i/ù/à.*

1. L'allbero......
2. L'esercizi.......
3. La strad.......
4. Il fratell.......
5. La madr.......
6. Il poet.......
7. La bambin.......
8. Il fior.......
9. Il dentist.......
10. Il professor.......
11. La professoress.......
12. Il programm.......
13. Il giornal.......
14. Il cinem.......
15. La sintes.......
16. La libert.......
17. La giovent.......
18. La television.......
19. La radi.......
20. La situazion.......
21. L'attric.......
22. L'attor.......
23. La man.......
24. La rivoluzion.......

2. Put in the correct form of the definite article.

1. Lo........ sport
2. .... foto
3. .... film
4. .... tennis
5. .... azione
6. .... soluzione
7. .... tesi
8. .... tema
9. .... mercoledì
10. .... Austria
11. .... Norvegia
12. .... domenica
13. .... Monte Bianco
14. .... Mississippi
15. .... Mediterraneo
16. .... Baviera.

3. Complete the words with the correct endings *a/o/e* and appropriate article.

1. La............ ragazza... italiana che vive con me è molto simpatica.
2. .... gatt... di mia zia si chiama Tom.
3. Alice abita in...... cas...... nel centr...... di New York.
4. Non trovo più ...... chiav...... della macchin...... .
5. ...... padr...... di Davide è tedesco.
6. Anna esce con .... nuovo ragazz...... .
7. Jim è uno sudent...... americano.
8. Michael Ende, l'autor...... del libr...... *La storia infinita* è morto recentemente.

4. Correct the mistakes. Some sentences are correct, others have one mistake.

1. Mia moglie non è italiana. Va bene
2. Il Lombardia è una regione molto grande. ....
3. La gatta di mia nonno ha tre gattini. ....
4. L'italiano è una lingua difficile. ....
5. La fiore che preferisco è la rosa. ....
6. Il mano destra mi fa male. ....
7. Devo comprare una sapone per lavare i vestiti. ....
8. In tv c'è un serie di film molto interessanti. ....
9. L'Italia si trova in un situazione difficile. ....
10. L'anno prossimo vado in vacanza in Spagna. ....

	SINGULAR		PLURAL	
MASCULINE	**-O**	il telefon**o**	**-I**	i telefon**i**
	-E	il can**e**	**-I**	i can**i**
	-A	il sistem**a**	**-I**	i sistem**i**
FEMININE	**-A**	la scuol**a**	**-E**	le scuol**e**
	-E	la chiav**e**	**-I**	le chiav**i**
	-TA'	la libert**à**	**-TÀ**	le libert**à**
	-TU'	la virt**ù**	**-TÙ**	le virt**ù**
	-I	la cris**i**	**-I**	le cris**i**
	-O	la man**o**	**-I**	le man**i**

Nouns that do not change:

	SINGULAR	PLURAL
Nouns ending with a consonant, and foreign words in general	**il** film	**i** film
monosyllable nouns	**il** re	**i** re
shortened nouns	**la** foto	**le** foto

	SINGULAR			PLURAL	
MASCULINE	**-IO** **-IO**	**il** figl**io** **lo** z**io**	➜	**-I** **-II**	**i** figl**i** **gli** z**ii**
	-CO **-GO** *(accent on the second syllable from the end)*	**il** cuo**co** */'kwɔko* **l'**albɛr**go** */al'bɛrgo/*	➜	**-CHI** **-GHI** *(accent on the second syllable) from the end)*	**i** cuo**chi** */'kwɔki/* **gli** albɛr**ghi** */al'bɛrgi/*
	-CO **-GO** *(accent on the (third syllable from the end)*	**il** medi**co** */'mɛdiko/* **lo** psicolo**go** */psi'kɔlogo/*	➜	**-CI** **-GI** *(accent on the (third syllable from the end)*	**i** medi**ci** */'mɛditʃi/* **gli** psicolo**gi** */psi'kɔlodʒi/*
FEMININE	**-CA** **-GA**	**la** ban**ca** **la** dro**ga**	➜	**-CHE** **-GHE**	**le** ban**che** **le** dro**ghe**
	-CIA	**la** farma**cia**	➜	**-CIE**	**le** farma**cie**
	-CIA **-GIA** *(after a vowel)*	**la** cami**cia** **la** vali**gia**	➜	**-CIE** **-GIE** *(after a vowel*	**le** cami**cie** **le** vali**gie**
	-CIA **-GIA** *(after a consonant)*	**l'**ar**ancia** **la** pio**ggia**	➜	**-CE** **-GE** *(after a consonant)*	**le** ar**ance** **le** pio**gge**

Many nouns ending in **-co** and **-go** do not follow the given plural rule, e.g.: **l'**ami**co**, **gli** ami**ci**.

Can you remember the ponethic symbols? See Appendix 1.
Can you remember how to write the sounds */tʃo/*, */ki/*, etc. in Italian? See Appendix 2.

1. Complete the words with the correct plural endings and put in the correct form of the definite article.

1. Le bambin e
2. ......esercizi.......
3. ......strad.......
4. ......fratell.......
5. ......madr.......
6. ......poet.......
7. ......alber.......
8. ......fior......
9. ......dentist.......
10. ......professor.......
11. ......professoress.......
12. ......programm.......
13. ......giornal.......
14. ......cinem.......
15. ......sintes.......
16. ......television......
17. ......radi......
18. ......situazion......
19. ......attric......
20. ......attor......
21. ......man......
22. ......rivoluzion......

2. Rewrite the words in the plural form and put in the correct form of the definite article.

1. Lo zio .... Gli zii ....
2. Il figlio ....
3. L'albergo ....
4. Il medico ....
5. La droga ....
6. La farmacia ....
7. La pioggia ....
8. Il film ....
9. La libertà ....
10. La foto ....
11. Lo sport ....

3. Look at the pictures. Write the singular and plural form of the noun with the definite article.

1.

2.

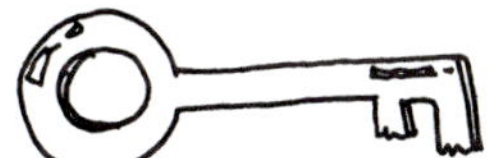
3.

4.

5.

6.

7.

8.

1. singolare .... il bambino ....
   plurale .... i bambini ....
2. singolare ....
   plurale ....
3. singolare ....
   plurale ....
4. singolare ....
   plurale ....
5. singolare ....
   plurale ....
6. singolare ....
   plurale ....
7. singolare ....
   plurale ....
8. singolare ....
   plurale ....

The following nouns have irregular plural forms:

SINGULAR		PLURAL
l'uomo	*man*	**gli** uom**ini**
il dio	*god*	**gli** de**i**
l'uovo	*egg*	**le** uov**a**
il paio	*pair*	**le** pai**a**

Some parts of the body are masculine in the singular form, but feminine in the plural form:

SINGULAR		PLURAL
il ginocchi**o**	*knee*	**le** ginocchi**a**
il bracci**o**	*arm*	**le** bracci**a**
il dit**o**	*finger*	**le** dit**a**
il sopracciigli**o**	*eyebrow*	**le** sopraccigli**a**
l'oss**o**	*bone*	**le** oss**a**
il labbr**o**	*lip*	**le** labbr**a**

Some very common nouns are only used in the plural form:

i pantaloni	*trousers*
le mutande	*briefs*
gli occhiali	*glasses*

Some very common nouns are only used in the singular form:

la gente	*people*
la frutta	*fruit*
la fame	*hunger*
la sete	*thirst*

1. Look at the pictures. Write the singular and plural form of the noun with the correct form of the definite article.

1

2

3

4

5

6

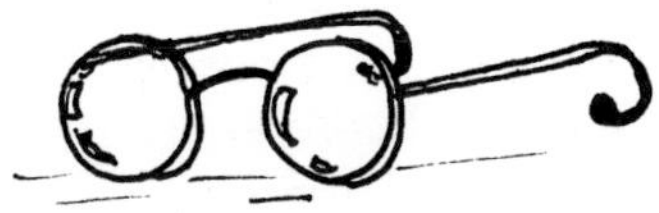

7

8

1. singolare ......l'uovo......
   plurale ......le uova......
2. singolare ....
   plurale ....
3. singolare ....
   plurale ....
4. singolare ....
   plurale ....
5. singolare ....
   plurale ....
6. singolare ....
   plurale ....
7. singolare ....
   plurale ....
8. singolare ....
   plurale ....

	SINGULAR			PLURAL	
MASCULINE	-O -E	**il** bambin**o** brav**o** **l'**eserciz**io** facil**e**	➜ ➜	-I -I	**i** bambin**i** brav**i** **gli** eserciz**i** facil**i**
FEMININE	-A -E	**la** bambin**a** brav**a** **la** lezion**e** facil**e**	➜ ➜	-E -I	**le** bambin**e** brav**e** **le** lezion**i** facil**i**

Adjectives ending in **-A**:

masculine plural changes to **-I**: **Il** simbol**o** socialist**a** **-I** simbol**i** socialist**i** *(The socialist symbols)*

feminine plural changes to **-E**: **La** politic**a** liberist**a** **-Le** politich**e** liberist**e** *(Liberalist politics)*

Adjective ending in **-co** and **-go** follow the same rules as nouns that end in **-co** and **-go**. See Unità 8.

Adjectives can be placed **before** or **after** a noun.
If the adjective is *longer* than the noun it is usually positioned *after* the noun.

The adjectives **bello**, **quello** and **buono.**
If the adjectives **bello** or **quello** are placed *before* the noun, they follow the rules of the *definite article.*

		SINGULAR		PLURAL		
MASCULINE	**il** bambino **lo** stadio **l'**albero	**il bel** bambino **il** bel**lo** stadio **il** bel**l'**albero	que**l** bambino quel**lo** stadio quel**l'**albero	**i** bambini **gli** stadi **gli** alberi	**i** be**i** bambini **i** be**gli** stadi **i** be**gli** alberi	que**i** bambini que**gli** stadi que**gli** alberi
FEMININE	**la** ragazza **l'**idea	**la** bel**la** ragazza **la** bel**l'**idea	quel**la** ragazza quel**l'**idea	**le** ragazze **le** idee	**le** bel**le** ragazze **le** bel**le** idee	quel**le** ragazze quel**le** idee

The adjective **buono** follows the rules of the *indefinite article.*

		SINGULAR
MASCULINE	**un** bambino **uno** studente	**un** buo**n** bambino **un** buo**no** studente
FEMININE	**un** artista **una** ragazza **un'**amica	**un** buo**n** artista **una** buo**na** ragazza **una** buo**n'**amica

If **bello** or **buono** are placed *after* the noun they act like normal **-A** or **-O** ending adjectives:

– Mio figlio è un bimb**o** buon**o**, non piange quasi mai. *(My son is a really good baby, he hardly ever cries)*
– In questo bosco ci sono tanti alber**i** bell**i**. *(There are lots of lovely trees in this forest)*

Quello as a demonstrative adjective, see Unità 12. **Quello** as a demonstrative pronoun, see Unità 13.

Study the following sentence.

– Parma è una città **molto tranquilla**. *(Parma is a very quiet town).*

The adjective (3) is always placed after the noun (1) when it is modified by an adverb (2):
(1) (2) (3)

– Ecco un monumento **estremamente interessante**.
(Now there's an extremely interesting monument)

1. Look at the pictures and complete the sentences with the adjectives from the box below.

1. Roberta è bionda e .... **2.** Silvana è .... e .... **3.** Stefano ha la maglietta e i pantaloni ....

4. L'esame è ...., ma .... **5.** I due giovani sposi sono molto .... **6.** Il professore è molto .... e ....

lungo	felice	facile	severo	biondo	grasso	basso	carino	sporco	antipatico

2. Choose the correct form of the adjective to complete the sentences.

1. Passami una penna nera .
a nero b nere **c nera** d neri.

2. Conosco molti ragazzi ....
a tedesche b tedesco c tedesci d tedeschi.

3. Silvia ha un .... appartamento con quattro camere.
a bel b bell' c bello d bell.

4. Mia sorella è sempre ....
a allegra b allegre c allegri d allegro.

5. Stasera in televisione c'è un film molto ....
a bel b bello c bell' d begli.

6. Mio fratello ha una macchina ....
a verda b verde c verdo d verdi.

3. Correct the mistakes. Some sentences are correct, others have one mistake.

1. La strada dove vive tuo cugino è molto buia. va bene
2. Ho comprato degli occhiali nuovi. ....
3. Mia moglie ha gli occhi marrone e i capelli castani. ....
4. Il partito socialisto italiano è nato nel 1892. ....
5. Tua figlia è una studentessa intelligenti. ....
6. Quel albero è pieno di fiori. ....
7. Che belli occhi che hai! ....
8. Cecilia è una buon amica di Stefania. ....
9. Vivo in città tranquilla e molto bella. ....
10. La birra fredda è molto buona, caldo non si riesce a bere. ....

Possessive adjectives and possessive pronouns have the same form.

	MASCULINE		FEMININE	
	SINGULAR	**PLURAL**	**SINGULAR**	**PLURAL**
I persona sing.	**mio**	**miei**	**mia**	**mie**
II persona sing.	**tuo**	**tuoi**	**tua**	**tue**
III persona sing.	**suo**	**suoi**	**sua**	**sue**
I persona plur.	**nostro**	**nostri**	**nostra**	**nostre**
II persona plur.	**vostro**	**vostri**	**vostra**	**vostre**
III persona plur.	**loro**	**loro**	**loro**	**loro**

Study the following sentences.

- **Il** mi**o** amic**o** Fulvio è medico. *(My friend Fulvio is a doctor)*
- **La** mi**a** amic**a** Anne è francese. *(My friend Anne is Frenck)*

The possessives change according to gender and number of the possessed noun.
E.g.: if the noun is masculine and singular (amic**o**), the possessive form is **il** mi**o**.

Loro does not change form. – Ecc**o** là **le loro** ragazz**e**. *(Their girls friends are over there)*

How do you distinguish between a **possessive adjective** and a **possessive pronoun**?

The possessive adjective is followed by the noun that is being referred to.
The possessive pronoun replaces the noun.

Possessive adjectives (before a noun).

- **La mia casa** ha tre piani. *(My house is on three floors).*
- **Il loro cane** è molto pericoloso con gli estranei. *(Their dog is very dangerous with strangers).*

Possessive pronouns (substitute a noun):

- **La casa** di Mario ha sette piani, **la mia** tre. *(Mario's house is on seven floors, mine is on three).*
- Il **cane** del Signor Bianchi non fa male mai a nessuno, invece **il loro** è molto pericoloso. *(Mr Bianchi's dog never hurts anyone, but theirs is very dangerous).*

In some cases the possessives adjective is placed **after** the noun. For example:

- Vieni a casa mia stasera? *(Are you coming to my house this evening?)*
- Mamma mia! *(My goodness!)*

The *definite article* is usually required before the possessive adjectives ad pronouns.

The definite article is generally *omitted* with *singular* nouns referring to members of the family (padre, madre, sorella, etc.) but required when used in the *plural* form.

- **Mia** madre si chiama Paola. *(My mother's name is Paola)*
- **I miei** nonni sono molto vecchi. *(My grandparents are very old)*

With **loro** the article is required even with nouns referring to the family:

- **La loro** madre è molto giovane. *(Their mother is very young).*

Proprio is used instead of **suo** and **loro** when

the subject is *nessuno, tutti (no one, everyone)* or other *indefinit pronouns.* (See Appendix 3):

- **Nessuno** deve pensare solo ai **propri** affari. *(No one should think only about their own interests)*

when the subject is not mentioned, in other words the sentence construction is *impersonale* (See Appendix 3):

- **È** importante ripensare ai **propri** errori. *(It is important to reconsider ones own mistakes)*

1. Rewrite the following in the plural form.

1. La tua casa ....*le tue case*..........
2. Il mio amico ....
3. La nostra macchina ....
4. Il suo libro ....
5. Il vostro ufficio ....
6. Il loro giornale ....

2. Complete the sentences with the correct form of the possessive adjective.

1. Dormo sempre nel ......*mio*...... letto.
2. La figlia di Antonio e Laura si chiama Anna, il .... figlio Nicola.
3. Questo è il .... cappello; l'ho comprato a Parigi.
4. Giulia insegna in una scuola elementare; .... marito è barbiere.
5. Claudia e io amiamo la musica. Il .... genere preferito è il blues.
6. Voi siete argentini, ma i .... nonni erano italiani.
7. Ti piace il .... lavoro?
8. L'estate prossima andiamo al mare con i .... amici.
9. Domani parlerò con la .... direttrice per dirle che sono stanco di lavorare per lei.
10. Luigi abita al secondo piano; .... cugina al primo piano.

3. Complete the answers with the correct possessive pronoun.

1. Questa macchina è di Carlo? No, non è ......*la sua*......; è di Antonella.
2. Sandra è la sorella di Fausto? Sì, è .... sorella, ed è la moglie di Angelo.
3. Sei sicuro che il mio appuntamento sia alle 10? No, il mio è alle 10, ... è alle 10,30.
4. Guarda! La madre dei fratelli Acerbi! No, non è .... madre. Lei è a Roma in questo periodo.
5. Ricordati di chiamarmi oggi pomeriggio. Va bene, ma dammi .... numero di telefono.
6. Le mie vacanze sono andate molto bene e le vostre? .... sono state bellissime.

4. Join the sentences using a possessive adjective and by adding e or *ma* where possible.

1. La casa di Mauro è in Via Van Gogh; l'ufficio di Mauro è in Via Brambilla.
La casa di Mauro è in Via Van Gogh e il suo ufficio è in Via Brambilla
2. I Menozzi vivono in Germania. Il sogno dei Menozzi è di tornare in Italia.
....
3. La sorella di Roberto lavora in una fabbrica. La madre di Roberto è pensionata.
....
4. Questa lettera è per tuo fratello; non conosco l'indirizzo di tuo fratello.
....
5. Mi piacciono i formaggi francesi. Il prezzo dei formaggi francesi è abbastanza alto.
....
6. Quelle sono le nostre biciclette. Le biciclette di Susanna e la tua sono in garage.
....
7. La zia di Simona e Mario è simpatica. Le cugine di Simona e Mario sono insopportabili.
....
8. Parma è una città dell'Emilia Romagna. Gli abitanti di Parma si chiamano parmigiani.
....

Demonstrative adjectives: **questo** (this, these)

SINGULAR	*this*		**PLURAL**	*these*
MASCULINE	*before a consonant* **questo**	*before a vowel* **quest'**	**MASCULINE**	**questi**
FEMININE	*before a consonant* **questa**	*before a vowel* **quest'**	**FEMININE**	**queste**

Quello *(that, those)*

SINGULAR	*that*		**PLURAL**	*those*
MASCULINE				
before a consonant	**quel**	quel bambino	**quei**	quei bambini
before S + consonant , Z, PS, GN, X	**quello**	quello studente	**quegli**	quegli studenti
before a vowel	**quell'**	quell'albero	**quegli**	quegli alberi
FEMININE				
before a consonant	**quella**	quella casa	**quelle**	quelle case
before a vowel	**quell'**	quell'ape	**quelle**	quelle api

▶ **Quello** used as an *adjective* behaves like the definite article (See Unità 5) and the adjective **bello** (See Unità 10).

Study the picture.

Questo is used for people and things which are *close* to the speaker.

Study the picture.

Quello is used for people and things which are at a *distance* from the speaker.

▶ *The article* is *not* used with the demonstrative adjectives.

Apart from **questo** and **quello** there are other less common demonstrative adjectives such as:

codesto used in some regions of Italy or in bureaucratic language to talk about an object at a *distance* from the speaker but *close* to the listener.

– Egregio Direttore, mi rivolgo a **codesto** Istituto per...
(Dear Sir, I'm writing to this Institute in order to...)

1. Rewrite the following in the plural form.

1. Questa festa ....queste........ ....feste........
2. Quest'idea ....
3. Questo compagno ....
4. Questa domanda ....
5. Questa classe ....
6. Questo studente ....
7. Questa lettera ....
8. Questo numero ....
9. Quest'albero ....
10. Quest'appartamento ....

2. Use *quello* instead of *questo* in both the singular and plural forms.

1. ...Quella... festa ....quelle........ ....feste........
2. .... idea ....
3. .... compagno ....
4. .... domanda ....
5. .... classe ....
6. .... studente ....
7. .... lettera ....
8. .... numero ....
9. .... albero ....
10. .... appartamento ....

3. Look at the pictures and complete the sentences.

Demonstrative pronouns: **questo** and **quello** *(this, that)*.

	SINGULAR *this/that*		PLURAL *these/those*
MASCULINE	**questo** **quello**	**MASCULINE**	**questi** **quelli**
FEMININE	**questa** **quella**	**FEMININE**	**queste** **quelle**

The *demonstrative pronouns* take the place of a noun.

The *article* is *not* used with the demonstrative pronouns.

Study the picture.

The pronoun **quello** - but not **questo** - is used to avoid the repetition of a noun.

Study the picture.

Quello - but not *questo* - is used before relative pronouns.

Apart from *questo* and *quello* there are other less common demonstrative pronouns:

- **codesto**: used in some regions of Italy or in bureaucratic language to talk about an object at a *distance* from the speaker but *close* to the listener.
- **ciò:** is used instead of *quello* or *questo* when the meanings is *questa* or *quella cosa. (This or that thing/what).*
  - **Ciò** (quello) **che** mi dici mi rende felice! *(What you're telling me makes me very happy!)*

1. Look at the pictures and complete the sentences.

2. Complete the sentences with the correct demonstrative pronoun.

1. Ti presento mio fratello e .questa...................... è sua moglie.
2. Guarda laggiù c'è un piccolo lago e .... è il Monte Bianco.
3. ....che volevo dirvi è che l'anno prossimo vado in pensione.
4. Non mi ricordo bene .... che mi hai detto.
5. Riesci a leggere quel cartello là in fondo e .... più piccolo di fianco?
6. Ecco a Lei, Signore: questo è il suo passaporto e .... è il biglietto aereo.

3. Put the words into the right order.

1. Mattina/devo/scuola/andare/a/questa.
   Questa mattina devo andare a scuola
2. Tua/ciò/personalità/che/crea/sempre/la/è/problemi.
   ....
3. Sempre/quello/voglio/che/faccio.
   ....
4. Direttore,/egregio/Istituto/invio/a/codesto/curriculum vitae/il/mio.
   ....
5. Quella/questa/mia/di/è/è/la/Flavio/casa/e.
   ....
6. Chi/quelle/queste/di/sono/scarpe/e?
   ....

4. Answer the following questions.

1. Quali film preferisci? ...Quelli....... d'avventura.
2. Quali macchine ti piacciono? .... da corsa.
3. Chi sono quei ragazzi? .... che giocano con me a calcio.
4. Dove sono le mie foto? .... del mare sono sul tavolo.
5. Come si chiamano le tue colleghe? .... che lavorano nel mio ufficio si chiamano Luisa e Camilla.
6. Cosa vuoi mangiare? .... che mangi tu?

Vorrei *(would like)* is used to express a wish or ofter someting, while **potrei** *(could)* is used to ask for permission or to make a request.

vorr**ei**	potr**ei**
vorr**esti**	potr**esti**
vorr**ebbe**	potr**ebbe**
vorr**emmo**	potr**emmo**
vorr**este**	potr**este**
vorr**ebbero**	potr**ebbero**

These verb endings belong to the *conditional*. See Unità 49 and 50.

Study the picture.

1) *What would you like to eat?*
I'd like a plate of spaghetti with a tuna sauce, please.

2) *Giovanni and Sandra would like to go to the seaside on Sunday. What would you like to do?*
I don't know yet.

3) *This seat is free, isn't it? Could I sit here, please?*
Of course!

4) *Could you tell me where the station is, please?*

1. Write an appropriate sentences in each of the speech bubbles.

2. Complete the sentences.

1. Mi ...potresti........ passare l'acqua per favore?
2. .... un gelato alla fragola, per favore. E uno per mia figlia al cioccolato.
3. Pino e io .... andare al mare, ma non abbiamo molti soldi quest'anno.
4. Mi scusi, Signor Vigile, mi .... indicare dov'è Piazza Navona, per favore?
5. Come, scusi? .... ripetere, per favore?
6. Giovanni .... cambiare lavoro, ma non è facile trovare un buon posto.
7. Cosa .... fare da grande? Lo stesso lavoro di tuo padre?
8. Cosa .... mangiare? Spaghetti alla bolognese per tutti e due?
9. Mi scusi, ... fumare qui?
10. Scusate, ... fare un po' di silenzio, per favore?

3. Complete the dialogue.

Dal salumiere

- Signora buongiorno?
- Buongiorno, ..vorrei........ 200 grammi di prosciutto di Parma, per favore.
- Nient'altro?
- ......2...... farmi provare quella mortadella?
- Certamente, ...3...... provare anche quest'altro tipo.
- No, va bene quello!
- Le piace?
- È molto buona; ne ......4...... 100 grammi.
- Poi?
- Basta così, grazie ......5...... pagare con il bancomat?
- Sì, certo.

The cardinal numbers:

0 zero
1 uno
2 due
3 tre
4 quattro
5 cinque
6 sei
7 sette
8 otto
9 nove
10 dieci
11 undici
12 dodici
13 tredici
14 quattordici
15 quindici
16 sedici
17 diciassette
18 diciotto
19 diciannove
20 venti
21 ventuno
22 ventidue
23 ventitré
24 ventiquattro
25 venticinque
26 ventisei
27 ventisette
28 ventotto
29 ventinove
30 trenta
40 quaranta
50 cinquanta
60 sessanta
70 settanta
80 ottanta
90 novanta
100 cento
102 centodue
200 duecento
1000 mille
2000 duemila
10.000 diecimila
100.000 centomila
1.000.000 un milione
1.000.000.000 un miliardo

When a cardinal number is used as an adjective it is usually placed *before* the noun it is referring to.

– Questo libro ha **trecentoventidue** pagine.
(This book has three hundred and twenty-two pages)

The cardinal numbers are invariable except in the following cases:

x = per
: = diviso
– = meno
+ = più
= = uguale

uno has a feminine form: **una**;

– Guarda, **una** stella cadente! *(Look! A shooting star!)*

mille has an irregular plural form: mila;

– Questa casa costa circa **quattrocentomila** euro. *(A coffee and an ice-cream comes to tour thousand)*

zero, milione and **miliardo** all have regular plural forms: **cinque zeri** *(five noughts)*, **due milioni** *(two million)*, **tre miliardi** *(three billion)*.

– Secondo un rapporto dell'Organizzazione Mondiale della Sanità nel 2020 saranno sette miliardi gli esseri umani con problemi derivanti dalla malnutrizione.
– *According to a report by the World Health Organisation, in the year 2020 seven billion people will be suffering from problems caused bu malnutrition)*

The cardinal numbers are written as one word, except for the figures with **milione** and **miliardo**; in such cases the words are written separately with an **e** *(and)* between the two numbers.

– Quella villa è molto cara, costa un **milione** e **duecentomila** euro.
(That villa is very expensive, it costs one million two hundred thousand euro)

▶ When writing a cheque the numbers are written together as one word without using an **e** *(and)*. This includes amounts with the words **milioni** and **miliardi**.

▶ When the words **milione** and **miliardo** are followed by a noun, the preposition **di** is used.

– Milano ha circa due milioni **di** abitanti. *(Milan has about two million inhabitants)*

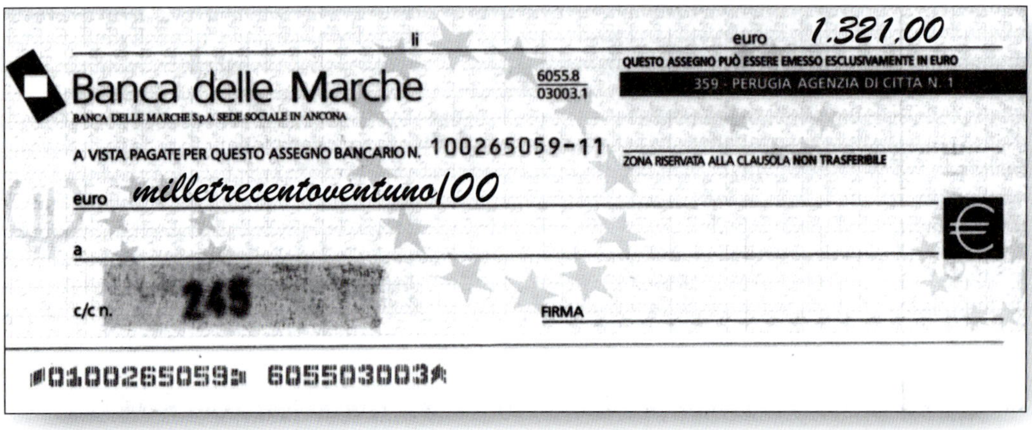

Numbers in Italian are masculine.

– **Il cinque** è il mio numero fortunato. *(Five is my lucky number)*

1. Write the numbers in words.

1. 1.321 ...*milletrecentoventuno*...
2. 20 ...
3. 15 ...
4. 56.418 ...
5. 5.000.000.000 ...
6. 86 ...

2. Write the words in numbers.

1. quarantacinque ...*45*...
2. settecentodiecimila ...
3. quattro milioni ...
4. dodici virgola nove ...
5. milletrecentoventicinque ...
6. un miliardo ...

3. Write the sums in words.

1. 8 x 9 = 72 ...*otto per nove uguale settantadue*...
2. 6 + 2 = 8 ...
3. 18 : 2 = 9 ...
4. 200.000 – 40.000 = 160.000 ...
5. 6 x 6 = 36 ...
6. 82 – 31 = 51 ...

The ordinal numbers:

1° primo	***(first)***	***11° undicesimo***
2° secondo	***(second)***	***12° dodicesimo***
3° terzo	***(third)***	***13° tredicesimo***
4° quarto	***(fourth)***	***20° ventesimo***
5° quinto	***(fifth)***	***21° ventunesimo***
6° sesto	***(sixth etc.)***	***22° ventiduesimo***
7° settimo		***23° ventitreesimo***
8° ottavo		***100° centesimo***
9° nono		***1.000° millesimo***
10° decimo		***1.000.000° milionesimo***

When an ordinal number is used as an adjective it is usually placed *before* the noun it is referring to.

– Abito al **terzo** piano.
(I live on the third floor.)

The ordinal numbers are placed *after* the names of kings, popes, etc.

– Ecco il ritratto dell'imperatore Carlo **V**.
(There's the portrait of the Emperor Charles V.)

The ordinal numbers are formed by adding the ending **-esimo** to the cardinal number, remembering to remove the final vowel of the latter: ventiquattresimo.

Whit the number **-tre** the final vowel is kept: ventritr**ee**simo.

Ordinal numbers have *masculine*, *feminine*, *singular* and *plural* forms, like normal adjectives ending in **-o** and **-a**.

– Prenda **la** second**a** strad**a** a destra!
(Take the second street on your right!)

Fractions are formed by using a *cardinal* number followed by an *ordinal* number.

2/3 = due terzi. *(Two thirds.)*
5/11 = cinque undicesimi. *(Five elevenths.)*

Exception: 1/2 = un mezzo. *(A half.)*

When you want to talk about an approximate quantity, without stating a precise number, the following words are used:

una decina = circa dieci *(about ten)*
una ventina, trentina, ecc. = circa venti, trenta, ecc. *(about twenty, thirty, etc.)*
un centinaio, un migliaio = circa cento, mille. *(about a hundred, a thousand.)*

Plural: alcune decine, centinaia, migliaia. *(Tens, hundreds, thousands.)*

1. Correct the following ordinals where necessary.

1. 3° prima ....*terzo*........
2. 13° undicesimo ....
3. 8° terzo ....
4. 23° tredicesimo ....
5. 9° quarto ....
6. 20° ventesimo ....
7. 5° quinto ....
8. 21° ventunesimo ....
9. 6° sesto ....
10. 34° trentaquattresimo ....
11. 7° settimo ....
12. 1000° centesimo ....
13. 8° ottavo ....
14. 100° millesimo ....
15. 9° nono ....
16. 11° decimo ....

2. Write the numbers in words.

1. 1/3 ....*un terzo*........
2. 5% ....
3. 8° ....
4. 10° ....
5. 1° ....
6. Papa Giovanni XXIII ....

3. Find a synonym for the following expressions.

1. Circa dodici ....*una dozzina*........
2. Circa dieci ....
3. Circa cento ....
4. Circa mille ....
5. 300 o 400 ....
6. 3000 o 4000 ....

There are two ways of telling the time: one is used in everyday Italian and the other for more official situations (times of trains, planes, cinema, theatre, radio and TV programmes, etc.).

Look at the example below. Can you work out the rule?

le due e dieci
le dieci e cinque
l'una e venti
le sette meno cinque
le otto meno venti

le due e dieci
le dieci e cinque
le tredici e venti
le diciotto e cinquantacinque
le diciannove e quaranta

For official times the twenty-four hour clock is used, i.e. 19.00 *"le diciannove". 20.50 "le venti* e *cinquanta"*; while in more colloquial situations it is more common to say *le sette, le nove meno dieci.*

When telling the time cardinal numbers are used (uno, due, tre, ecc.).

When telling the time the plural form of the verb is used: - **Sono le** due e dieci, le undici e cinque, le otto meno venti, etc. *(It's ten past two, five past eleven, twenty to eight,* etc.*).*

The single form of the verb is required only in one case: - **È l'**una, l'una e cinque, l'una meno venti, etc. *(It's one o'clock, five past one, twenty to one,* etc.*).*

When telling the time the *definite article* (il, lo, la, etc.) is always needed before the number on the hour.

Sono **le** tre. *(It's three o'clock).*
È **l'**una e dieci. *(It's ten past one).*

You can ask the time in various ways. Two very common forms are:

Che ora è? **Che ore sono?** *(What's the time?)*

Mezzogiorno and **mezzanotte** *(midday* and *midnight)*:

1 - È **mezzogiorno** = ore 12.00 *(It's midday)* 2 - È **mezzanotte** = ore 24.00 *(It's midnight)*

With **mezzogiorno** and **mezzanotte** the singular form of the verb is used and the article is omitted..

In official situations the following forms are used: 1 - Sono le dodici. *(It's twelve o'clock.)* 2 - Sono le ventiquattro. *(It's twenty-four hundred hours.)*

Tra le ore e i minuti occorre normalmente mettere
e *before* the half hour: *6.25* sei **e** venticinque *(twenty-five past six)*
meno *dopo* la mezz'ora: *11.40* dodici **meno** venti *(twenty to twelve)*

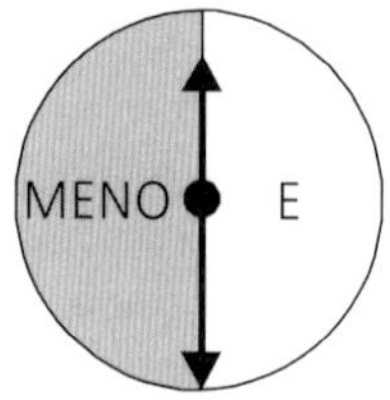

For the following times you say:

2.15 **due e un quarto** *(a quarter past two)*
2.45 **tre meno un quarto** * *(a quarter to three)*
2.30 **due e mezza** *(half past two)*

* Sometimes *due* ***e tre*** *quarti* or *un quarto* ***alle*** *tre* are used.
The form with **meno** is frequently substituted by **alle**:
5.50 dieci **alle** sei. *(ten to six)*; *9.40* venti **alle** dieci *(twenty to ten).*

The preposition used with time expressions is **a/alle/all'**; see Unità 23.

A mezzogiorno in estate fa molto caldo. *(It is very hot in summer at midday)*
Vado sempre a letto **alle** undici e mezza. *(I always go to bed at half past eleven)*
Pranzo solitamente **all'**una e un quarto. *(I usually have lunch at a quarter past one)*

1. Write the times in words.

1. 4.10. Le quattro e dieci
2. 10.15. ....
3. 1.05. ....
4. 10.00. ....
5. 6.50. ....
6. 11.40. ....
7. 2.45. ....
8. 8.30. ....

2. Look at the clocks and write the times in words.

1. Le quattro meno venti
2. ....
3. ....
4. ....
5. ....
6. ....

3. Look at the pictures and correct the verbs or the times where necessary.

1. Salvatore si alza alle sette e un quarto. Va bene
2. Salvatore fa ginnastica alle sette e venti. ....
3. Salvatore pranza alle sette e mezza. ....
4. Salvatore prende l'autobus alle otto meno dieci. ....
5. Salvatore arriva in ufficio alle otto e venti. ....
6. Salvatore comincia a lavorare alle dodici e mezza. ....
7. Salvatore arriva a casa alle sei meno un quarto. ....
8. Salvatore cena alle otto. ....
9. Salvatore guarda la televisione alle undici. ....

4. Answer the following questions.

1. A che ora ti svegli? ....
2. A che ora fai colazione? ....
3. A che ora inizi a lavorare o a studiare? ....
4. A che ora torni a casa? ....
5. A che ora ceni? ....
6. A che ora vai a letto? ....

Study the pictures.

To talk about the **date** cardinal numbers are used:

Oggi è il **nove** ottobre 2000. *(Today it the nine of October 2000).*

Except for when it is the first day of the month.

Il **primo** maggio è la Festa del Lavoro. *(The first of May is May Day).*

Look at the picture.

What preposition do you use with the date? **No preposition** is needed with the **date**. See Unità 27.

The **year** is usually written in numbers but read as *one word.*

– 1995 ➜ **millenovecentonovantacinque**

or you can use an *abbreviated* form if it is clear which century is being referred to:

– L'89 (l'**ottantanove**) è stato l'anno della caduta del muro di Berlino. *('89 was the year the Berlin wall fell).*

When referring to a decade, for example the years between 1980 and 1989, you can say:

– **Gli anni Ottanta.** *(The Eighties).*

You can talk about **centuries** in two ways, either using the **cardinal numbers** (for centuries after the year one thousand) usually written with a capital letter:

– Il **Quattrocento** è il secolo del Rinascimento in Italia. ➜ **1400**
(The fifteenth century is the century of the Renaissance in Italy).

or with ordinal numbers:

– Il **quindicesimo** secolo è il secolo del Rinascimento in Italia. ➜ **1400**
(The fifteenth century is the century of the Renaissance in Italy).

With **years** and **centuries** the preposition **in** is used in its combined form with the article **nel/nell'**. See Unità 23 and 27.

– Mi sono sposato **nel** 1992. *(I got married in 1992).*
– Colombo "scopri" l'America **nel** quindicesimo secolo (**nel** Quattrocento).
(Columbus "discovered" America in the fifteenth century) (in the fourteen hundreds).
– **Nell'**Ottocento l'Italia era un paese molto povero. *(In the eighteen hundreds Italy was a very poor country).*

1. Write the dates in words.

1. 30/3/1992 trenta marzo millenovecentonovantadue
2. 12/1/1923 ....
3. 1/5/1653 ....
4. 2/1/1229 ....
5. 15/8/1998 ....
6. 9/7/1888 ....
7. 22/10/1960 ....
8. 5/2/1912 ....

2. Complete the sentences with either a preposition or the definite article or both where necessary.

1. Nel 1982 l'Italia ha vinto il mondiale di calcio.
2. Sono nato .... ottobre.
3. Mia sorella è nata .... 1980.
4. Sono arrivato in Germania .... dieci di ottobre.
5. Garibaldi è vissuto .... diciannovesimo secolo.
6. .... primo maggio è la Festa del Lavoro.

3. Guess the year or the century. Write your answers in words.

1. È vissuto Napoleone ....
2. È finita la seconda guerra mondiale ....
3. C'è stata la rivoluzione sovietica ....
4. Colombo è arrivato in America ....
5. È vissuto Giulio Cesare ....

4. Look at the pages from Lino's diary and write suitable sentences.

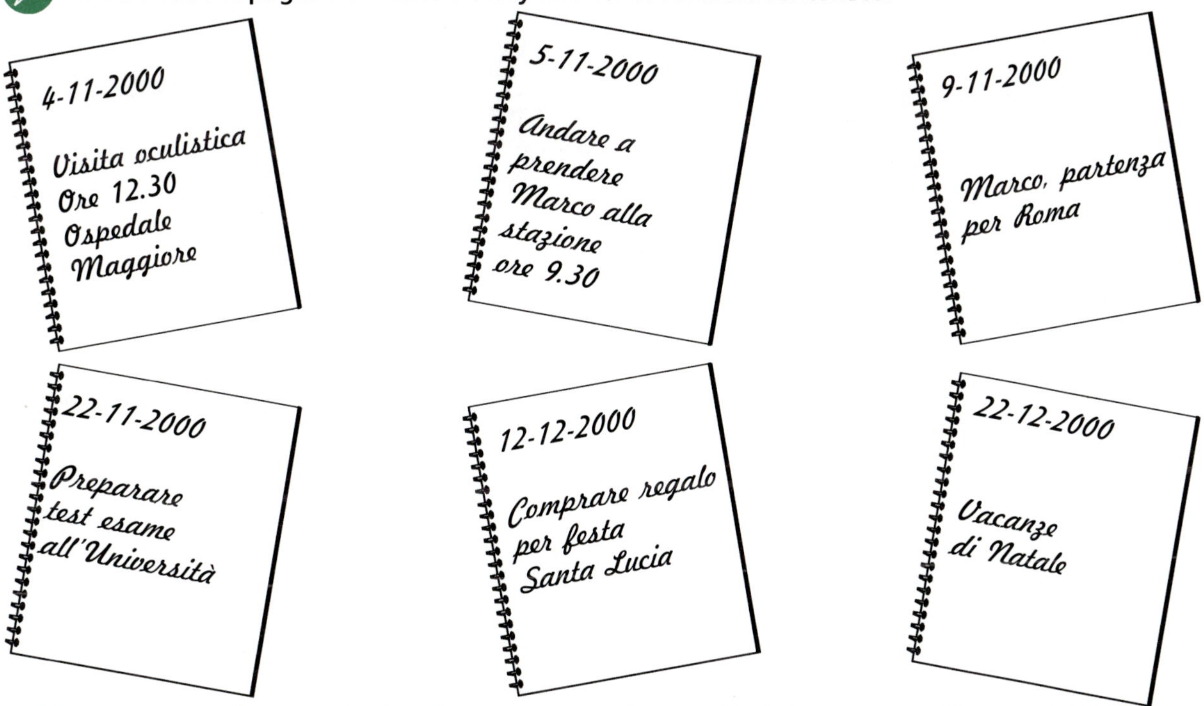

1. Il quattro novembre duemila Lino ha una visita oculistica alle dodici e mezzo all'Ospedale Maggiore.
2. ....
3. ....
4. ....
5. ....
6. ....

Chi? *(Who?)*

Study the pictures.

Chi is used to ask about a person's identity.
It is invariable and only used for people.

Question words can follow prepositions.
e.g.: **di chi?** *(Whose?)*

Che cosa? *(What?)*

Che cosa is invariable and only used for things.

- **Che** or **cosa** can be used instead of **Che cosa**.
  – **Che** mangiamo oggi? **Cosa** mangiamo oggi?
  (What are we going to eat today?).

Quale? *(Which? What?)*

Quale changes with the plural form and becomes **quali**.

- **Che** can be used instead of **quale**.
  – **Che** libro stai leggendo?
  (What book are you reading?)
- Before **è** (the verb to be) **qual** is used.
  – **Qual** è l'indirizzo della tua scuola?
  (What's the address of your school?)

Quanto? *(How much? how many?* etc.)

Quanto changes with gender and number. It is used to ask about **quantity**. It acts as a pronoun and an adjective. Do you remember the difference between an adjective and a pronoun? See Appendix 3.

Adjective	Pronoun
Quanto tempo ci vuole da Roma a Napoli in treno? *(How long does is take from Rome to Naples by train?)* **Quanta** carne mangi alla settimana? *(How much meat do you eat a week?)* **Quanti** amici hai in Italia? *(How many friends have you got in Italy?)* **Quante** sigarette fumi ogni giorno? *(How many cigarettes do you smoke a day?)*	**Quanto** costa la tua nuova macchina? *(How much is your new car?)* **Per quanti** hai preparato stasera? *(How many people have you cooked for tonight?)*

- Before doing the exercises, see Unità 20.

1. Complete the sentences with the missing question words.

1. *Chi* è quel ragazzo? È il fratello di Giovanni?
2. .... piangi?
3. .... sei nato? A Vienna vero?
4. .... anni hai?
5. .... sei tornato dalle vacanze? La settimana scorsa?
6. .... libri preferisci? I libri di narrativa o di saggistica?
7. .... è quella macchina? È di tua madre?
8. .... vuoi bere? Una birra?

2. Match the questions and answers.

1. *Dove vai quest'estate?*
2. Perché non esci con noi sabato sera?
3. Quanto costa una bottiglia di olio di oliva?
4. Chi è l'autore dei Promessi Sposi?
5. Quando parti per Roma?
6. Come sta tua nonna?
7. Quale film ti è piaciuto di più quest'anno?
8. Cosa fai questo fine settimana?

a Non molto bene. Sai, ha già 88 anni.
b Alessandro Manzoni.
c *Penso di andare in Portogallo.*
d Circa 6 euro, penso.
e Vorrei andare al cinema.
f Un film con Massimo Troisi, "Il Postino".
g Perché ho promesso a mia moglie di andare al ristorante.
h Venerdì prossimo.

3. Read the answers and write the questions.

1. *Come si chiama* ?
Mirella Chiari.
2. .... ?
A Pesaro in Via Rubini 8.
3. .... ?
Sono farmacista.
4. .... ?
Di solito prendo l'autobus.
5. .... ?
Mi piace molto leggere e fare delle passeggiate.
6. .... ?
Ho due figli, un maschio e una femmina.
7. .... ?
Gloria ha 6 anni e Paolo 4.
8. .... ?
Normalmente sono io che pulisco in casa. Mio marito invece cucina.

4. Answer the following questions.

1. Qual è la capitale del Brasile? *Brasilia*
2. Chi ha scritto la *Divina Commedia?* ....
3. Dov'è Belgrado? ....
4. Quando è vissuto A. Lincoln? ....
5. Quanti anni è durata la Prima Guerra Mondiale? ....
6. Come si dice "bistecca" in inglese? ....

Come? *(How?)*

Come is used to ask about the **way** something is done or the **way** someone feels.
Study the picture.

Perché? *(Why?)*

Perché is used to ask for a **reason**.
"**Perché** non mi hai chiamato ieri sera?" "**Perché** sono tornata a casa alle due questa notte".
("Why didn't you call me yesterday evening?" "Because I got home at two o'clock last night.")

▶ **Perché** is used in both the question and the answer.

Quando? *(When?)*

Quando is used to ask about **time**.
"**Quando** sei tornata? Alle due?" "Sì, ma perché ti arrabbi?"
("When did you get back? At two o'clock?" "Yes, but why are you angry?")

Dove? *(Where?)*

Dove is used to ask about **place**, whether involving movement or state.
See Appendix 3: expressions of place.

Da dove? *(Where from?)*

Da dove is used to ask about a person's place of origin.

■ Some question words can be used to make exclamations.

1. Put the words into the right order form questions.

1. Sei/così/ieri/tornato/perché/sera/tardi? *Perché sei tornato così tardi ieri sera?*
2. Tua/lavora/sorella/dove? ....
3. Mangiato/a/ieri/pranzo/cosa/hai? ....
4. Guadagni/mese/quanto/al? ....
5. La/che/si vede/casa/di chi/laggiù/è? ....
6. Quella/carina/da dove/ragazza/viene/così? ....
7. Comincia/quando/il/di/spagnolo/corso? ....
8. Puoi/di/pensare/come/questo/me? ....

2. Put in the missing words to complete the letter.

Cara Alicia,

Come va? Ti scrivo dopo tanto, ...2....... non ho mai tempo per pensare agli amici.
È iniziata la primavera ......3....... bello!
Finalmente posso uscire in bicicletta. E lì, ...4..... è il tempo? .....5..... comincia a fare caldo? .....6..... tempo ti rimane prima di finire il tuo corso?
Noi stiamo bene, stiamo programmando le vacanze estive. L'anno scorso siamo andati in Norvegia. ....7....... è bello quel paese!
Quest'anno vorremmo andare in Egitto. E tu? ....8....... ti piacerebbe fare? ....9....... vorresti andare?
Scusami per la fretta, ma ora devo già uscire. ....10....... vita orribile! Lavoro, lavoro, e ancora lavoro!
.......11.......stress!
.......12....... vieni a trovarci? Spero di rivederti presto.

Un abbraccio
Filippo

3. Correct the mistakes where necessary.

1. Chi è quella macchina? *Di chi*
2. Da dove vive tua zia? ....
3. Quanto si dice "dog" in Italiano? ....
4. Quando finisci di lavorare normalmente? ....
5. Quanto stupido! Ho dimenticato l'appuntamento. ....
6. Cosa fratelli hai? ....
7. Chi fa Gianni? ....
8. Quali paesi vorresti visistare? ....

4. Write suitable exclamations.

1. Ci sono 20° sotto zero oggi! *Che freddo*!
2. Ho vinto 10 milioni al totocalcio! ....!
3. Ho visto la mostra sul surrealismo spagnolo! ....!
4. Ho provato le melanzane alla parmigiana di mia zia! ....!
5. A Londra ieri c'erano più di 30 gradi! ....!
6. Ho preso un brutto voto nell'esame, ma non era per niente facile; anzi, ...!

- Various groups of adverbs exist, some express **manner**, **quantity**, or **doubt,** others are used to **deny** or **confirm** something, etc.
- Adverbs of manner are usually formed from the adjective. Look at the following table.

Adjective	*Adverb formation feminine form of the adjective*	*Adverb*
fredd**o** *(cold)*	fredd**a** **+ mente**	fredd**amente** *(coldly)*
brev**e** *(brief)*	brev**e** **+ mente**	brev**emente** *(briefly)*
faci**le** *(easy)*	facil **+ mente**	faci**lmente** *(easily)*
regola**re** *(regular)*	regola**r** **+ mente**	rego**larmente** *(regular)*

– Ieri ho visto Giovanna. Mi ha salutato molto **freddamente.**
(I saw Giovanna yesterday. She said hello to me very coldly.)

▶ Some adverbs are irregular:

Adjective		*Adverb*	
buono	*(good)*	**bene**	*(well)*
cattivo	*(bad)*	**male**	*(badly)*
leggero	*(light, slight)*	legge**rm**ente	*(lightly, slightly)*
violento	*(violent)*	violen**te**mente	*(violently)*

– Sergio dice che l'esame è andato **bene**. *(Sergio says the exam went well.)*

- **Confirming** and **denying** adverbs.

Apart from sì (yes), there are many other words that can be used to confirm something, e.g.
certamente, certo, sicuramente, davvero, esattamente, ecc. *(certainly, of course, surely, really, exactly,* etc.*)*

To deny something, *no* and *non* are used. *Non* is followed by a verb and the rest of the sentence.
"Sai nuotare?" "**No, non mi** piace l'acqua."
("Can you swim?" "No, I don't like water.")

▶ In colloquial language *non* can be made stronger by adding the word *mica*.

"Sei stato tu a rompere il vetro della finestra!" "**No**, **non** è **mica** colpa mia; mi hanno spinto!"
("It was you who broke the window!") ("No, it really wasn't my fault, they pushed me!")

- Adverbs of **doubt**.

Forse, magari, probabilmente, ecc. *(maybe, perhaps, probably,* etc.*)*

– "Che cosa fai questo fine settimana?" "Non lo so ancora. **Forse** domani sera esco con Davide o **magari** domenica lo invito a cena a casa mia".
("What are you doing this weekend?" "I'm not sure yet. Maybe I'll go out with Davide tomorrow evening or perhaps I'll invite him to dinner at my place on Sunday.)

- Study the position of the adverbs in the following examples.

– Ho lavorato **duramente** questa settimana. *(I've worked hard this week.)*

– Mi sembra che il tuo vestito sia **leggermente** corto. *(I think your dress is just slightly on the short-side.)*

Adverbs are usually placed *after* the verb. See Unità 22 for the adverbs of frequency.

1. Change the adjectives into adverbs.

1. Dolce *dolcemente*
2. Difficile ....
3. Facile ....
4. Artistico ....
5. Grande ....
6. Assurdo ....
7. Forte ....
8. Debole ....
9. Antico ....
10. Nuovo ....
11. Particolare ....
12. Caldo ....

2. Complete the sentences with an adverb from the box below.

1. Sono in grande difficoltà; *difficilmente* riuscirò a finire il lavoro per domani sera.
2. Che cos'ha tua sorella? L'ho salutata e lei mi ha risposto molto ....
3. L'esame era molto difficile; secondo me è andato ....
4. Il quadro è quasi dritto; muovilo .... verso destra.
5. Che bella scrittura! Tutte le lettere si capiscono ....
6. Che uomo romantico! Mi parla sempre così ....

appassionatamente, freddamente, leggermente, perfettamente, male, difficilmente.

3. Mach the sentences from the columns.

1. *Hai visto la partita ieri sera?*	a Certamente. Ecco qua.
2. Genova è in Lombardia.	b Forse. Dipende dal tempo. Fa ancora molto freddo.
3. Mi può prestare una penna, per favore?	c Sì, è proprio buono.
4. Vai al mare questo fine settimana?	d Mi piacerebbe, ma non ho proprio tempo!
5. Ho visto Claudio ieri sera con una nuova ragazza.	e *Certo, lo sai che le vedo tutte!*
6. Tua figlia ha rotto un braccio a un suo amichetto.	f Non ancora. Probabilmente lo finirò domenica.
7. Hai sentito il vino che ti ho dato?	g Ancora! Non ricordi proprio niente di quello che hai studiato!
8. Hai finito il libro che ti ho prestato?	h Non so, magari lo dovrò fare io.
9. Chi scriverà la lettera per il direttore?	i Non è mica vero. Lei è stata con me tutto il giorno.
10. Vieni al cinema stasera?	l Impossibile! Sicuramente non era lui. È l'uomo più fedele che conosca.

Adverbs of **quantity**.

+++	**molto, tanto, parecchio**	*very much, a lot (of), a load (of)*
++	**abbastanza, piuttosto**	*enough, quite, rather*
+	**un po'**	*a little*
-	**poco**	*little*
−−	**niente**	*not... at all*

– Ho studiato **molto**; mi fa male la testa. *(I've studied a lot; I've got a headache)*
– Fa già **abbastanza** caldo, domani vado al mare. *(It's already quite warm, tomorrow I'm going to the seaside)*

Study the picture.

Troppo *(too/too much)* is used to indicate excessiveness

Frequency adverbs.

sempre	*(always)*
quasi sempre	*(almost always)*
solitamente, normalmente	*(usually, normally)*
spesso	*(often)*
talvolta, a volte	*(sometimes, occasionally)*
raramente	*(rarely)*
quasi mai	*(hardly ever)*
mai	*(never)*

Adverbs are usually placed *after* the verb..

Some adverbs of frequency (*mai, sempre, spesso, quasi mai, quasi sempre*) can be placed between the auxiliary verb and the past participle in compound tense forms.

– Ho **sempre** pensato che l'Italia fosse un paese di gente bassa e con i capelli scuri.
(I always thought that Italy was a nation of small people with dark hair)

– Non sono **quasi mai** andato in montagna da piccolo, ma adesso mi piace molto.
(When I was small I hardly ever went to the mountains, but now I like going there a lot)

See Unità 62 for the comparative form of the adverb.

1. Answer the questions using the adverbs from the box below.

1. Ti alzi spesso alle 6 del mattino? ....
2. Fai colazione? ....
3. Lavori anche il sabato? ....
4. Mangi spesso carne di maiale? ....
5. Vai al cinema? ....
6. Lavi i piatti? ....
7. Ti stiri i vestiti? ....
8. Vai spesso a fare la spesa? ....
9. Bevi spesso il vino? ....
10. Vai spesso a letto dopo mezzanotte? ....

sempre, quasi sempre, solitamente, spesso, a volte, raramente, quasi mai, mai

2. Look at the chart and the box below. Write sentences using the correct adverbs of frequency.

	Sandra e Giovanni	Paola	Luisa	Tu e la tua famiglia
Andare a teatro	✓	✓	✘	
Andare in vacanza	✓✓	✘	✓	
Mangiare al ristorante	✓✓	✘	✓	
Comprare dei regali	✓✓✓	✓✓	✓✓	
Praticare uno sport	✓✓✓	✓	✓	
Leggere libri	✓	✘	✓	
Fare shopping	✓✓✓	✓✓	✓✓	

1. Sandra e Giovanni ....
2. Sandra e Giovanni ....
3. Paola ....
4. Paola ....
5. Luisa ....
6. Luisa ....
7. Tu e la tua famiglia ....
8. Tu e la tua famiglia ....

✘ mai, quasi mai, ✓ raramente, a volte; ✓✓ spesso, solitamente; ✓✓✓ quasi sempre, sempre

3. Answer the following questions using an adverb of quantity.

1. Ti piace la musica classica? ....
2. Ti piace guardare la televisione? ....
3. Ti piace la cucina cinese? ....
4. Ti piace viaggiare? ....

4. Complete the sentences with an adverb of quantity.

1. *Lui è molto* grasso, ma è anche alto.
2. Ho studiato ...., ma non è ancora ....
3. Ho mangiato .... a pranzo e ho già fame.
4. Ieri sera ho bevuto .... e adesso ho il mal di testa.
5. Stamattina c'è stato il terremoto, ma io non ho sentito ....
6. In estate fa .... caldo nella Pianura Padana.

Prepositions in Italian:
di *(of)*, **a** *(to, at)*, **da** *(from)*, **in** *(in)*, **con** *(with, by)*, **su** *(on)*, **per** *(for)*, **tra/fra** *(among, between)*.

When the prepositions **a, da, di, in, su** are used together with the definite article, compound words are formed.

	il	*lo*	*l'*	*la*	*i*	*gli*	*le*
a	**al**	**allo**	**all'**	**alla**	**ai**	**agli**	**alle**
da	**dal**	**dallo**	**dall'**	**dalla**	**dai**	**dagli**	**dalle**
di	**del**	**dello**	**dell'**	**della**	**dei**	**degli**	**delle**
in	**nel**	**nello**	**nell'**	**nella**	**nei**	**negli**	**nelle**
su	**sul**	**sullo**	**sull'**	**sulla**	**sui**	**sugli**	**sulle**

– Vai spesso **al** cinema?
(Do you often go to the cinema?)

– **Nella** mia strada vivono molti extracomunitari.
(Lots of foreigners live in my street)

The preposition **con** may also have a form:

con + *il* = **col** but also **con il**

con + *i* = **coi** but also **con i**

In modern Italian it is more common to use **con il**/etc. instead of the combined form.

– Fa molto freddo. Esci **con il** cappotto!
(It's really cold. Put your coat on to go out!)

1. Put in the correct form of combined preposition. Use the prepositions in brackets.

1. Sull' albero (su).
2. .... cinema (a).
3. .... bambino (di).
4. .... Germania (da).
5. .... pomeriggio (in).
6. .... amici (a).
7. .... autobus (su).
8. .... psicologo (da).

2. Put the words into order.

1. Giornale/articolo/sul/oggi/di/c'è/interessante/molto/un
Sul giornale di oggi c'è un articolo molto interessante
2. Ancora/un po'/nel/c'è/frigorifero/latte/di?
....
3. Mio/appena/è/gruppo/preferito/uscito/disco/del/il/nuovo.
....
4. Mesi/di/esco/in/nei/primavera/spesso/bicicletta.
....
5. Ieri/un/sulle/programma/visto/specie/ho/in/d'estinzione/via.
....
6. È/casa/famiglia/della/Anna/quella/la/di.
....
7. Tempi/Romani/Parma/stata/è/fondata/ai/dei.
....
8. Luca/verrà/Spagna/dalla/mese/il/prossimo/trovarci/a.
....

3. Answer the following questions.

1. Di chi è quella moto? (di) Dell' amico di Giovanni.
2. Dove passate le vacanze di Natale? (a) .... mare, in Sicilia.
3. A chi telefoni? (a) .... idraulico.
4. Da dove viene Diego? (da) .... Colombia.
5. Dove si comprano i francobolli? (da) .... tabaccaio.
6. Quando sei nato? (in) .... 1971.

4. Complete the sentences.

1. C'è un gatto sul tetto.
2. Ho un vaso di fiori .... balcone.
3. Quella macchina è .... zio di Susy.
4. È il libro .... vicina di Maurizio.
5. Mia suocera lavora .... reparto di ortopedia .... ospedale di Padova.
6. Ieri sera sono andato .... cinema.
7. Il professore sta parlando .... differenze tra il passato prossimo e l'imperfetto.
8. .... calde sere d'estate è bello uscire a mangiare un gelato con gli amici.

Prepositions of place and movement.

Do you understand these two concepts? See Appendix 3: expressions of place.
For the use of the definite article, see Unità 5. For prepositions with the definite article, see Unità 23.

IN (*In*, at, to)

- To indicate position.
  - **Nel** tuo zaino ci sono troppi libri. *(There are too many books in your rucksack)*
- With shops, places of work and public offices, etc.
  - Claudio è **in** ufficio. *(Claudio is in the office)*
  - **Nella** macelleria di Piazza Garibaldi si può comprare dell'ottima carne. *(You can buy excellent meat at the butcher's in Piazza Garibaldi)*
  - Stasera Sandra e io andiamo **in** pizzeria. *(Sandra and I are going to the pizzeria tonight)*
  - I francobolli si comprano **in** posta o **in** tabaccheria. *(You can buy stamps at the post-office or at the tobacconist's)*
  - Ogni domenica alle ore 10 vado alla messa **nella** chiesa di Sant'Antonio. *(I go to mass at St. Antony's every Sunday at 10 o'clock)*

▶ See Unità 25 **da** for the use of: vado **dal** macellaio/vado **in** macelleria. *(I'm going to the bucher's)*

- With the names of continents, countries, regions and large islands.

▶ Without the definite article.
  - Chi viene **in** Europa ha la possibilità di visitare molti paesi ricchi di storia. *(Whoever comes to Europe can visit many countries rich in history)*
  - Mi piacerebbe vivere **in** Portogallo per un po' di tempo. *(I'd like to live in Portugal for a little while)*
  - **In** Emilia Romagna il tasso di disoccupazione è molto basso. *(The rate of unemployment in Emilia Romagna is very low)*
  - L'anno scorso ho trascorso le vacanze **in** Madagascar. *(Last year I spent my holidays in Madagascar)*

- With the names of squares, roads, etc.

▶ Without the definite article.
  - Abito **in** Via dei Pini. *(I live in Via dei Pini)*
  - **In** Piazza del Duomo a Parma ci sono opere artistiche di grande valore. *(There are great works of art in Parma's Piazza del Duomo)*

▶ With parts of the house.
  - Gianni è sceso **in** garage a pulire la bicicletta. *(Gianni has gone down to the garage to clean his bike)*
  - Preferisco mangiare con gli amici **in** soggiorno, perché **in** cucina c'è poco spazio. *(I'd rather eat with my friends in the living-room, as there is little room in the kitchen)*
  - **Nei** bagni inglesi normalmente non c'è il bidè. *(There isn't usually a bidet in an English bathroom)*

- With the following expressions:
  - **In** centro. **In** periferia. **In** campagna. **In** montagna. *(In the centre. In the suburbs. In the country. In the mountains.)*

A *(At, in)*

- With the names of cities, towns, villages and small islands.
  - Abito **a** Padova. *(I live in Padova)*
  - Quest'anno vado **a** Spoleto per il festival. *(I'm going to Spoleto for the festival this year)*
  - Non so cosa darei per vivere **all**'Isola d'Elba. *(I'd give anything to live on Isola d'Elba)*
- With the word **casa**.
  - Questa sera resto **a** casa. *(I'm staying at home this evening)*
  - Domani siamo invitati a cena **a** casa di Carlo. *(We've been invited to dinner at Carlo's house tomorrow)*
- Con le seguenti espressioni:

  A scuola. **All**'università. **Al** cinema. **A** teatro. **Al** mercato. **Al** ristorante. **Allo** stadio. **Al** mare.
  (At school. At university. At the cinema. At the theatre. At the market. At the restaurant. At the stadium. At the seaside)
  A destra. **A** sinistra. *(On the left. On the right)*
  All'estero. (Abroad) **Al** telefono. *(On the telephone)*

1. Choose the correct preposition.

1. Mariella vive ....*in*.... Argentina. a/in
2. .... gelateria Tropical fanno dei gelati squisiti. in/nella
3. .... appartamento di Stefano ci sono due bagni. in/nell'
4. .... Bologna c'è l'università più vecchia del mondo. a/in
5. Abito .... Via del Casale 12. a/in
6. Mi piace molto viaggiare .... estero. nell'/all'
7. Domani andiamo a cena .... casa di Veronica. a/nella
8. Vivere .... periferia è meno caro che vivere .... centro. in/a, in/a.

2. Complete the sentences with the correct preposition.

1. Mia cugina ha una casa ....*in*.... centro.
2. .... ristorante "Al Mare" si mangia dell'ottimo pesce.
3. Claudia vive .... Napoli.
4. I bambini vanno .... scuola alle 8.
5. Lorenzo va .... Australia in gennaio.
6. Di solito passo le vacanze .... montagna.
7. Giovanni deve essere .... suo ufficio alle 9.
8. Sono molti i posti che vorrei visitare .... America.

3. Match the sentences from the columns.

1. *Passo le vacanze di Natale*	a in ufficio.
2. Il Presidente delle Repubblica vive	b in una fabbrica di bottiglie di plastica.
3. Cristiano incontra i suoi clienti	c *in montagna.*
4. La scuola di lingue si trova	d in soggiorno.
5. Il ragazzo di Simona lavora	e a Roma.
6. La sera guardo spesso la televisione	f nella salumeria di Tonino.
7. Ho comprato dell'ottimo prosciutto	g all'università.
8. Negli Stati Uniti costa moltissimo studiare	h in Via Casa Bianca 66.

Movement - place of origin.

DA *(From)*

- Vengo **da** Londra, la più bella città d'Europa. *(I come from London, the most beautiful city in Europe)*
- Karl è tedesco, viene **da** Norimberga. *(Karl is German, he comes from Nurnberg)*

DA used together with a person's name or a profession or personal object pronoun takes on the meaning of **a casa di, nel negozio/ufficio/ecc. di**. *(at someone's house, shop, office, etc.)*

- Stasera vengo **da** te, ma prima passo **da** Roberto.
  (I'm coming to your house tonight, but I'm going to stop off at Robert's before)
- Sarò **dal** dentista alle 4 oggi pomeriggio. *(I'll be at the dentist's at 4 o'clock this afternoon)*

When talking about shops you can use either the shop owner's profession or the kind of shop in question.

- Vado **dal** macellaio. or: – Vado **in** macelleria. *(I'm going to the butcher's)*

DA... A... *(From........ to)*

- In treno si va **da** Milano **a** Bologna **in** due ore. *(It takes two hours from Milano to Bologna by train)*

SU *(On)*

Il gatto è **sulla** sedia.
(The cat is on the chair)

SOTTO *(Under)*

Il gatto è **sotto** la sedia.
(The cat is under the chair)

FRA/TRA *(Among, between)*

Il gatto dorme **tra** le sedie.
(The cat is sleeping between the chairs)

DIETRO *(Behind)*

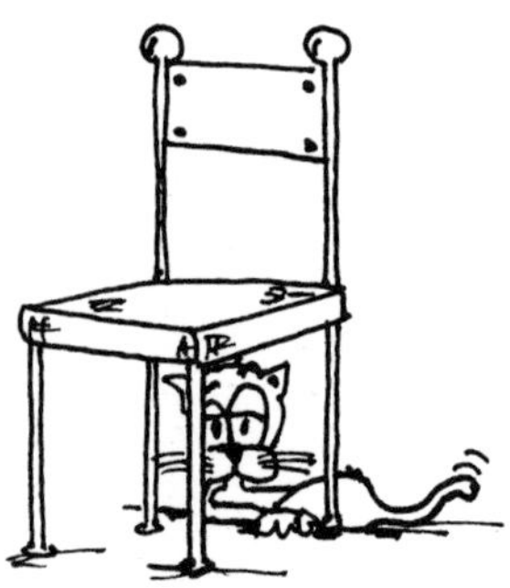

Il gatto è **dietro** la sedia.
(The cat is behind the chair)

DAVANTI A *(In front of)*

Il gatto gioca **davanti allo** specchio.
(The cat is playing in front of the mirror)

DENTRO *(In, inside)*

Il gatto dorme **dentro** la scatola.
(The cat is sleeping in/inside the box)

FUORI *(Outside)*

Il gatto dorme **fuori della** finestra.
(The cat is sleeping outside the window)

1. Complete the sentences with the correct form of the preposition DA.

1. Andiamo dal.......... dottore?
2. Jean viene .... Parigi.
3. Domani sono a cena .... mia nonna.
4. Questo è un registratore che viene .... Giappone.
5. Puoi andare .... fornaio a comprare un po' di pane.
6. Puoi passare .... me stasera?

2. Complete the sentences with the correct form of the preposition SU.

1. C'è un libro sul.......... banco.
2. Oggi c'è una fitta nebbia .... Pianura Padana.
3. Non c'è vita .... Luna.
4. Ho affittato una casetta .... quella collina.
5. D'inverno c'è spesso molta neve .... montagne della Valle d'Aosta.
6. Ci possono stare due persone .... mio motorino.

3. Look at the picture and choose the correct preposition to complete the sentences.

1. Il gatto è sulla.......... sedia.
Sulla, sotto la, davanti alla, tra le.

2. Il gatto è .... la sedia.
Fra, dietro, dentro, sotto.

3. Il gatto è .... la sedia.
Dentro, su, davanti, dietro.

4. Il gatto gioca .... specchio.
Dietro lo, davanti allo, dentro lo, sullo.

5. Il gatto dorme .... le sedie.
Fuori, davanti, tra, dietro.

6. Il gatto dorme .... la scatola.
Dietro, dentro, su, davanti.

ACCANTO A *(Next to)*

Il gatto è **accanto alla** finestra.
(The cat is next to the window)

DI FIANCO A *(Beside/side by side)*

I due gatti sono uno **di fianco all'**altro.
(The two cats are side by side)

PER/ATTRAVERSO *(Through, accross)*

Mi piace camminare **per/attraverso** il centro di Roma.
(I like walking through the centre of Roma)

FINO A *(Until, up to, as far as)*

Vada diritto **fino al** semaforo e poi volti a destra.
(Go straight on until the traffic lights and then turn right).

LUNGO *(Along)*

Che bello camminare **lungo** i canali di Venezia!
(Isn't it lovely walking along the canals in Venice)

VICINO A *(Near/Close to)*

LONTANO DA *(Far from)*

Milano si trova **vicino a** Torino. Venezia si trova **lontano da** Palermo.
(Milan is near Turin) (Venice is far from Palermo)

SOPRA *(On, above, over)*

Il libro è **sopra** il tavolo.
(The book is on the table)

1. Look at the pictures and choose the correct preposition to complete the sentences.

1. Il gatto è ...accanto... alla finestra.
   Fino, attraverso, lungo, accanto.

2. Il due gatti sono uno .... all'altro.
   Per, di fianco, attraverso, lungo.

3. Mi piace camminare .... il centro di Roma.
   Accanto, fino, per, lontano.

4. Vada dritto .... semaforo e poi volti a destra.
   Lungo, per, vicino, al, fino al.

5. Che bello camminare .... i canali di Venezia!
   Vicino a, lontano da, fino a, lungo.

6. Milano è .... Torino.
   Lungo, vicino a, per, di fianco.

2. Complete the sentences with one of the following prepositions of place: a, da, in, su, per, tra.

1. La giacca è ..sul....... letto.
2. Vivo .... Bologna.
3. Juan è spagnolo, viene .... Madrid.
4. Rimini è .... Romagna.
5. A che ora parti .... la Scozia?
6. Stasera vado .... ristorante.
7. Per andare .... Milano .... Roma, si passa .... Bologna.
8. Appena sono entrato .... casa, ho visto il regalo per il mio compleanno.
9. Il barbiere è laggiù, ... il giornalaio e il bar.
10. .... suo ufficio ci sono tre computer.
11. Devo andare .... medico perché ho spesso il mal di testa.
12. Chi è quella ragazza seduta .... Renzo e Simone?
13. L'estate scorsa ho trascorso le vacanze .... Monte Rosa.
14. Chicago è .... Stati Uniti.
15. Non è più possibile salire .... Torre di Pisa.

3. Complete the sentences with one of the following expressions of place: lungo, di fianco, vicino, lontano, davanti, dietro, dentro.

1. ...Dentro.... un vecchio baule di mia nonna ho trovato delle foto bellissime.
2. I vecchi passano molto tempo seduti .... una finestra.
3. Molte barche scendono spesso .... il fiume Po.
4. È brutto passare le vacanze di Natale .... da casa.
5. Bisogna stare .... agli amici nei momenti di difficoltà.
6. .... alla mia casa c'è un piccolo giardino.

A *(At)*

- When talking about the time.

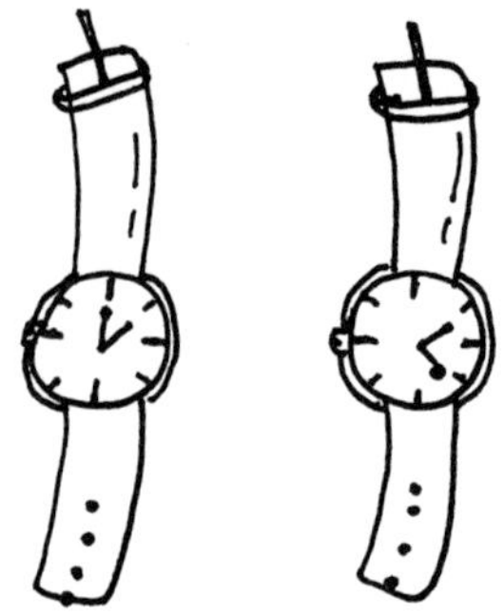

– Mi sveglio spesso **alle** 7. *(I often wake up at 7)*

IN *(In)*

- With the months of the year.

– Sono nato **in** ottobre. *(I was born in October)*

See Unità 17 for the time.

▶ Study the example.

– Sono nata **il** 20 dicembre 1971. *(I was born on the 20th of December 1971)*

When the full date is given a preposition is **not** required.

- With the seasons.
  – **In** primavera è bello fare passeggiate in campagna. *(In spring it's lovely going for walks in the country)*
- With years.
  – **Nel** 1995 il mese di maggio è stato molto brutto. Pioveva ogni giorno.
  (In 1995 the month of May was terrible. It rained every day)
- With centuries.
  – Ippolito Nievo è vissuto **nel** XIX secolo. *(Ippolito Nievo lived in the 19th century)*

▶ With the days of the week a preposition is **not** required.

– Linuccio ha fatto un esame **mercoledì** 14 giugno 1995. *(Linuccio did an exam on Wednesday 14th June 1995)*

When talking about repeated events the definite article is used before the day of the week.

– La domenica non si lavora. *(You don't work on Sundays)*

- **In** is also used to express the time necessary to do something.

– Ho fatto i compiti **in** due ore. = ci ho messo due ore a fare i compiti
(I did my homework in two hours = it took me two hours to do my homework)

– Si va da Perugia ad Assisi **in** 20 minuti. = ci vogliono 20 minuti da Perugia ad Assisi.
(You can go from Perugia to Assisi in 20 minutes = it takes 20 minutes from Perugia to Assisi)

PER *(For)*

- **Per** is used to talk about the length of time.

– Vado in vacanza **per** due settimane.
(I'm going on holiday for two weeks)

- It is also used for special holiday periods.
  – **Per** Natale vorrei andare a sciare. *(I'd like to go skiing for Christmas)*

TRA/FRA *(In/within)*

- **Tra** or **fra** are used to indicate the period between the present moment of time and the beginning of a future event.

– **Fra** venti minuti devo tornare a lavorare.
(I have to go back to work in twenty minutes)

1. Complete the sentences with a time preposition where necessary.

1. Il film inizia ...*alle*... 8,30.
2. I corsi all'università finiscono .... maggio.
3. Vado spesso a letto .... mezzanotte.
4. .... Pasqua vado in Spagna.
5. Molti italiani .... inverno fanno la settimana bianca.
6. Finirò questo libro .... un anno.
7. Sono nato .... il 16 ottobre.
8. .... sabato serà andrò al cinema.
9. Ho avuto l'influenza e non sono andato a lavorare .... una settimana.
10. Mio nonno era nato .... XIX secolo.

2. Correct the sentences where necessary.

1. Ieri sono andato a lavorare a 8.
   Ieri sono andato a lavorare alle 8
2. In 1985 sono stato in vacanza in Iugoslavia.
   ....
3. Giovedì finisco di lavorare al mezzogiorno.
   ....
4. In Natale molti italiani vanno in chiesa.
   ....
5. Le rose nascono fra primavera.
   ....
6. Fra due ore torno a casa.
   ....
7. In treno si va da Milano a Roma in cinque ore.
   ....
8. A Venerdì sera vado sempre in palestra.
   ....

3. Answer following questions about yourself.

1. Quando vai solitamente in vacanza?
   ....
2. A che ora ti svegli di solito la domenica?
   ....
3. A che ora vai a letto di solito alla sera?
   ....
4. In che mese è cominciato il corso d'italiano?
   ....
5. In che anno sei nato?
   ....
6. Quand'è il tuo compleanno?
   ....
7. Per quante ore alla settimana riesci a studiare l'italiano?
   ....
8. In che giorni hai lezione d'italiano?
   ....

DA *(Since/for)*

- **Da** is used to indicate the beginning of an action which is still happening in the present.

  – Costantino studia **dal** 1977. = Costantino ha cominciato a studiare nel 1977.
  (Constantino has been studying since 1977 = Constantino began to study in 1977)

▶ N.B. In Italian the verb is used in the present indicative.

DI *(In)*

- With parts of the day.

  – **Di** mattino è bello stare a letto. *(It's nice staying in bed in the morning)*

DA... A... *(From.......... to)*

- **Da... a** is used to indicate the length of time, specifying both the starting and finishing time.

– Ho dormito **dalle** 11 di ieri sera fino **all'**una di oggi pomeriggio.
(I slept from 11 o'clock last night until 1 o'clock this afternoon)

FINO A *(Until)*

- **Fino a** is used to indicate the moment an on going action comes to an end.

– Ieri sera ho guardato la TV **fino alle** 2.30.
(I watched TV until 2.30 last night)

PRIMA *(Before)*

– **Prima di** andare in vacanza./**Prima delle** vacanze, Giorgio Rossi era molto depresso.
(Before going on holiday/Before his holiday, Giorgio Rossi was very depressed)

▶ **Prima** is followed by the preposition **di**. If the word **prima** is followed by a verb, then usually the *infinitive* of the verb is used, but if the subject of the two sentences changes, then it is necessary to use *prima + che + subjunctive*. See Unità 70 and 89.

– **Prima che** Giovanna arrivi, Patrizia pulirà la casa.
(Before Giovanna arrives. Patrizia will clean the house.)

DURANTE *(During)* **MENTRE** *(While)*

– **Durante** le vacanze Giorgio Rossi pensava al suo futuro.
(During his holiday Giorgio Rossi thought about his future)
– **Mentre** era in vacanza, Giorgio Rossi pensava al suo futuro.
(While he was on holiday, Giorgio Rossi thought about his future)

▶ **Durante** is followed by a noun. **Mentre** is followed by a complete sentence; the accompanying verb is never used in the infinitive form.

DOPO *(After)*

– **Dopo** le vacanze/**Dopo** essere tornato dalle vacanze, la vita di Giorgio Rossi è cambiata completamente.
(After his holiday/After returning from his holiday, Giorgio Rossi's life changed completely.)

▶ If the word **dopo** is followed by a verb, then usually the *perfect infinitive* form of the verb is used, but if the subject of the two sentences changes, then it is necessary to use *dopo + che + indicative*. See Unità 88.

– **Dopo che** sua madre era arrivata, Paolo uscì a far la spesa.
(After his mother arrived, Paolo went out to do some shopping)

1. Choose the correct preposition to complete the sentences.

1. Costantino studia *dal*..........1977. — Dal, per, di, fra.
2. Ho dormito .... 11 di ieri sera fino .... una di oggi pomeriggio. — Per di, dalle all', fino a dall', in a.
3. Ieri sera ho guardato la TV .... 2.30. — Prima, dopo, fino alle, durante.
4. .... andare in vacanza, Giorgio Rossi era molto depresso. — Dopo, mentre, di, prima di.
5. .... le vacanze Giorgio Rossi pensava al suo futuro. — Mentre, durante, fino a, prima.
6. .... le vacanze la vita di Giorgio Rossi è cambiata completamente. — Fino a, dopo, prima, mentre.

2. Complete the sentences with one of the following time prepositions: di, a, da, in, per, fra.

1. *Nel*........ 1994 non è mai nevicato.
2. Ti ricordi che .... tre settimane è il compleanno di Elisa?
3. L'autunno dura .... settembre .... dicembre.
4. Gioco a calcio .... quando ero bambino.
5. .... notte mi piace leggere fino a tardi.
6. La lezione inizia .... 8.30.

3. Complete the sentences with one of the following time expressions: prima, dopo, mentre, durante, fino a.

1. *Dopo*....... un anno in Africa, Ilaria è tornata in Italia.
2. .... la recita un attore è caduto e lo spettacolo è stato interrotto.
3. Devo andare in banca .... di partire per le vacanze.
4. Lavoro .... sabato e poi starò in ferie per dieci giorni.
5. .... la pasta cuoce, bisogna mescolarla più volte.
6. .... aver ascoltato l'ultimo disco del mio gruppo preferito, sono corso a comprarlo.

4. Read the answers and write the questions.

1. *Da quando studi italiano*..?
   Dal 1992.
2. ....?
   Da giovedì.
3. ....?
   Dal 1995.
4. ....?
   Da quando ero bambino.
5. ....?
   Dall'estate scorsa.
6. ....?
   Dalle 5 di questo pomeriggio.
7. ....?
   Di pomeriggio.
8. ....?
   Di notte.

In this unit a lot of terminology is used. Don't worry about it too much!
Study the examples carefully and check with Appendix 3.

DI *(of, about, than, by)*

- Questa è la casa **di** Mario. *(This is Mario's house)* → *possession*
- Un disco **di** Luciano Pavarotti. *(A record by Luciano Pavarotti)* → *author*
- Una lattina **di** birra. *(A can of beer)* → *category*
- Una scultura **di** legno. *(A wooden sculpture)* → *material*
- Un gatto **di** sette chili. *(A cat weighing 7 kilos)* → *size*
- Un vecchio **di** 90 anni. *(A 90-year old man)* → *age*
- Silvia mi ha parlato **del** suo viaggio. *(Silvia told me about her trip)* → *topic*
- Giovanni è più giovane **di** Marco. *(Giovanni is younger than Marco)* → *comparison* (See Unità 59).

A *(to, at, with)*

- Ho dato l'invito **a** Giuseppe. *(I gave the invitation to Giuseppe)* → *indirect object*
- Non sono mai salito su un treno **a** vapore. *(I've never been on a steam train)* → *means*
- Nadia si è sposata **a** 25 anni. *(Nadia got married at 25)* → *age*
- Una maglietta **a** righe. *(A striped T-shirt)* → *kind*
- Un piatto di spaghetti **al** burro e un gelato **al** limone. *(A plate of spaghetti with butter and lemon flavoured ice-cream)* → *flavour and kind of disk*

DA *(from, out of, by)*

- Ho comprato un costume **da** bagno blu. *(I've bought a blue swimming costume)* → *purpose*
- **Da** piccolo volevo fare il medico. *(When I was little I wanted to be a doctor)* → *condition*
- Una banconota **da** 10 euro. *(A 10 euro banknote)* → *amount*
- Ieri ho pianto **dalla** rabbia. *(I cried out of anger yesterday)* → *cause*
- La Divina Commedia è stata scritta **da** Dante. *(The Divine Comedy was written by Dante)* → *agent* (See Unità 75).

▶ With **lontano** and **diverso** *(far from* and *different from/to)*

- Napoli è diversa **da** Milano. *(Naples is different from Milan)*
- Palermo si trova lontano **da** Torino. *(Palermo is far from Turin)*

1. Complete the sentences with the correct form of the preposition DI.

1. Questa è la borsa ..del......... tuo professore.
2. Qual è il nome .... quello studente.
3. Dov'è la macchina .... caffè?
4. Ho letto un articolo interessante sulla terza pagina .... giornale .... oggi.
5. Ieri ho visitato il museo .... arte moderna.
6. Ti ricordi l'indirizzo .... tua sorella?
7. Mi passi quella bottiglia .... vino, per favore?
8. Sta facendo freddo, mi sono messo una maglia .... lana.
9. Carla mi ha raccontato .... sua esperienza in Cina.
10. Fausto è più basso .... sua amica.

2. Complete the sentences with the correct form of the preposition A.

1. Ho detto tutto .alla........ tua ragazza.
2. Hai telefonato .... Ditta Fraschetti?
3. L'anno prossimo passerò le vacanze su una barca .... vela.
4. Che buona la tua torta .... cioccolato!
5. Hai offerto qualcosa da bere .... tuoi amici?
6. Silvio si è laureato .... 23 anni.
7. Guarda quella ragazza con la camicia .... quadri: è mia sorella.
8. Sai preparare la pizza .... quattro formaggi?

3. Complete the sentences with the correct form of the preposition DA.

1. ....Da....... chi è stata composta l'*Aida*?
2. Gianni ha comprato una bicicletta .... corsa.
3. Sono andato in banca a ritirare un assegno .... un milione.
4. Cosa farai .... grande?
5. La polizia è stata chiamata .... vicini di casa.
6. Tremavo .... paura.

4. Complete the sentences with the correct preposition. Choose from DI, A, DA.

1. ....Di........... chi è quel libro?
2. Hai parlato .... tua madre .... tuo nuovo progetto?
3. Ho preso le tue scarpe .... ginnastica.
4. Per fare la pasta .... pizza ci vuole un po' .... lievito.
5. .... quanti anni sei sposata?
6. Ti piace la mia giacca .... cotone .... righe?
7. Michela mi vuole parlare .... sua storia con Mario.
8. In Italia si può prendere la patente .... guida .... 18 anni.
9. In quel ristorante fanno delle tagliatelle .... funghi buonissime.
10. Ho dato il regalo .... matrimonio .... Francesca e Beppe.

In this unit a lot of terminology is used. Don't worry about it too much!

Study the examples carefully and check whit Appendix 3.

IN *(By)*

- Vado spesso all'università **in** bicicletta.
  (I often go to university by bike) ➜ *means of transport*

CON *(With)*

- Domani esco **con** Natalia.
  (I'm going out with Natalia tomorrow) ➜ *company*
- Luigi parla **con** un forte accento siciliano.
  (Luigi speaks with a strong Sicilian accent) ➜ *manner.*
- Un bimbo **con** i capelli ricci.
  (A boy with curly hair) ➜ *kind*
- Mi piace bere un bicchiere di rum **con** ghiaccio.
  (I like drinking rum with ice) ➜ *union*

Senza is the opposite of ***con***

- Mi piace bere il rum **senza** ghiaccio. *(I like drinking rum without ice)*

SU *(About, on)*

- Ieri ho visto un film **su** Malcolm X.
  (Yesterday I saw a film about Malcolm X) ➜ *topic*
  Sandra è ormai **sulla** trentina.
  (Sandra is about thirty now) ➜ *a rough estimate of age, prices and quantity*

PER *(In order to, for)*

- Bisogna lavorare **per** vivere
  (You need to work in order to live) ➜ *purpose*
- Ho comprato una macchina usata **per** 10 milioni.
  (I bought a second-hand car for 10 million) ➜ *price*
- Ogni giovane deve studiare **per** il proprio futuro.
  (Every young person has to study for his own future) ➜ *advantage/disadvantage*

With the following expressions:

per esempio,	*(for example)*
per caso,	*(by chance)*
per fortuna,	*(fortunately)*
per piacere/favore,	*(please)*
per telefono.	*(on the phone)*

FRA/TRA *(Among, between, out of)*

- **Fra** i libri che ho letto di recente "Los pasos pedidos" è il più interessante.
  (Out of all the books I've read recently "Los pasos perdidos" is the most interesting) ➜ *partitive*

1. Complete the sentence with either IN or CON and a word from the box below.

1. Mi piace uscire la sera *con gli amici* .
2. La maggior parte degli italiani va a lavorare ....
3. Chi è quel ragazzo .... ?
4. Da Milano a Londra ci vuole un'ora e mezza ....
5. Carina quella ragazza .... !
6. Lo preferisce .... ?
7. Carlos parla italiano .... brasiliano.
8. Gli studenti spesso non ascoltano ....

attenzione	i capelli biondi	macchina	ghiaccio	accento	aereo	tua sorella	gli amici

2. Complete the sentences with the correct form of either SU or PER.

1. Quel signore deve essere già *sulla* settantina.
2. Sto leggendo un libro .... indios del Brasile.
3. Ho comprato un regalo .... mio fratello.
4. Ho venduto il mio computer .... ottocentomila lire.
5. Rifletti .... quello che ti ho detto!
6. Mi puoi chiamare alle otto .... favore?
7. Filippo lavora .... una società multinazionale.

REVISION EXERCISE: PREPOSITIONS

3. Complete the sentences, where necessary, with one of the following prepositions: DI, A, DA, IN, CON, SU, PER, TRA/FRA.

1. Robert viveva *in* Italia, ma poi è tornato *negli* Stati Uniti.
2. Domani arriva la ragazza .... Piero.
3. Mi piace molto viaggiare .... treno.
4. Hai telefonato .... tua madre?
5. Hai parlato .... il tuo capo?
6. Ho venduto la mia vecchia casa .... duecento milioni?
7. Sono andato .... cinema .... un vecchio amico.
8. .... primavera nascono le foglie .... alberi.
9. L'anno prossimo andiamo .... Berlino.
10. Ieri sera ho fatto una passeggiata .... centro.
11. .... Giovedì c'è la finale .... Coppa Uefa.
12. Dopo la partita andremo .... mangiare una pizza.
13. Questa sera vado .... cena .... Luca.
14. Ci sono tanti pregiudizi nei confronti .... persone .... i capelli rossi.
15. Devo andare .... salumiere, ma non ne ho voglia.
16. Ho comprato un disco .... il compleanno .... Stefano.
17. La Seconda Guerra Mondiale è finita .... Italia .... il 25 Aprile 1945.
18. Vado .... vacanza .... due settimane.
19. Quando torno .... vacanze, dovrò partire .... la Spagna .... lavoro.
20. .... due ore finirò questo lavoro e andrò finalmente .... casa .... Marzia.

Study the picture.

– Oggi a pranzo **ho mangiato** un buon piatto di pesce.
(At lunch time today I ate a lovely plate of fish)

The **passato prossimo** is formed with the present indicative of *essere* or *avere* + the *past participle* of the main verb.

Many verbs have a regular form of the **past participle**.

-ARE	cantare *(sing)*	cant**ato**
-ERE	credere *(believe)*	cred**uto**
-IRE	dormire *(sleep)*	dorm**ito**

Here is a list of the irregular **past participles** of many common verbs.

accendere *(turn on)*	*acceso*	mettere *(put)*	*messo*	risolvere *(solve)*	*risolto*
aprire *(open)*	*aperto*	morire *(die)*	*morto*	rispondere *(answer)*	*risposto*
bere *(drink)*	*bevuto*	muovere *(move)*	*mosso*	rompere *(break)*	*rotto*
chiedere *(ask)*	*chiesto*	nascere *(be born)*	*nato*	scegliere *(choose)*	*scelto*
chiudere *(close)*	*chiuso*	nascondere *(hide)*	*nascosto*	scrivere *(write)*	*scritto*
correggere *(correct)*	*corretto*	offrire *(offer)*	*offerto*	succedere *(happen)*	*successo*
correre *(run)*	*corso*	perdere *(lose)*	*perso (perduto)*	togliere *(remove)*	*tolto*
cuocere *(cook)*	*cotto*	piacere *(like)*	*piaciuto*	tradurre *(translate)*	*tradotto*
decidere *(decide)*	*deciso*	piangere *(cry)*	*pianto*	uccidere *(kill)*	*ucciso*
dire *(say/tell)*	*detto*	porre *(place)*	*posto*	vedere *(see)*	*visto (veduto)*
dividere *(divide)*	*diviso*	prendere *(take)*	*preso*	venire *(come)*	*venuto*
essere *(be)*	*stato*	ridere *(laugh)*	*riso*	vincere *(win)*	*vinto*
fare *(do/make)*	*fatto*	rimanere *(stay)*	*rimasto*	vivere *(live)*	*vissuto*
leggere *(read)*	*letto*				

Past participle agreements.

Study the following examples.

– Gloria **è** andat**a** in discoteca sabato sera. *(Gloria went to the disco on Saturday evening)*
– **Siamo** tornat**i** dalle vacanze da poco e ora non abbiamo voglia di lavorare.
(We haven't been back from our holidays for long and now we don't feel like working)

When **essere** is used the *past participle* agrees with the *subject,* both in number (singular or plural) and gender (masculine or feminine).

Osserva l'esempio: – Cinzia **ha** ordinat**o** una birra gelata. *(Cinzia has ordered a really cold beer)*
When **avere** is used there is usually no need for past participle agreement.

When the *past participle* follows a *direct object* the agreement is optional.

– **Vi** hanno sentit**o/i** cantare giovedì sera a teatro. *(They heard you sing at the theatre on Thursday evening)*

Exception: When the pronouns **lo, la, l', li, le,** are used with **avere**, then the agreement is necessary.

1. Write the correct form of the past participle for the following regular verbs.

1. Mangiare ....mangiato........
2. Parlare ....
3. Credere ....
4. Finire ....
5. Visitare ....
6. Ripetere ....
7. Studiare ....
8. Vendere ....

2. Write the correct form of the past participle for the following irregular verbs.

1. Aprire ....aperto........................
2. Correre ....
3. Chiedere ....
4. Risolvere ....
5. Chiudere ....
6. Dire ....
7. Essere ....
8. Fare ....
9. Prendere ....
10. Scrivere ....
11. Rispondere ....
12. Mettere ....

3. Rewrite the sentences using the passato prossimo. Take care with the verb agreements.

1. Questa sera gioco a calcio con i miei amici.
   Ieri sera ho .giocato a calcio con i miei amici...... .
2. L'estate prossima Luca va in Venezuela.
   L'estate scorsa Luca è ....
3. Stasera guardo la televisione.
   Ieri sera ho ....
4. Oggi fa bello.
   Ieri ha ....
5. Penso a te tutti i giorni.
   Ieri ho ....
6. Entriamo a scuola alle 8.
   Ieri siamo ....
7. Franca arriva domani alle 6.
   .... è .... ieri alle 6.
8. Domani i tuoi genitori partono per la Francia.
   Ieri .... sono ....

4. Complete the sentences with the correct ending of the past participle.

1. Ieri sera ho mangiat..o.... una pizza.
2. Giovanna è andat......... in montagna domenica scorsa.
3. Simona e Roberto si sono sposat......... in marzo.
4. Abbiamo vist......... un film interessante ieri sera.
5. Ho comprat......... un vestito nuovo.
6. Vi ha chiamat......... Mirella?
7. Hai sentito Sandra? Sì, l'ho chiamat.......... stamattina.
8. Siamo andat......... a Parigi, ma non siamo salit.......... sulla Tour Eiffel.

The **passato prossimo** is used to talk about actions related to present time.

- It is used to talk about actions that take place in an unfinished time period.

- It is used to express a finished action that took place in the distant past but which still has some result in the present.
  - Ieri sera **ho mangiato** troppo e non **sono riuscito** a dormire tutta la notte!
    (I ate too much yesterday evening and didn't sleep all night)

▶ In Northern Italy, the passato prossimo is used in spoken language, instead of the passato remoto, to talk about a past action. The passato remoto is now used mainly for written Italian.
  - Sette anni fa **sono andato** in Nicaragua. *(I went to Nicaragua seven years ago)*

When forming the **passato prossimo**, the auxiliary verb **essere** is used in the following cases:

- With **intransitive verbs.** These are verbs that do not have a direct object. (See Appendix 3).
  The majority of these verbs fall into the following categories:
  - **verbs indicating movement** ➜ andare, arrivare, tornare, ecc. *(go, arrive, return,* etc.*)*
  - **verbs indicating state** ➜ stare, rimanere, ecc. *(be, stay,* etc.*)*
  - **verbs indicating a change of state** ➜ diventare, nascere, morire, ecc. *(become, be born, die,* etc.*)*
- **reflexive verbs:** – **Mi sono** appena **alzato** e sono già stanco. *(I have just got up and I'm tired already)*
- ***essere*** is also used with other verbs:
  - **Sono bastati** dieci minuti per tornare a casa.
    (I only needed 10 minutes to get home) ➜ bastare *(be enough/need)*
  - Mi è **piaciuta** molto la festa di sabato sera.
    (I like the party on Saturday evening a lot) ➜ piacere *(like)*

Essere is also used with the following common verbs:
sembrare *(seem),* parere *(seem/think),* accadere/succedere *(happen),* costare *(cost),* mancare *(miss),* dipendere *(depend),* dispiacere *(displease/mind),* toccare *(touch),* occorrere *(to be necessary).*

▶ See Unità 31, for the **subject** and **past participle** agreements.

When forming the **passato prossimo**, the auxiliary verb **avere** is used in the following cases:

- with **transitive verb**. These are verbs which are followed by a direct object. (See Appendix 3):
  - Ieri **ho mangiato** le prime fragole della stagione. *(Yesterday I ate the first strawberries of the season.)*

With some werbs the auxiliary **avere** is required when the verb is used transitively, i.e. verb + direct object.
  - **Ho** cominciato il mio nuovo libro la settimana scorsa. *(I started my new book last week)*
  - **Ho** finito il primo e ora prendo un piatto di carne ai ferri.
    (I've finished the first course and I'll have some grilled meat now)

However, when such verbs are used intransitively, i.e. the verb is not followed by an object, then the auxiliary **essere** is used.
  - Il film **è** cominciato mezz'ora fa. *(The film started half an hour ago)*
  - Il corso **è** finito in anticipo oggi. *(The course finished early today)*

Here is a list of other verbs that can take either the auxiliary **essere** (when used intransitively) or **avere** (when used transitively): scendere *(go down/get off)*, salire *(go up/get on)*, passare *(go past)*, continuare *(continue)*, bruciare *(burn)*, saltare *(jump)*, cambiare *(change)*, aumentare *(increase)*, diminuire *(reduce, decrease)*.

Study the following examples:
  - Ieri non **sono** potuto **andare** al mare, perché pioveva.
    (Yesterday I wasn't able to go to the seaside because it was raining).
  - **Ho** dovuto **mangiare** tutto, per non offendere il cuoco.
    (I had to eat everything, so as not to offend the cook)

With the verbs **potere**, **volere**, and **dovere** the auxiliary required depends on the verb that follows.

▶ In spoken Italian the auxiliary verb **avere** is used more and more frequently regardless of the verb that follows.

1. Put the words into order and rewrite the sentences with the correct verb form.

1. Ieri/coca/fredda/bere/male/stare/e/una.
   Ieri ho bevuto una coca fredda e sono stato male .
2. Italia/scorso/molti/visitare/l'/l'/turisti/anno.
   ....
3. Fare/delle/bellissime/in/vacanze/mia moglie/ed/Sardegna/io.
   ....
4. Praga/vedere/museo/a/un/interessante/molto/Silvia.
   ....
5. Divorziarsi/mese/il/Barbara/scorso.
   ....
6. Ieri/fabbriche/rimanere/le/chiuse/sciopero/per.
   ....
7. Aspettare/ieri/Federica/io/alle/ma/10/fino/non/arrivare/sera.
   ....
8. Questa/vedere/mio/mattina/cugino/alla/autobus/dell'/fermata.
   ....

2. Complete the letter with the verbs from the box below. Use the present or passato prossimo.

Caro Tom,
Come ....*va*.....? ....2.............. la tua lettera questa mattina e ti scrivo immediatamente.
E così ....3............... l'università e hai trovato un lavoro in Mozambico. Ti piace? E i tuoi genitori cosa ....4.............. della tua nuova vita? Sicuramente non deve essere facile per loro sapere che tu ....5.............., in un paese così lontano. Io ....6................ bene. ....7.............. anch'io un nuovo lavoro che mi ....8.............. molto, anche se non ho molto tempo libero. Ieri per esempio ....9............. di lavorare alle 8 di sera e ....10............. a casa stanchissimo. Alle ....11............ a letto e ....12............ fino alle 7 questa mattina. Scrivimi presto e buona fortuna!

dormire	andare	ricevere	abitare	stare	finire	trovare	pensare	piacere	finire	arrivare	andare

3. Read the answers and write the question.

1. *A che ora ti sei svegliato* ?
   Questa mattina alle 8. Ma di solito alle 7.
2. .... ?
   Sì, ho preso un caffè e ho mangiato una brioche.
3. .... ?
   No, ho preso l'autobus.
4. .... ?
   No, sono rimasto in ufficio, perché ho ricominciato alle 2.
5. .... ?
   Alle 7. Ho fatto un'ora di straordinario.
6. .... ?
   Alle 7,30.
7. .... ?
   Un piatto di spaghetti al pomodoro e un po' di formaggio.
8. .... ?
   Alle 11.

Regular verbs

I - ARE: cantare *(sing)*		II - ERE: vedere *(see)*		III a - IRE: sentire *(hear)*		III b - IRE: finire *(finish)*	
(io)	cant - **avo**	(io)	ved - **evo**	(io)	sent - **ivo**	(io)	fin - **ivo**
(tu)	cant - **avi**	(tu)	ved - **evi**	(tu)	sent - **ivi**	(tu)	fin - **ivi**
(lui, lei)	cant - **ava**	(lui, lei)	ved - **eva**	(lui, lei)	sent - **iva**	(lui, lei)	fin - **iva**
(noi)	cant - **avamo**	(noi)	ved - **evamo**	(noi)	sent - **ivamo**	(noi)	fin - **ivamo**
(voi)	cant - **avate**	(voi)	ved - **evate**	(voi)	sent - **ivate**	(voi)	fin - **ivate**
(loro)	cant - **avano**	(loro)	ved - **evano**	(loro)	sent - **ivano**	(loro)	fin - **ivano**

The verbs *essere* and *avere*

AVERE *(have)*		ESSERE *(be)*	
(io)	**avevo**	(io)	**ero**
(tu)	**avevi**	(tu)	**eri**
(lui, lei)	**aveva**	(lui, lei)	**era**
(noi)	**avevamo**	(noi)	**eravamo**
(voi)	**avevate**	(voi)	**eravate**
(loro)	**avevano**	(loro)	**erano**

Irregular verbs

DIRE *(say)*	(io)	**dicevo**	**FARE** *(do, make)*	(io)	**facevo**	**PORRE** *(put/place)*	(io)	**ponevo**
	(tu)	**dicevi**		(tu)	**facevi**		(tu)	**ponevi**
	(lui, lei)	**diceva**		(lui, lei)	**faceva**		(lui, lei)	**poneva**
	(noi)	**dicevamo**		(noi)	**facevamo**		(noi)	**ponevamo**
	(voi)	**dicevate**		(voi)	**facevate**		(voi)	**ponevate**
	(loro)	**dicevano**		(loro)	**facevano**		(loro)	**ponevano**
TRADURRE *(translate)*	(io)	**traducevo**	**TRARRE** *(pull, draw)*	(io)	**traevo**			
	(tu)	**traducevi**		(tu)	**traevi**			
	(lui, lei)	**traduceva**		(lui, lei)	**traeva**			
	(noi)	**traducevamo**		(noi)	**traevamo**			
	(voi)	**traducevate**		(voi)	**traevate**			
	(loro)	**traducevano**		(loro)	**traevano**			

▶ Also: **bevevo.** *(I drank)*

When using the imperfect the main stress falls on the second syllable from the end, for example:
io dicevo, noi cantavamo, voi eravate, ecc. *(I said, we sang, you were,* etc.*)*

▶ The third person plural (**loro**) has the stress on the third vowel from the end, for example:
loro dicevano, cantavano, erano, ecc. *(they said, sang, were,* etc.*)*

1. Write the verbs in the correct form of the imperfect.

1. Chiedere *io chiedevo*
2. Parlare ....
3. Andare ....
4. Mangiare ....
5. Finire ....
6. Partire ....
7. Dovere ....
8. Fare ....
9. Dire ....
10. Essere ....

2. Mark the stress on the verbs.

1. Andav**à**mo.
2. Sentivo.
3. Ascoltavate.
4. Correvi.
5. Bevevano.
6. Era.
7. Guardavano.
8. Prendeva.

3. Complete the sentences with the correct form of the imperfect. Use the verbs from the box below.

1. Quando *avevo* 12 anni, ... in una squadra di baseball.
2. All'età di 28 anni Nicola .... ancora all'università.
3. Da piccoli mio fratello ed io .... spesso le vacanze sul Lago di Garda.
4. La mia famiglia tanti anni fa .... una casetta in collina.
5. Giulio .... così innamorato di Elena che le .... sempre lettere lunghissime.
6. Questa mattina quando mi sono alzato, ...
7. Da bambino .... in centro.
8. Camilla .... 20 sigarette al giorno; poi improvvisamente ha smesso.

passare	nevicare	fumare	avere	abitare	giocare	andare	essere	avere	scrivere

■ The **imperfect** is used in the following cases:

● Study the examples..

1 2
- Mentre **facevo** colazione, è arrivata (arrivò) mia madre.
  (While I was having breakfast, my mother arrived)

1 2
- **Studiavo** all'Università di Firenze, quando scoppiò (è scoppiata) la Seconda Guerra Mondiale.
  (I was studying at Florence University, when the Second World War broke out)

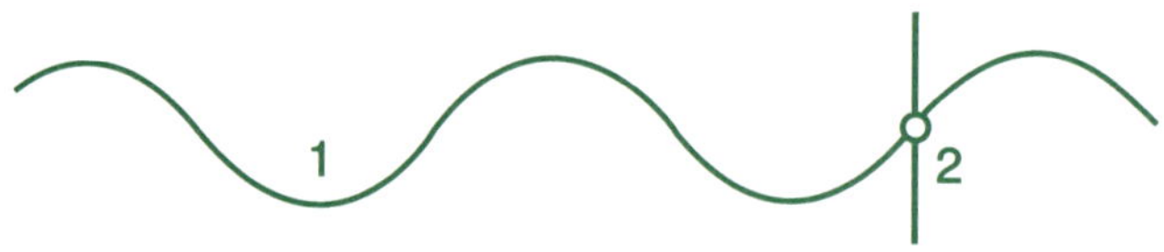

To talk about an on-going action in the past, "interrupted" by another event (the latter expressed with the **passato remoto** or **passato prossimo**).

● Study the examples.

- Quando **ero** piccolo, **andavo** spesso a giocare a calcio.
  (When I was young, I often used to/would often go and play football)
- D'estate mi **piaceva** leggere libri in giardino.
  (In the summer I used to enjoy reading books in the garden)

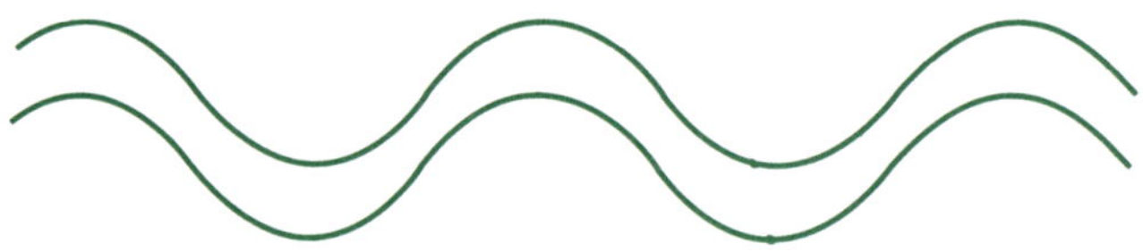

To talk about a habitual or repeated action in the past.

● Study the examples.

- Mentre **lavoravamo**, il cane ci **guardava** e **scodinzolava**.
  (While we are working, the dog was wagging ist tail and watching us)
- Federico **dormiva**, Laura **stirava** e nessuno **si preoccupava** del piccolo Alfredo, che **piangeva**.
  (Federico was sleeping, Laura was ironing and no one bothered about little Alfredo, who was crying)

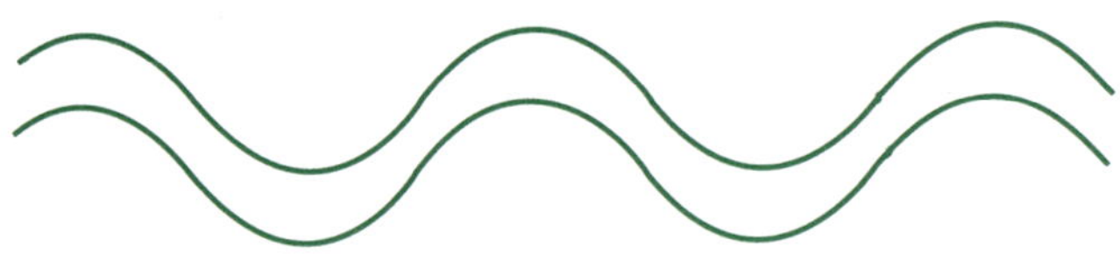

To talk about two or more actions taking place simultaneously in the past over an indefinite time period.

● For the use of the imperfect in a hypothetical clause, see Unità 74.

● For the use of the structure STARE + gerund with the imperfect, see Unità 52.

1. Match the sentences from the columns.

1. *Mentre tornavo a casa,*
2. Quando era bambina
3. Mentre facevo la doccia,
4. In estate mio padre lavorava
5. Ieri sera mentre leggevo il giornale,
6. Quando andavo a scuola,
7. Quando il film è cominciato,
8. Appena smetteva di lavorare,

a e noi bambini andavamo al mare.
b è arrivato Amilcare.
c arrivavo spesso in ritardo.
d *ho incontratro Francesco e suo padre.*
e Fernando andava subito in bar.
f è andata via la luce.
g Cristina andava spesso in piscina.
h c'erano poche persone nel cinema.

2. Put the words into order and rewrite the sentences using the correct verb forms.

1. Quando /film/guardare/d'amore/Isabella/piangere.
Quando guardava film d'amore, Isabella piangeva
2. Quando/Lorenzo/partire/madre/essere/sempre/sua/triste.
...
3. Mentre/la/preparare/ieri/cena/tagliarsi/un/dito/sera/mi.
...
4. Bello/essere/parlare/mio/con/nonno/perché/sempre/storie/interessanti/raccontare/delle.
...
5. Mentre/magiare/arrivare/Tommaso/sera/ieri/noi.
...
6. Ogni/mia/sera/leggere/madre/guardare/mio/televisione/la/padre/noi/e/compiti/fare/i.
...

3. Correct the mistakes where necessary.

1. Quando ho avuto 16 anni, andavo spesso in discoteca.
Quando avevo 16 anni, andavo spesso in discoteca
2. Prendevo la patente a 18 anni.
...
3. Mentre Lucia mi ha baciato, è arrivata la mia ragazza.
...
4. Ieri sera camminavo per il centro, quando ho visto un ragazzo che rubava una bicicletta.
...
5. Questa mattina c'era il sole e contemporaneamente è piovuto.
...
6. Quando iniziava la Seconda Guerra Mondiale, mia mamma aveva un anno.
...

4. Complete the sentences.

1. Da piccolo *mi piaceva molto la Nutella*
2. Mentre Gabriele cantava, Paola ...
3. Quando faceva bel tempo, ...
4. Mia nonna mi ha telefonato mentre ...
5. Quando andavo a scuola ...
6. Quando gli italiani erano più poveri ...
7. Sono andato a Parigi mentre ...
8. Quando la vedevo, ...

Study the picture.

– Alessandro Manzoni **scrisse** I Promessi Sposi nel XIX secolo.
(Alessandro Manzoni wrote The Betrothed in the 19th century)

Regular verbs

I - ARE: cantare *(sing)*	**II - ERE: vendere** *(sell)*	**III a - IRE: sentire** *(hear)*	**III b - IRE: finire** *(finish)*
(io) cant - **ai**	(io) vend - **ei**	(io) sent - **ii**	(io) fin - **ii**
(tu) cant - **asti**	(- **etti**)	(tu) sent - **isti**	(tu) fin - **isti**
(lui, lei) cant - **ò**	(tu) vend - **esti**	(lui, lei) sent - **ì**	(lui, lei) fin - **ì**
(noi) cant - **ammo**	(lui, lei) vend - **é**	(noi) sent - **immo**	(noi) fin - **immo**
(voi) cant - **aste**	(- **ette**)	(voi) sent - **iste**	(voi) fin - **iste**
(loro) cant - **arono**	(noi) vend - **emmo**	(loro) sent - **irono**	(loro) fin - **irono**
	(voi) vend - **este**		
	(loro) vend - **erono**		
	(- **ettero**)		

Even with the third person plural, the word stress is placed on the first vowel of the ending for the **passato remoto**. for example: cantarono, vendettero, sentirono, etc. (not cantarono, etc.).

Verbs *essere* and *avere*

AVERE		**ESSERE**	
(io)	**ebbi**	(io)	**fui**
(tu)	**avesti**	(tu)	**fosti**
(lui, lei)	**ebbe**	(lui, lei)	**fu**
(noi)	**avemmo**	(noi)	**fummo**
(voi)	**aveste**	(voi)	**foste**
(loro)	**ebbero**	(loro)	**furono**

Common irregular verbs

bere *(drink)*	*bevvi/bevetti*	mettere *(put)*	*misi*	scrivere *(write)*	*scrissi*
cadere *(fall)*	*caddi*	nascere *(be born)*	*nacque*	spegnere *(put out)*	*spensi*
chiedere (ask)	*chiesi*	perdere *(lose)*	*persi*	stare *(be, stay)*	*stetti*
conoscere *(know)*	*conobbi*	prendere *(take)*	*presi*	tenere *(hold)*	*tenni*
correre *(run)*	*corsi*	rendere *(return)*	*resi*	vedere *(see)*	*vidi*
dare *(give)*	*diedi (detti)*	rispondere *(answer)*	*risposi*	venire *(come)*	*venni*
decidere *(decide)*	*decisi*	rompere *(break)*	*ruppi*	vivere *(live)*	*vissi*
fare *(make/do)*	*feci*	sapere *(know)*	*seppi*	volere *(want)*	*volli*

In most cases only **io**, **lui/lei**, **loro**, adopt the irregular forms, while the other persons maintain the infinitive stem.

Io *ruppi*	noi rompemmo
tu rompesti	voi rompeste
lui *ruppe*	loro *ruppero*

The **passato remoto** is used to talk about an action completely finished in the past and which does not continue into the present.

– Alla fine degli anni sessanta l'uomo **mise** piede sulla luna. *(Man first walked on the moon at the end of the 60s)*

In Northern and some central parts of Italy, the **passato prossimo** is used in spoken language instead of the **passato remoto** to express past actions. The **passato remoto** is now mainly used in written Italian.

– La prima volta che **sono andato** a Parigi avevo 17 anni. *(The first time I went to Paris I was 17)*
– La prima volta che **andai** a Parigi avevo 17 anni. *(The first time I went to Paris I was 17)*

1. Put the verbs in the correct form of the passato remoto.

1. Vendere *io vendetti*......................................
2. Perdere ....
3. Correre ....
4. Andare ....
5. Avere ....
6. Aspettare ....
7. Essere ....
8. Ritornare ....
9. Potere ....
10. Dare ....
11. Stare ....
12. Vedere ....
13. Volere ....
14. Rompere ....

2. Mark the stress on the verbs.

1. Ascolt**ò**.
2. Discussi.
3. Parlasti.
4. Abitarono.
5. Veniste.
6. Finirono.
7. Parlai.
8. Ritorno.

3. Put the verbs in brackets into the correct form of the passato remoto or imperfect.

Tutto *iniziò*................ (iniziare) alle 7 un mattino d'inverno, quando il postino ....2............ (suonare) e ....3............ (dare) a Luigi la "cartolina".
Da settimane ormai ....4............... (sapere) che ....5............. (dovere) arrivare.
Gli amici ogni giorno gli ....6............. (dire): "Tranquillo! Ti manderanno in Sicilia!".
A Luigi la Sicilia ....7.............. (piacere). Lo ....8............. (affascinare) la sua gente e il sapore mediterraneo. Per lui figlio della nebbia, la Sicilia ....9.............. (essere) il sole, il calore, la vita.
Peccato che il suo paese ....10............. (essere) a più di mille chilometri.
Quel giorno ....11.............. (rendersi conto) immediatamente che qualcosa non era andato come si pensava. ....12............. (mettersi) il cappotto e ....13............. (uscire) di casa. ....14............ (andare) subito al bar, ma non ....15............ (esserci) nessuno; in un attimo ....16............. (pensare) che cosa fare ....17............ (decidere) di andare da Massimo: sicuramente stava lavorando. Nella fabbrica ....18........... (esserci) molto rumore: "Leggi qui!", ...19.......... (urlare). "Luigi, ti hanno esonerato dal servizio militare! Non devi più partire", ...20......... (rispondere) Massimo, felice.

In Italian there are two aspects of the past: the **imperfect** and the **perfect** *(passato prossimo* and *passato remoto).*

The **imperfect** is used to talk about a finished action in the past, seen as if it were an on-going event, i.e. happening around a certain time. – Ieri alle 23,15 **guardavo** una partita alla televisione. *(I was watching a football match on television at 23.15 yesterday).*	The **passato prossimo** or **passato remoto** are used to talk about a finished action in the past, but not seen as if it were an on-going event. – **Ho vissuto** in Inghilterra per vari anni. *(I lived in England for several years)* The duration of the action is not important: if the action is finished, then the **passato prossimo** or **passato remoto** is used. – La schiavitù in America **durò** diversi secoli. *(Slavery lasted for several centuries in America)*
The **imperfect** is used to talk about an on-going action in the past, "interrupted" bt another event. – Mentre **guardavo** la televisione, **è andata** via la corrente. *(While I was watching television, the electricity was cut off)* – Quando **è arrivata** sua madre, Luca **dormiva**. *(When his mother arrived, Luca was sleeping)* Note that **mentre** *(while)* is followed by the **imperfect**.	The **passato prossimo** or **passato remoto** are used to talk about an action that interrupts another on-going event in the past. – Quando **è arrivata** sua madre, Luca **dormiva.** *(When hir mother arrived, Luca was sleeping)* – Mentre **guardavo** la televisione, **è andata** via la corrente. *(While I was watching the television, the electricity was cut off)* Note that **quando** *(when)* is followed by the **passato prossimo** or **passato remoto.**
The **imperfect** is used to talk about simultaneous on-going actions in the past. – Mentre lui **guardava** la TV, sua moglie **leggeva** un libro e il piccolo **dormiva**. *(While he was watching television, his wife was reading a book and the little one was sleeping).*	The **passato prossimo** or **passato remoto** are used to talk about finished actions which take place one after the other. – Ieri sera **ho guardato** una partita, poi **ho fatto** la doccia e **sono andato** a letto. *(Last night I watched a match, then I had a shower and went to bed)*
The **imperfect** is used to talk about habitual or repeated actions in the past. – Da piccolo mi **piaceva** andare al mare in estate, ma non **sopportavo** la montagna. *(When I was young I used to like going to the seaside in the summer, but I couldn't stand going to the mountains)*	The **passato prossimo** or **passato remoto** are used to talk about one-off actions in the past, i.e. neither habitual or repeated events. – Mi **è piaciuto** molto il viaggio in Giappone. *(I enjoyed the trip to Japan very much)*

1. Put the verbs in brackets into the correct verb forms.

1. Quando Silvano ...*è uscito/uscì*............ (uscire), ...*pioveva*....... (piovere).
2. L'idraulico .... (arrivare), mentre i Bianchi .... (cenare).
3. Ieri alle 10 di sera mia moglie .... (leggere) e io .... (preparare) la cena.
4. .... (io studiare) latino per cinque anni.
5. Il Medioevo .... (durare) molti secoli.
6. Mentre voi .... (essere) in piscina, io .... (andare) a casa vostra.
7. Quando .... (suonare) alla porta, Linda .... (dormire).
8. Da piccolo mi .... (piacere) leggere, ma non .... (sopportare) di fare i compiti.
9. Domenica scorsa .... (io svegliarsi) alle 10, ... (fare) colazione e poi .... (pulire) la casa.
10. Sabato sera .... (io vedere) un film di Ken Loach che mi .... (piacere) molto.
11. Quando Franco .... (avere) l'incidente, la strada .... (essere) bagnata.
12. Cosa .... (tu fare), quando ti .... (chiamare)?

2. Read the answers and write the questions.

1. *Cosa hai fatto ieri sera*..?
Sono andato al cinema con alcuni amici.
2. ....?
In bicicletta. Era una serata calda.
3. ....?
No, dopo siamo andati in pizzeria.
4. ....?
Sì, il film era molto interessante.
5. ....?
No, lei non è venuta; non stava bene.
6. ....?
Aveva un po' di mal di testa.
7. ....?
Non lo sapevi? Sì, si è sposata un mese fa.
8. ....?
È andata in Giamaica.

3. Answer the following questions.

1. Cosa hai fatto nell'estate 1995?
....
2. Sei mai stato in Portogallo?
....
3. Quanti anni avevi quando hai cominciato a studiare l'italiano?
....
4. Cosa facevi d'estate quando andavi a scuola?
....
5. Facevi dello sport da piccolo? Che sport praticavi?
....
6. Dov'eri l'anno scorso per l'ultimo dell'anno?
....

Regular verbs

I - ARE: cantare *(sing)*		II - ERE: credere *(believe)*		III a - IRE: sentire *(hear)*		III b - IRE: finire *(finish)*	
(io)	cant - **erò**	(io)	cred - **erò**	(io)	sent - **irò**	(io)	fin - **irò**
(tu)	cant - **erai**	(tu)	cred - **erai**	(tu)	sent - **irai**	(tu)	fin - **irai**
(lui, lei)	cant - **erà**	(lui, lei)	cred - **erà**	(lui, lei)	sent - **irà**	(lui, lei)	fin - **irà**
(noi)	cant - **eremo**	(noi)	cred - **eremo**	(noi)	sent - **iremo**	(noi)	fin - **iremo**
(voi)	cant - **erete**	(voi)	cred - **erete**	(voi)	sent - **irete**	(voi)	fin - **irete**
(loro)	cant - **eranno**	(loro)	cred - **eranno**	(loro)	sent - **iranno**	(loro)	fin - **iranno**

For the future the regular verbs belonging to group I change the **A** of the infinite -ARE into an **E,** for example: parl**e**rò *(I'll speak)*, asp**e**tterò *(I'll wait)*, etc.

Verbs *essere* and *avere*

AVERE		ESSERE	
(io)	**avrò**	(io)	**sarò**
(tu)	**avrai**	(tu)	**sarai**
(lui, lei)	**avrà**	(lui, lei)	**sarà**
(noi)	**avremo**	(noi)	**saremo**
(voi)	**avrete**	(voi)	**sarete**
(loro)	**avranno**	(loro)	**saranno**

Irregular verbs

Verbs that drop the infinitive vowel.	and**a**re *(go)* dov**e**re *(must)* pot**e**re *(can)* sap**e**re *(know)* ved**e**re *(see)* viv**e**re *(live)*	and**rò** dov**rò** pot**rò** sap**rò** ved**rò** viv**rò**
*Verbs that drop the infinitive vowel and change the **l** or the **n** of the stem into **rr**.*	rima**ne**re *(stay)* te**ne**re *(hold, keep)* ve**ni**re *(come)* vo**le**re *(want)*	rima**rr**ò te**rr**ò ve**rr**ò vo**rr**ò
	b**e**re *(drink)*	be**rrò**
*Verbs that maintain the infinitive **a**.*	d**a**re *(give)* f**a**re *(do, make)* st**a**re *(be, stay)*	d**a**rò f**a**rò st**a**rò

With verbs ending in -**CARE** and -**GARE** an **H** is added before the **E**, for example: spie**gare** *(explain)* → spie**gherò**, cer**care** *(look for)* → cer**cherò**.
Verbs ending in -**CIARE** and -**GIARE** drop the **I**, for example: annun**ciare** *(announce)* → annun**cerò**, man**giare** *(eat)* → man**gerò**.

The **future simple** is used:

- to talk about future events seen from the present:

- to talk about future uncertainty or doubts:
  – Che cosa **penseranno** di me i tuoi genitori? *(What will your parents think of me?)*
- **to express a supposition**:
  – **Sarai** stanco, ti porto a letto! *(You must be tired, I'll take you to bed!)*

In Italian the **present indicative** is often used instead of the **future simple**:
– Quest'estate **vado** in Turchia. *(This summer I'm going to Turkey)*

1. Rewrite the sentences using the correct form of the future simple.

1. Oggi fa bello. Domani ......*farà bello*......
2. Vado spesso al cinema ....
3. Mi ricordo di te ....
4. Abbiamo fame ....
5. I miei amici stanno bene ....
6. Leggo il giornale ....
7. Patrizia studia l'inglese ....
8. Dobbiamo fare benzina ....

2. Look at Sara's diary and write sentences about her future plans.

1. Domani ....*ci sarà*.... l'esame d'italiano.
2. Quando .... al mare, mi ....
3. L'Italia .... meno di 60 milioni d'abitanti nel 2000.
4. Voi .... al vostro paese e noi .... qui.
5. Fra poche settimane .... l'inverno e ci si .... mettere vestiti pesanti.
6. .... a usare il computer e mi .... un cd-rom.
7. Se .... molto, non .... a tennis.
8. .... anche tu alla festa di compleanno di mio nipotino?

3. Complete the sentences with the correct form of the future simple. Use the verbs from the box below.

1. *Giovedì 10 novembre alle ore 17 Sara andrà dal dentista.*
2. ....
3. ....
4. ....
5. ....
6. ....
7. ....
8. ....
9. ....

avere restare tornare dovere imparare comprare venire giocare andare abbronzare piovere arrivare esserci

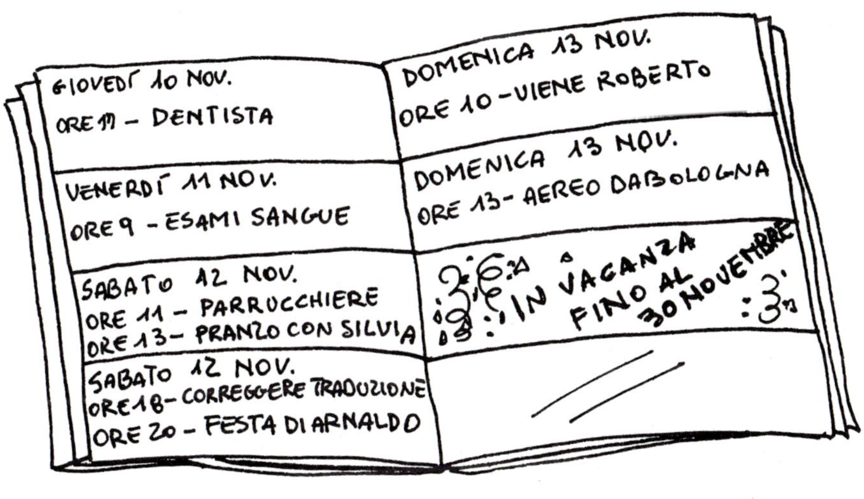

Do you remember what a personal pronoun is? See Appendix 3.

Subject pronouns.

	singular	*plural*
first person	**io**	**noi**
second person	**tu**	**voi**
third person	**egli, lui, esso** **ella, lei, essa**	**essi, esse, loro**

The subject pronoun is not often used in Italian.

- Ho chiamato Carlo e gli ho detto della nuova casa. *(I called Carlo and told him about the new house)*

However, in some cases it is necessary.

- when the speaker wants to *contrast* the two subjects in question:
  - **Lui** sa l'inglese, ma **lei** non capisce nemmeno una parola. *(He speaks English but she doesn't understand a word)*
- when the speaker wants to emphasise the subject; in such cases the subject pronouns is often placed after the main verb;
  - Me l'ha detto **lei**, ma non ci credo. *(She told me but I don't believe it)*
- when **anche**, **neanche**, **neppure**, **nemmeno** *(also, neither)* are used.
  - **Anche noi** vogliamo provare a giocare a squash. *(We would also like to try a game of squash)*

In modern Italian **lui** and **lei** are used much more than **egli**, **ella**, **essa**. In the plural form **loro** takes the place of **essi** and **esse**.

Esso is used for things or animals.

In Italian the subject pronoun **tu** is used when there is an *informal* relationship between the two speakers. When the relationship is more *formal* then the polite form **lei** is used.

Study the picture.

Lei (the polite form) is used for both masculine and feminine genders. It is usually written with a capital letter (**Lei**).

In modern Italian the plural subject pronoun **voi** is almost always used for both polite and informal situations.

The subject pronoun **Loro** is rarely used nowadays as the plural polite form.

1. Rewrite the sentences in the plural form.

1. Io non sono inglese.
...*Noi non siamo inglesi*.................................
2. Lei lavora in un ufficio.
....
3. Tu parli bene l'italiano.
....
4. Io non conosco il turco.
....
5. Lui vive a Bruxelles.
....
6. Io gioco a calcio due volte alla settimana.
....

2. Rewrite the sentences using the personal pronoun instead of the noun.

1. *Sabrina* abita in una bella casa in collina.
...*Lei abita in una bella casa in collina*...........................
2. Domani *Claudia ed io* andiamo a casa di mia madre.
....
3. *Rino* parte oggi pomeriggio per Firenze.
....
4. *Tu e Ignazio* mi avete stancato.
....
5. *Vittoria* ha cominciato ad andare all'asilo.
....
6. *I Raimondi* vengono stasera a cena da noi.
....

3. Complete the sentences with the subject pronoun.

1. ....*Tu*............ sei l'amico di Sonia?
2. .... devo uscire. Signora, ... non può restare qui.
3. .... andiamo a casa, ... restate ancora un po'?
4. .... sono principiante in russo, ma .... invece lo conosci già bene.
5. .... hanno una casa di tre stanze da letto mentre .... viviamo in quattro in 50 metri quadrati.
6. .... non si ricorda di me, ma .... mi ricordo di lui.

Do you understand what is meant by "subject" and "object"? See Appendix 3.

Object pronouns have both stressed and unstressed forms. If you want to know why, see Appendix 3. Otherwise you need only learn which are which.

Object pronouns

Stressed forms

		singular	plural
first person		**me** *(me)*	**noi** *(us)*
second person		**te** *(you)*	**voi** *(you)*
third person	*masculine*	**lui, (esso)** *(him, it)*	**loro, (essi)** *(them)*
	feminine	**lei, (essa)** *(her, it)*	**loro, (esse)** *(them)*
	reflexive	**sé** *(oneself, etc.)*	**sé** *(themselves)*

Lui, lei, loro are used for people; **esso**, **essa**, **essi**, **esse** for both things or people.

Stressed object pronouns are used:

- when preceded by a preposition, i.e. as **indirect object pronouns.**

- to emphasise a person expressed with the object pronoun in the sentence.

  – Hai visto **me** o mio fratello ieri al supermercato?
  (Did you see me or my brother at the supermarket yesterday?)

Study the example..

  – **Prima di te** ho avuto colleghi insopportabili. *(The colleagues I had before you were unbearable)*

The stressed object pronouns are usually preceded by **di** when used with prepositions such as: *dentro, fuori, prima, dopo, sopra, sotto, senza, contro*.

Sé is the **reflexive** form for the third person singular and plural.

Sé can be made more emphatic by **se stesso/a/i/e**.
Note that with the form **se stesso** there is no accent on **sé**.

  – Lui pensa solo a **sé (se stesso)** e non si interessa mai agli altri.
  (He only thinks about himself and never takes other people into consideration).

1. Complete the sentences with the correct personal pronoun.

1. Lui si ricorda di me, ma ......io...... non mi ricordo di ......lui...... .
2. Lei si ricorda di te, ma .... non ti ricordi di ....
3. Noi ci ricordiamo di voi, ma .... non vi ricordate di ....
4. Tu conosci loro, ma .... non conoscono ....
5. Voi conoscete lui, ma .... non conosce ....
6. Io conosco lei, ma .... non conosce ....
7. Lei ama lui, ma .... non ama ....
8. Loro pensano a te, ma .... non pensi a ....

2. Complete the sentences with the correct stressed object pronoun.

1. Chi hai chiamato? ......Me...... o mio fratello?
2. Hai visto Flavio o hai solamente parlato con ....?
3. Ho ancora sonno. Ti avevo detto di svegliare Giorgio, non ....
4. Penso spesso a Lorenza, ma lei non pensa a ....
5. Cerca di stare bene con .... stesso e poi cambierai la tua vita.
6. Sono arrivato prima io, quindi ora tocca a ...., poi Signora toccherà a ....!
7. Le generazioni future che verranno dopo di .... conosceranno un mondo diverso.
8. Pensate meno a .... stessi, se volete avere più amici.
9. Spero che Alice torni presto, senza di .... sono triste.
10. Sopra di .... vive una famiglia con cui non andiamo molto d'accordo.

Can you remember the difference between a direct and indirect object pronoun? See Appendix 3.

Unstressed object pronouns are the most common. They are used as direct and indirect object pronouns when there is no need to give special emphasis to the pronoun.

Unstressed direct object pronouns

		singular	*plural*
first person		**mi** *(me)*	**ci** *(us)*
second person		**ti** *(you)*	**vi** *(you)*
third person	*masculine*	**lo/l'** *(him, it)*	**li** *(them)*
	feminine	**la/l'** *(her, it)*	**le** *(them)*
	reflexive	**si** *(oneself, etc.)*	**si** *(themselves)*

Unstressed pronouns are used as the direct object in a sentence. The direct object pronoun answers the question **chi**? and **che cosa**?

– Claudio, **ti** ho chiamato ieri, ma non eri in casa. (**Ti** = the person who was called, i.e.Claudio).
(Claudio, I called you yesterday but you weren't at home)

– Quanti anni ha tua madre?
– *How old's your mother?*
– Non **lo** ricordo.
– *I don't remember.*
Si usa **lo** per sostituire un'intera frase.
Lo *is used to substitute a complete sentence.*

Unstressed indirect object pronouns

		singular	*plural*
first person		**mi** *(me)*	**ci** *(us)*
second person		**ti** *(you)*	**vi** *(you)*
third person	*masculine*	**gli** *(him, it)*	**loro/gli** *(them)*
	feminine	**le** *(her, it)*	**loro/gli** ***(them)***
	reflexive	**si** *(oneself, etc.)*	**si** *(themselves)*

Unstressed pronouns are used as the indirect object pronoun in a sentence, where the preposition *a* is not expressed. The indirect object pronoun answers the questions: **a chi**? **a che cosa**?

– Ho visto Silvio e **gli** ho detto di telefonare a Luca. *(**Gli** – the person who was told to phone Luca, i.e. Silvio).*
(I saw Silvio and told him to telephone Luca)

The masculine and feminine form of the third person plural for the indirect object pronoun is **loro.** However, in modern Italian **gli** is often used instead of **loro** again for both sexes.

– I miei genitori mi hanno chiesto quando penso di sposarmi. Ho risposto **loro** che non lo sapevo
Gli ho risposto che non lo sapevo.
(My parents have asked when I am thinking of getting married. I told them that I didn't know.)

Unstressed object pronouns are placed:

- **before** the verb, when used in an indicative, conditional or subjunctive sentence.
  – **Mi** dai un bicchiere d'acqua, per favore? *(Can you give me a glass of water, please?)*
  – **Ti** piacerebbe, andare in vacanza in Madagascar? *(Would you like to go to Madagascar on holiday?)*
  – Signora, **mi** dica, come fa a mantenersi così in forma? *(Tell me, how do you manage to keep so fit?)*

- after the verb, when used with an infinitive, a participle, a gerund or imperative. (II person. sing. and plural).
  – Sarebbe bello conoscer**la** meglio, ma ha un marito molto geloso.
  (It would be nice to get to know her more, but her husband is very jealous)
  – Silvana ha accettato il contratto di lavoro propost**ole**. *(Silvana accepted the contract they proposed)*
  – Parlando**gli**, forse potrei capire il suo punto di vista. *(Talking to him, maybe I could understand his point of view)*
  – Lascia**mi** in piace, ti prego, non vedi che sto lavorando! *(Leave me alone, can't you see I'm working!)*

When the infinitive is used with an unstressed pronoun the final **e** of the verb is dropped.

parlar**e** + **gli** → parla**rgli** *(Speak to him)*
legger**e** + **lo** → legger**lo** *(Read it)*

With *dovere, potere, sapere* and *volere* two constructions are possible:

Voglio conoscer**la** or **La** voglio conoscere *(I want to meet her)*

1. Tick whether the underlined unstressed object pronouns are direct or indirect.

	Compl. oggetto (chi/che cosa?)	Compl. di termine (a chi/a che cosa?)
1. Ho visto tua mamma e le ho dato la tua cartolina.	☐	☒
2. Telefona a Giuliana e chiedile come sta.	☐	☐
3. Mi piace molto la birra.	☐	☐
4. Dove sei? Non ti vedo più.	☐	☐
5. Chiamatemi quando arrivate a Rimini.	☐	☐

2. Put in the correct object pronoun.

1. Roberto ....lo............................
2. A Sara ....
3. Carla e me ....
4. Al bambino ....
5. I tuoi genitori ....
6. La casa ....
7. Agli studenti ....
8. A te ....

3. Complete the sentences with the correct unstressed direct object pronoun.

1. Ho bisogno di parlare con Giorgia, ma non so se stasera ....la.......... vedrò.
2. Ho visto un armadio che mi piace; .... voglio comprare.
3. Dov'è la mia scarpa? Non .... trovo!
4. Non mi piacciono i film del terrore, non andrò mai a veder ....
5. Ieri sera ho studiato molto le preposizioni, ma oggi non .... so già più.
6. Sono finite le uova, scendo a comprar ....!
7. Quando visito un museo interessante, ... consiglio sempre ai miei amici.
8. Hai fatto un'altra torta? .... posso assaggiare?

4. Complete the sentences with the correct unstressed indirect object pronoun.

1. Chiama Giovanni; ....gli........... devi dire di venire a cena da noi domani.
2. Hai visto Anita? .... devo parlare urgentemente.
3. Se vedo Giulio e Federica, ... do le foto di questa estate.
4. Per il tuo compleanno, ... regalerò un buon libro.
5. Per il compleanno di mia moglie, ... pagherò una vacanza in Senegal.
6. Amiamo molto la natura e .... piace fare lunghe passeggiate nei boschi.
7. Luca, ... va di passare il fine settimana in Toscana?
8. .... posso offrire qualcosa da bere o preferite un gelato?

5. Complete the sentences with the correct unstressed object pronoun and add the ending to the past participle.

1. Hai letto il libro che ...ti........... ho dat................ ?
2. Avete visto il video che .... ho prestat.................?
3. No, non .... abbiamo ancora vist................ .
4. Le pile del registratore si sono scaricate e .... ho già ricomprat............ .
5. Ho regalato a mia figlia una bambola e lei .... ha rott.............. subito.
6. Ho visto Filippo e .... ho raccontat................ tutto.
7. Ho perso il portafoglio sull'autobus e .... hanno telefonato subito.
8. Che fortuna! Chi .... ha ritrovat.............?

Look at the picture.

Alzarsi and **lavarsi** are both reflexive verbs. Study the table below.

io	**mi** *(myself)*	lavo
tu	**ti** *(yourself)*	lavi
lui/lei	**si** *(himself/herself)*	lava
noi	**ci** *(ourselves)*	laviamo
voi	**vi** *(yourselves)*	lavate
loro	**si** *(themselves)*	lavano

Reflexive verbs consist of a reflexive pronoun together with the verb.

With compound tenses reflexive verbs always take the auxiliary verb **essere**.

For the past participle agreements with the verb **essere**, see Unità 31.

Some common reflexive verbs.

addormentarsi *(fall asleep)*	fidarsi *(trust)*
alzarsi *(get up)*	incontrarsi *(meet each other)*
ammalarsi *(take ill)*	lavarsi *(get washed)*
arrabbiarsi *(get angry)*	pettinarsi *(comb one's hair)*
bagnarsi *(get wet)*	riposarsi *(rest)*
chiamarsi *(be called)*	rompersi *(break)*
fermarsi *(stop)*	sedersi *(sit down)*

Some transitive verbs (see Appendix 3) become reflexive in order to emphasise meaning.

- Ieri sera **mi sono** mangiato una pizza favolosa e **mi sono** bevuto una birra alla spina squisita!
  (Yesterday evening I devoured a wonderful pizza and downed some excellent beer!)
- Ieri sera **ho** mangiato una pizza favolosa e **ho** bevuto una birra alla spina squisita!
  (Yesterday evening I ate a wonderful pizza and drank some execellent beer!)

The position of the reflexive pronouns follows the rules of the unstressed object pronouns. See Unità 40.

1. Complete the sentences with the reflexive pronoun.

1. Dario, a che ora ......ti...... svegli di solito?
2. .... fate la barba tutti i giorni?
3. .... lavo sempre con l'acqua calda.
4. A colazione .... mangiamo sempre due uova.
5. Non .... ricordate il nostro indirizzo?
6. Dove .... incontrano i tuoi amici?
7. Molti studenti .... addormentano in classe.
8. Lucia .... pettina con cura.

2. Rewrite the sentences from exercise 1 using the correct form of the passato prossimo.

1. Dario, a che ora ......ti sei svegliato...... ieri?
2. .... la barba questa mattina?
3. .... con l'acqua calda.
4. A colazione .... due uova, questa mattina.
5. Ieri sera non .... il nostro indirizzo?
6. Dove .... i tuoi amici questa mattina?
7. Molti studenti .... in classe lunedì mattina.
8. Lucia .... con cura ieri mattina.

3. Put the words into order and rewrite the sentences using the correct verb forms.

1. Ieri/alzarsi/Paola/9/alle.
   Ieri Paola si è alzata alle 9
2. Susanna/ieri/addormentarsi/tardi/sera.
   ....
3. Bambini/facilmente/piccoli/ammalarsi/i.
   ....
4. L'autobus/fermarsi/ieri/non/mattina.
   ....
5. Sorella/con/arrabbiarsi/ieri/me/mia.
   ....
6. Scorso/anno/rompersi/Valeria/braccio/l'/un.
   ....
7. È/questo/libero/posto?/sedersi/potere?
   ....
8. Come/tuoi/i/chiamarsi/nipoti?
   ....

4. Read the answers and write the questions. Use the verbs from the box below.

1. ....? Alle 7, tranne il lunedì.
2. ....? No, è stata la parrucchiera.
3. ....? Sì, ho dormito un paio d'ore.
4. ....? Davanti al cinema, ti va bene?

pettinarsi, svegliarsi, lavarsi, bagnarsi, fidarsi, arrrabbiarsi, incontrarsi, rompersi, riposarsi, ammalarsi.

Ci is used

- with the meaning of **qui, lì** (*here, there*) in order to substitute a noun of place determining state or movement.

  – Sei mai stata a Roma? - Sì, **ci** sono andata due anni fa.
  (Have you ever been to Rome? - Yes, I went there two years ago.)

  Study the example.

  – Oggi **a scuola c'**erano due studenti nuovi.
  (There were two new students at school today.)

- With verbs that take the prepositions **a** *(pensare a) (think about)*, **su** *(contare su) (count on)*, it then means **a/su questo/ciò, a/su lui/lei/loro.**

  – Hai pensato **al** regalo per Roberto? - **Ci** ho pensato, ma non mi è venuto in mente niente.
  (Did you think about a present for Roberto? - Yes, I thought about it, but nothing came to mind).
  – Posso contare **sulla** tua presenza al congresso? - Sì, **ci** puoi contare.
  (Can I count on your presence at the congress? - Yes, you can count on it.)

Vi can be used instead of **ci**, but mainly in written language.

– È gradita la Sua presenza al ricevimento. La preghiamo di portar**vi** altra persona di suo gradimento.
(You are warmly invited to the reception. You are welcome to bring other guests of your choice.)

Sometimes in spoken language, **ci** is used without any particular meaning; for example with the verb **avere**, especially where the answer to a question contains the pronouns (**lo, la, l', li, le**).

– Hai ancora la tua mazza da baseball? - No, non **ce l'**ho più.
(Have you still got your baseball bat? - No, I haven't got it any more.)

See Unità 44: **ci** + pronouns.

Ne is used

- to replace an object noun or a whole sentence introduced by **di** or **da**, to give the meaning of **di/da questo/a di/da lui/lei/loro, da questo luogo**.

  – Ti ricordi **di** Elsa? – Sì, me **ne** ricordo bene.
  (Do you remember Elsa? - Yes, I remember her well.)

  – Chi mi ha detto che tornerai in Germania presto? Ah, sì, me **ne** ha parlato Gianni.
  (Who told me you are going back to Germany soon? Ah, yes, Gianni told me about it.)

  – Sono stato a Perugia, **ne** sono appena tornato.
  (I've been to Perugia, I've just got back)

  When there is a compound tense, the past participle does not agree with the object introduced by **di**.

  – Avete parlato **di** musica ieri sera? No, non **ne** abbiamo parlat**o**.
  (Did you talk about music yesterday evening? No, we didn't talk about it.)

1. Complete the sentences with CI or NE.

1. Vivo a Parma e ....ci....... sto bene.
2. Sono andato in piazza, ma non .... erano i miei amici.
3. Mi piacerebbe andare in Indonesia, perché chi .... è stato mi ha detto che è molto bella.
4. Io non ho visto niente e non .... so nulla.
5. Se non hai comprato lo zucchero, ... penso io.
6. Per andare a Napoli da Roma .... vogliono tre ore.
7. Sono stanco di questo lavoro; non .... posso più.
8. Ci vediamo alle 8? Sì, ... puoi contare.
9. Io non mi ricordo di tua zia, ma mia madre se .... ricorda.
10. Chi ti ha detto che mi sposo? Me .... ha parlato Beppe.
11. Se te .... parlo, è perché ti voglio bene.
12. Non dò mai opinioni, se non .... sono sicuro.

2. Answer the questions using CI or NE.

1. Sei stato a Madrid?
Sì, ci sono stato
2. Hai parlato del tuo compleanno a mia madre?
Sì, ...
3. Stai pensando di andare in pensione l'anno prossimo?
Sì, ...
4. Posso contare sul tuo aiuto?
Sì, ...
5. Ti sei ricordata di andare al supermercato?
No, ...
6. Sei andato al cinema ieri sera?
No, ...
7. Come eri quando sei tornato da Napoli?
.... pieno d'entusiasmo.
8. Sei sicura di quello che dici?
Sì, ...
9. Quanto ci vuole per andare a Verona da Mantova?
.... mezz'ora.
10. Hai sentito parlare dell'ultimo libro di Tabucchi?
No, ...

Study the pictures.

1

2

Ne is used to indicate **part** of a quantity and take the place of a noun. In example number 1, **ne** replaces the word "**sigarette**". In the second example **ne** substitutes the word "**vino**".

3

4

In the first two examples only **part** of the quantity is expressed, in examples 3 and 4 the whole quntity is being expressed. When the whole quantity is expressed, i.e. **tutto**, then the pronouns **lo/la/li/le** are used instead of **ne**.

- When the concept expresses **zero** quantity, i.e. **niente** or **nessuno**, then **ne** is used.

  – Quanti film di Fellini hai visto? – Non **ne** ho visto **nessuno**.
  (How many of Fellini's films have you seen? - I haven't seen any of them.)
  – Quanto latte bevi ogni giorno? – Non **ne** bevo.
  (How much milk do you drink a day? - I don't drink any.)

- In compound tenses, even with the auxiliary *avere*, the past participle agrees with the noun replaced by **ne**.

  – Quant**i** libr**i** hai letto quest'estate? – **Ne** ho lett**i** cinque.
  (How many books have you read this summer? - I've read five)
  – Che disch**i** avete ascoltato alla festa? – **Ne** abbiamo ascoltat**i** alcuni latino-americani molto belli.
  (Which records did you listen to at the party? - We listened to some really nice Latin American ones.)
  – Quant**i** turist**i** arriveranno quest'anno in Italia? – Non si sa, ma finora **ne** sono arrivat**i** due milioni.
  (How many tourist will come to Italy this year? - We don't know, but/so far/two million tourists have come.)

▶ When the quantity expressed is *zero (nessuno, niente)*, the past participle agrees only in gender and not in number.

  – Hai visto **le ragazze** del corso d'italiano? - No, non **ne** ho ancora vist**a** **nessuna**.
  (Have you seen the girls on the Italian course? - No, I haven't seen anyone yet.)

- **Ne** is also used in specific expressions.

  – Non **ne** posso più, sono stanchissimo. *(I can't take anymore, I've had it.)*

  – Non voglio più vivere in Italia, me **ne** vado, torno in Germania. *(I don't want to live in Italy anymore. I'm leaving, I'm going back to Germany.)*

  – Ho detto a Martino la verità e se **n'**è avuto a male. *(I told Martino the truth and he was really upset.)*

1. Answer the following questions.

1. Quante sigarette fumi ogni giorno?
Ne fumo .... 10.
2. Quanti soldi spendi ogni mese?
.... molti.
3. Quanti cucchiaini di zucchero prendi col caffè?
.... 2.
4. Quanta birra bevi?
.... tutta.
5. Compri molta carne ogni settimana?
No, ... molta.
6. Leggi libri classici?
No, ...
7. Quanti errori fai negli esercizi d'italiano?
.... pochi.
8. Ascolti molti dischi di musica lirica?
Sì, ... parecchi.
9. Compri molti giornali sportivi?
Sì, ... tutti.
10. Quanti film western guardi in tv?
.... nessuno.

2. Complete the questions and the answers using the correct form of the passato prossimo.

1. Quante sigarette *hai fumato* ieri?
Ne ho fumate .... 10.
2. Quanti soldi .... il mese scorso?
.... molti.
3. Quanti cucchiaini di zucchero .... col caffè?
.... 2.
4. Quanta birra ....?
.... tutta.
5. .... molta carne la settimana scorsa?
No, ... molta.
6. .... libri classici?
No, ...
7. Quanti errori .... negli esercizi d'italiano ieri?
.... pochi.
8. .... molti dischi di musica lirica ieri?
Sì, ... parecchi.

3. Complete the sentences with NE or LO/LA/LE/LI and add the correct ending to the past participle.

1. Mi piacciono molto i gelati, ma ora non ....*ne*..... voglio.
2. I tartufi sono buonissimi, ma non se .... trovano molti.
3. La tua torta era squisita: .... ho finit............ .
4. Il pacchetto di sigarette è già vuoto. .... hai fumat......... tutte?
5. Hai visto il telegiornale? Sì, ... vist........... tutto.
6. Hai letto il giornale oggi? Sì, ... ho lett......... tre.
7. Vuoi un po' di grappa? No, grazie. .... ho già bevut............ troppa.
8. Quante sigarette hai fumato oggi? Non .... ho fumat........... nessuna.
9. Mangi molto pane? No, non .... mangio.
10. Hai fatto gli esercizi di grammatica? Sì, ... ho fatt......... tutti.

		indirect							
		mi	*ti*	*gli/le*	*si*	*ci*	*vi*	*gli*	*si*
di	*lo*	me lo	*te lo*	*glielo*	*se lo*	*ce lo*	*ve lo*	*glielo*	*se lo*
r	la	me la	te la	gliela	se la	ce la	ve la	gliela	se la
e	li	me li	te li	glieli	se li	ce li	ve li	glieli	se li
tt	le	me le	te le	gliele	se le	ce le	ve le	gliele	se le
i	ne	me ne	te ne	gliene	se ne	ce ne	ve ne	gliene	se ne

- The ***i*** of **mi/ti/ci/vi/si** changes into an **e**, in front of another pronoun: **me lo**, etc.

- With combined pronouns the indirect object pronoun is placed before the direct object pronoun.

  – Chi ti ha dato quella bambola? - **Me l'**ha data la zia.
  (Who gave you that doll? - Aunty gave it to me.)

- Combined pronouns are written as two separate words, apart from the third person singular and plural **glielo**, etc.

  – Devi consegnare il libro a Renato. – **Gliel'**ho già spedito, **me lo** ha richiesto ieri per telefono.
  (You have to give the book to Renato. - I' ve already sent it off to him, he asked me for it yesterday on the phone.)

- When the pronouns follow a verb in the form of the *infinitive*, *gerund, imperative* or as a *participle*, they are joined to the actual verb.

  – **Diteglielo** voi a Sandro; io gliel'ho già ripetuto tre volte!
  (You tell Sandro; I've already repeated it to him three times.)

- With the infinitive the verb drops the final **e**.
  – Stasera c'è la prima dell'Aida! Te ne sei dimenticato? - No, ma hai fatto bene a ricorda**rmelo**.
  (It's the first performance of Aida this evening! Had you forgotten about it?
  No, but you did the right thing to remind me about it.)

- For the third person plural **gli** is commonly used nowadays. If **loro** is used, the sentence construction must be changel: the *direct object* pronoun **lo/la**/etc., is placed before the verb whereas the *indirect* object pronoun **loro** follows it.

  – Hai detto ai tuoi genitori che hai una ragazza nuova? – No, non **gliel'**ho ancora detto.
  Oppure: – No, non **l'**ho ancora detto **loro**.
  (Have you told your parents that you've got a new girlfriend? No, I haven't told them yet.)

Pronouns + Ci (place)

direct object pronouns	*mi*	*ti*	*lo*	*la*	*ci*	*vi*	*li*	*le*	*si*	*ne*
	mi ci	ti ci	ce lo	*ce la*	*no combination*	vi ci	*ce li*	ce le	**ci si**	*ce ne*

– Sei mai stato al Parco Ducale? – No, **mi ci** *porti tu?*
(Have you ever been to Parco Ducale? - No, will you take me there?)

1. Rewrite the sentences using the combined pronouns instead of the nouns in italics.

1. Ho dato *un libro a Giovanni*.
   Gliel'ho dato
2. *Ti* ho regalato *un disco*.
   ....
3. Il cameriere *mi* ha portato *il conto*.
   ....
4. Farò vedere *le foto a Carlo e Antonella*.
   ....
5. *Vi* ho detto *che vado in pensione*.
   ....
6. Fausto *ci* ha parlato *del suo nuovo lavoro*.
   ....
7. Miriam *vi* racconterà *la trama* del film.
   ....
8. *Ti* darò presto *mie notizie*.
   ....

2. Complete the sentences with the correct pronouns.

1. Silvano non vi ha parlato del suo libro, perciò ...ve ne... parlo io.
2. Dovrei prestare i soldi a mio cugino, ma non .... presterò.
3. Al mattino devo prendere una medicina, ma non .... ricordo mai.
4. Se vuoi un gelato, ... posso offrire.
5. Mio fratello aveva bisogno di trovare un appartamento in affitto e Pierluigi .... ha trovato.
6. Mi avete chiesto quanti anni ho, ma io non .... dirò.
7. Se vogliono sapere come finisce la storia, ... racconterò.
8. È meglio che tu non beva, ma se vuoi una birra, ... dò.

3. Answer the following questions.

1. Mi fai vedere il tuo passaporto?
   No, non te lo faccio vedere. La foto è orribile.
2. Puoi dare queste cartoline a Marta?
   No, ..., perché non la vedrò fino a mese prossimo.
3. Chi ti ha dato quei cioccolatini?
   .... Paolo.
4. Hai parlato ai tuoi genitori delle tue vacanze?
   Sì, ..., ma non erano molto interessati.
5. Ci sai dire dove vive Paolo?
   Mi dispiace, ...
6. Mi fai vedere la tua casa?
   Sì, ... subito.

4. Read the answers and write the questions.

1. Chi ti ha prestato i soldi? Me li ha prestati mio nonno.
2. ....? Ce ne ha parlato tuo marito.
3. ....? Accompagnamici tu! Ti prego.
4. ....? Ve lo ricorderò sicuramente.
5. ....? Me l'ha detto il professore. Io pensavo d'averlo fatto bene.
6. ....? Te la offro io.

With no preposition	*With a preposition*
CHE	CUI

Che and **cui** are *invariable* and are not used with an *article* (apart from the two cases below marked with *).

Che is *not* used with a preposition.

- Gli amici **che** abbiamo visto ieri sera sono simpatici. *(The friends (that) we saw yesterday evening are nice.)*
- Uno scrittore è una persona **che** scrive libri. *(A writer is a person who writes books.)*

Cui is used with a *preposition*.

- Il film **di cui** ti ho parlato è stato girato in Italia. *(The film (that) I spoke to you about was shot in Italy.)*
- La ragazza **con cui** sono andato in vacanza è partita per Londra.
  (The girl (who) I went on holiday with has left for London.)

When followed by **cui** the preposition **a** can be left out.

- La ditta **(a) cui** ho scritto ha sede in Svizzera. *(The firm (that) I wrote to is located in Switzerland.)*
- Il professore **(a) cui** hai parlato è molto disponibile. *(The professor (that) you spoke to is very helpful.)*

* When **cui** is placed between the definite article and the noun it expresses *possession (whose).*

- Il giovane, **il cui padre** lavora alla Fiat, sta facendo una ricerca sulla storia dell'automobile.
  *(The young man, **whose father** works for Fiat, is doing a research on the history of the car.)*
- Il pittore, **sulla cui arte** tanto si discute, è venezuelano.
  (The painter, whose art is so controversial, is Venezuelan.)

The article required depend on the noun which it refers to.

* **Il che** means e *questo* / e *ciò* (*which, this, that, it,* etc.)

- Ieri mi ha telefonato Carla; **il che** *(e questo/e ciò)* mi ha fatto molto piacere.
  (Carla telephoned me yesterday, which made me very happy.)

Chi means *le persone che, quelli che,* ecc. *(who, the people who, those who,* etc.*)*

The verbs is always used in the third person singular.

- **Chi** non lavora non mangia. *(If you dont work, you don't eat.)*
- Parlo solo con **chi** sa ascoltare. *(I only speak to those who know how to listen.)*
- **Chi** vuole frequentare il corso d'italiano deve iscriversi entro domani.
  (Whoever wishes to attend the Italian course must enrol by tomorrow.)

See Unità 19 for the interrogative **chi** (question word).

1. Match the job descriptions and rewrite the sentences below using the correct relative pronoun.

1. Il dottore		a) si usa a scuola
2. Il cane	è una persona....	b) cura gli ammalati
3. Il libro	è un oggetto.....	c) lavora in un ristorante
4. La gallina	è un animale....	d) si appende alla parete
5. Il quadro		e) ha le ali
6. Il macellaio		f) vende la carne
7. La cameriera		g) abbaia

1. *Il dottore è una persona che cura gli ammalati*
2. ....
3. ....
4. ....
5. ....
6. ....
7. ....

**2. Complete the sentences with a relative pronoun.
Use, where necessary, the following prepositions: DA, IN, CON, DI, A.**

1. Quello è il ragazzo *con cui* vivo.
2. L'appartamento............ abito è al terzo piano.
3. Mia zia, ... ho mandato una cartolina, mi ha telefonato ieri.
4. Il dentista .... sono andato ieri è molto caro.
5. L'attore, il .... ruolo preferito è quello del cattivo, deve ora recitare la parte di San Giuseppe.
6. In questa foto ci sono delle persone .... non ricordo il nome.
7. Ho rivisto l'amico, la .... foto è nel mio diario.

3. Complete the sentences using CHI (with or without a preposition) or IL CHE.

1. La tua amica mi ha mandato una cartolina; *il che* mi ha reso felice.
2. Ho saputo che è morto il mio scrittore preferito; .... mi ha fatto piangere.
3. .... vuole andare a casa, può uscire subito.
4. L'ufficio è aperto fino alle 13 .... vuole informazioni.
5. Bisogna chiederlo.....è più informato di noi.
6. Questa volta hai avuto fortuna, ... non vuole dire che ti andrà sempre bene.
7. La mia macchina, la presto solamente .... sa guidare bene.

3. Join the two sentences together using a relative pronoun.

1. Devo comprarmi un'auto nuova. Con un'auto nuova potrò andare in vacanza.
Devo comprarmi un'auto nuova, con cui potrò andare in vacanza.
2. Ho conosciuto un gruppo interessante di persone. Tra queste persone vi era un pittore famoso.
....
3. José ha deciso di tornare al suo paese. Ti ho parlato di lui questa mattina.
....
4. A Cuba passerei ogni inverno. Il suo clima è fantastico.
....
5. Hanno catturato tre ladri. I loro furti erano sempre sulle prime pagine dei giornali.
....
6. Spero di risparmiare un po' di soldi. Con quel denaro voglio fare un viaggio.
....
7. Quelle ragazze tedesche sono molto simpatiche. Si trovano in Italia in vacanza.
....
8. Questo è mio fratello Giovanni. Con lui gioco a calcio ogni settimana.
....
9. La ditta Telev produce telefoni cellulari. Ha sede a Torino.
....
10. Mio cuginetto è andato al cinema. Gli ho dato 10 euro.
....
11. Oggi ho rivisto un mio vecchio amico. E ciò mi ha fatto molto piacere.
....

Study the picture.

Relative pronouns may also be expressed with **quale/i**.
This form is more frequent in the written language.

	singular	*plural*
masculine	**il quale**	**i quali**
feminine	**la quale**	**le quali**

– Quelle sono le ragazze con **le quali** siamo andati al mare.
(Those are the girls (who) we went to the seaside with.)

These structures are variable and always require the definite article. They agree with the word they refer to in both gender and number.

With the prepositions **di**, **a**, **su**, **in**, compound forms of the prepositions with the definite article are formed; see Unità 23.

– Ho visto nuovamente gli studenti **ai quali** ho dovuto dare un cattivo voto.
(I have seen the students again who I had to give a bad mark to.)

It is sometimes necessary to use the structures with **quale/i** to avoid ambiguity.
Study the following example.

– Ieri ho visto Giovanni e sua nonna, **che** aveva appena comprato il pane.
(Yesterday I saw Giovanni and his grandmother, who had just bought some bread.)

The use of **che** in this case creates ambiguity. It is better to say:

– Ieri ho visto Giovanni e sua nonna, **la quale** aveva appena comprato il pane.
(Yesterday I saw Giovanni and his grandmother who had just bought some bread.)

Del quale expressing possession has the same construction as other prepositional phrases.

– Questo è il giovane, i genitori **del quale** lavorano con me.
(This is the young man whose parents work with me.)

Notice the different construction with **i cui**:

– Questo è il giovane, **i cui** genitori lavorano con me.

Il quale cannot be used as a direct object:

– Il ragazzo **che ho** conosciuto è giapponese.
~~il quale~~
(The boy (that) I met is Japanese.)

1. Rewrite the sentences using IL QUALE, etc. instead of CUI and CHE.

1. Quella è la ragazza con cui viviamo.
   ....Quella è la ragazza con la quale viviamo....
2. Ti ricordi come si chiama l'impiegato con cui abbiamo parlato?
   ....
3. Dove abita la signora di cui mi hai parlato?
   ....
4. Dove abita la professoressa per cui stai lavorando?
   ....
5. Gli studenti che non avranno con sé la carta d'identità non potranno sostenere l'esame.
   ....
6. Le persone a cui hai telefonato non mi sembrano molto affidabili.
   ....
7. La famiglia con cui hai vissuto si trasferirà in Olanda.
   ....
8. La commessa, il cui negozio mi hai consigliato, è amica di mio fratello.
   ....

2. Complete the sentences with a relative pronoun and a preposition, where necessary.

1. Ti ho portato i giornali ....che.... mi hai richiesto.
2. Sono arrivati i libri .... avete ordinato.
3. Non vorrei trovarmi mai nella situazione .... ti trovi tu ora.
4. Chi è l'attore .... mi ha parlato Gianna .... ha recitato in *Balla coi Lupi*?
5. Come si chiama la ditta .... lavora tuo padre?
6. Ecco il ristorante .... abbiamo mangiato ieri.
7. Mi dai il numero di telefono del ragazzo .... studi sempre?
8. La casa .... ti ho mostrato il progetto è troppo cara per me.

3. Correct the mistakes where necessary.

1. Conosci la signora anziana alla quale ci ha parlato di te?
   .....Conosci la signora anziana la quale ci ha parlato di te?
2. Come si chiama la ragazza del quale mi hai parlato?
   ....
3. E' il ballerino che abbiamo visto in teatro a Milano.
   ....
4. L'aereo con che sono tornato era in ritardo.
   ....
5. Il quale vuole partecipare alla festa deve portare una bottiglia di vino.
   ....
6. Dovrei dimagrire, il cui mi risulta difficile.
   ....
7. La città in cui vivo ha 200.000 abitanti.
   ....
8. Gli studenti, i cui esami non raggiungeranno la sufficienza, dovranno rifrequentare il corso.
   ....

4. Complete the article with the missing relative pronouns.

È mistero attorno all'autore della telefonata ...che..... i Carabinieri di Savona hanno ricevuto sabato notte. Una voce di donna ....2.......... parlava con un forte accento straniero e ....3.......... non ha voluto dire il proprio nome ha detto ai Carabinieri che in una delle vie principali della città, ...4.......... lei si trovava in quel momento, c'era un cadavere di un giovane uomo ai lati della strada. Una pattuglia dei Carabinieri, ...5.......... facevano parte gli agenti Rossi e Castellani, si sono diretti velocemente nella via ....6......... si parlava nella telefonata, ma nel momento ....7......... sono arrivati hanno visto solamente una donna ....8......... correva, ma nessun cadavere. I due agenti, ...9.......... hanno rincorso la donna senza raggiungerla, hanno dichiarato di non sapere il perché del comportamento della donna.

sarò **sarai** **sarà**	**partito/a,**	**avrò** **avrai** **avrà**	**mangiato**
saremo **sarete** **saranno**	**partiti/e**	**avremo** **avrete** **avranno**	**mangiato**

The **future perfect** is formed with the *future simple* of the auxiliaries *essere* or *avere* and the *past participle* of the verb.

Study the examples.

2000 * — 2002 * — 2003 *

Oggi dipendo dai miei genitori, ma **dopo che** mi **sarò laureato**, cercherò un lavoro.
(Now I depend on my parents but after I have graduated I will look for a job.)

ore 20.00 * — ore 20.10 *

Quando avrò finito di mangiare, farò una doccia. *(When I have finished eating, I will have a shower.)*

The **future perfect** expresses a future action which takes place before another relevant action in the future and is often introduced by **dopo che** or **quando**.

It is also used to express **uncertainty** or **doubt** referring to the *past*:

to express a **supposition** referring to the *past*:

– **Sarai stato** stanco ieri sera, dopo 4 ore in discoteca!
(You must have been tired last night after 4 hours in a disco!)

1. Write the verbs in the correct form of the future perfect.

1. Andrò ...Sarò andato...
2. Mangeremo ....
3. Visiteranno ....
4. Arriverai ....
5. Berrò ....
6. Nascerà ....
7. Ascolteranno ....
8. Sarete ....

2. Complete the sentences with the correct form of the future perfect. Use the verbs from the box below.

1. Non sento il rumore della lavatrice. ...Avrà finito... il lavaggio?
2. Dopo che Vittorio .... dalle vacanze, comincerà un corso di pittura.
3. Quando Linuccio .... il cane, andrà a cercare tartufi.
4. Che cosa .... Colombo quando arrivò in America?
5. Dopo che gli studenti .... la conferenza, dovranno fare un riassunto.
6. Mi comprerò un paio di pantaloni nuovi quando .... di pitturare la casa.
7. Che cosa .... tuo padre a tua madre, quando la vide dopo un anno?

finire tornare ascoltare addestrare dire pensare finire

3. Correct the sentences.

1. Andrò in America dopo che tornerà mio fratello dal suo viaggio di lavoro.
...Andrò in America dopo che sarà tornato mio fratello dal suo viaggio di lavoro...
2. Dopo che il Presidente della Repubblica leggerà il messaggio alla nazione, parleremo dei contenuti.
....
3. Mi ricorderò di lavare i piatti, dopo che finiremo di mangiare?
....
4. Mi avrete telefonato dopo che avrete cenato?
....
5. Che penserà di te la tua ragazza, quando ti ha visto con la tua compagna d'università?
....
6. Dopo che Lucia farà la doccia, si vestirà per uscire.
....
7. Non ci troveremo più a casa tua, dopo che partirai.
....
8. Nel 2010 non ci saranno state più molte specie animali, se non si cambieranno le leggi.
....

ero eri era	partito/a	avevo avevi aveva	mangiato
eravamo eravate erano	partiti/e	avevamo avevate avevano	mangiato

The **past perfect** is formed with the *imperfect* of the auxiliaries *essere* or *avere* and the *past participle* of the verb.

The **past perfect** is used to talk about an action which takes place *before* another event in the past expressed with the **passato prossimo/passato remoto** or **imperfect**.

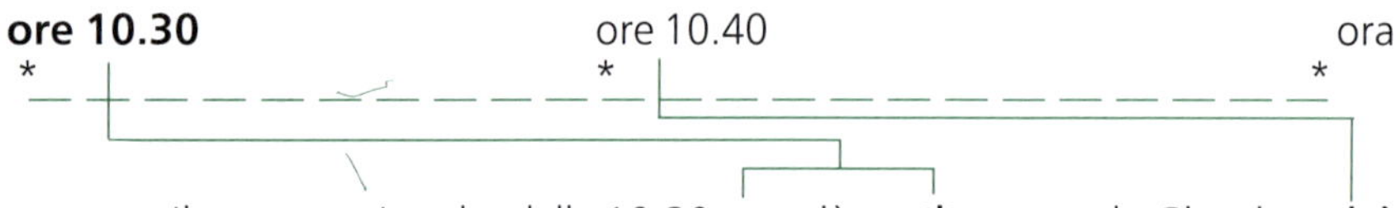

– Il treno per Londra delle 10.30 **era** già **partito**, quando Giorgio **arrivò** alla stazione.
(The 10.30 train to London had already left when Giorgio got to the station.)

When the **past perfect** is used with an *imperfect,* there is often a reference to repeated or habitual actions in the past.

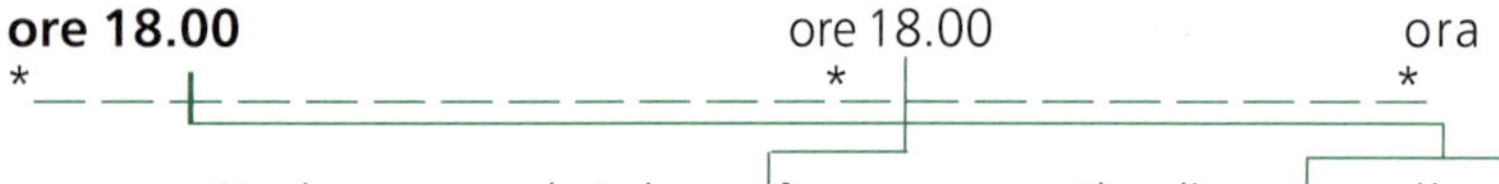

– Ogni sera quando Luisa **arrivava** a casa, Claudio **aveva** già **preparato** da mangiare.
(Every evening when Luisa got home, Claudio had already prepared the meal.)

– Dato che **aveva finito** di lavorare tardi, Silvia non **riuscì** ad andare al cinema.
(As she had finished work late, Silvia wasn't able to go to the cinema.)

Study the two previous examples.
Is the **past perfect** only used in main clauses?

It can be used both in the main clause and in subordinate clauses.

▶ See Unità 80 - The trapassato remoto.

1. Write the verbs in the correct form of the past perfect.

1. Mangiavo ....*aveva mangiato*........
2. Correvi ....
3. Dormivamo ....
4. Parlava ....
5. Salivate ....
6. Arrivavano ....
7. Salutavo ....
8. Lei andava ....

2. Match the sentences from the columns.

1. *Claudio aveva comprato la macchina da due giorni*
2. Non si erano visti da più di tre anni
3. Quando arrivò Francesca
4. Quando arrivai da Giulio
5. Aveva compiuto da poco 20 anni
6. Quando Pasquale arrivò alla stazione
7. Il nonno di Paolo raccontava spesso
8. La mattina dopo a scuola Susy mi diceva sempre

a aveva appena preso il caffè.
b quando la conobbi.
c cosa aveva fatto in guerra.
d *quando gliela rubarono.*
e il treno era già partito.
f avevo finito da poco di studiare.
g cosa aveva fatto la sera in discoteca.
h quando si incontrarono al cinema.

3. Put the verbs in brackets into the *passato prossimo, the imperfect or past perfect.*

1. Mio nipotino mi ....*chiedeva*..... (chiedere) spesso, cosa mi.......*era successo*....... (succedere) alla gamba.
2. Il film .... (cominciare), quando lui .... (arrivare) al cinema.
3. Un giorno i genitori di Piero gli .... (chiedere) come .... (guadagnare) tanti soldi.
4. Quando le .... (offrire) un caffè, mi .... (dire) che lo .... (già bere).
5. Ci .... (già conoscere) l'anno prima, ma non me ne .... (ricordare).
6. Giacomo non .... (ancora guadagnare) il suo primo stipendio, quando .... (ordinare) la moto nuova.
7. Il libro che .... (uscire) l'estate prima .... (essere) più interessante di quello pubblicato nel 1993.
8. Dato che Alex .... (finire) di lavorare, ... (andare) a fare una passeggiata.

4. Continue the sentences using the correct form of the *past perfect.*

1. Quando arrivai all'aeroporto, ...
2. Quando gli ho telefonato, ...
3. Quando sono arrivato a casa sua, ...
4. Quando è iniziata la partita, ...
5. Alla fine si capì chi ....
6. Non ricordavo cosa ....

Verbi regolari

I - ARE: cantare *(sing)*		II - ERE: credere *(believe)*		III a - IRE: sentire *(hear)*		III b - IRE: finire *(finish)*	
(io)	cant - **erei**	(io)	cred - **erei**	(io)	sent - **irei**	(io)	fin - **irei**
(tu)	cant - **eresti**	(tu)	cred - **eresti**	(tu)	sent - **iresti**	(tu)	fin - **iresti**
(lui, lei)	cant - **erebbe**	(lui, lei)	cred - **erebbe**	(lui, lei)	sent - **irebbe**	(lui, lei)	fin - **irebbe**
(noi)	cant - **eremmo**	(noi)	cred - **eremmo**	(noi)	sent - **iremmo**	(noi)	fin - **iremmo**
(voi)	cant - **ereste**	(voi)	cred - **ereste**	(voi)	sent - **ireste**	(voi)	fin - **ireste**
(loro)	cant - **erebbero**	(loro)	cred - **erebbero**	(loro)	sent - **irebbero**	(loro)	fin - **irebbero**

The conditional of regular and irregular verbs is formed in the same way as the future simple but with different endings.

Verbs *essere* and *avere*

AVERE		ESSERE	
(io)	**avrei**	(io)	**sarei**
(tu)	**avresti**	(tu)	**saresti**
(lui, lei)	**avrebbe**	(lui, lei)	**sarebbe**
(noi)	**avremmo**	(noi)	**saremmo**
(voi)	**avreste**	(voi)	**sareste**
(loro)	**avrebbero**	(loro)	**sarebbero**

Irregular verbs

Verbs that drop the infinitive vowel.	and**a**re *(go)* dov**e**re *(must, have to)* pot**e**re *(can, be able to)* sap**e**re *(know)* ved**e**re *(see)* viv**e**re *(live)*	an**drei** do**vrei** po**trei** sa**prei** ve**drei** vi**vrei**
*Verbs that drop the infinitive vowel and change the **l** or **n** of the stem into **rr**.*	rima**ne**re *(stay)* te**ne**re *(keep)* ve**ni**re *(come)* vo**le**re *(want)*	rima**rrei** te**rrei** ve**rrei** vo**rrei**
	bere *(drink)*	be**rrei**
*Verbs that maintain **the** infinitive **a**.*	d**a**re *(give)* f**a**re *(do, make)* st**a**re *(stay)*	d**a**rei f**a**rei st**a**rei

With verbs ending in **-CARE** and **-GARE** an **H** is added before the **E**, e.g.:

spie**gare** ➜ **spiegherei** *(explain)*
cer**care** ➜ **cercherei** *(look for)*

Verbs ending in **-CIARE** and **-GIARE** drop the **I**, e.g.:

annun**ciare** ➜ **annuncerei** *(announce)*
man**giare** ➜ **mangerei** *(eat)*

1. Rewrite the verbs in the correct form of the conditional.

1. Io parlo .... *parlerei* ....
2. Lui gioca ....
3. Noi corriamo ....
4. Voi sentite ....
5. Loro leggono ....
6. Tu scrivi ....
7. Noi cambiamo ....
8. Io fumo ....
9. Lei finisce ....
10. Io so ....
11. Lui ha ....
12. Tu vuoi ....
13. Noi diamo ....
14. Loro bevono ....

2. Correct the mistakes and rewrite the verbs in the correct form of the conditional.

1. Noi leggeremo .... *noi leggeremmo* ....
2. Tu saprasti ....
3. Lui serebbe ....
4. Io cantarei ....
5. Loro staressero ....
6. Voi mangiareste ....
7. Lui beverebbe ....
8. Tu veniresti ....
9. Lei volrebbe ....
10. Noi teneremmo ....
11. Io andrerei ....
12. Lei doverebbe ....
13. Voi cercarete ....
14. Noi spiegeremmo ....

The **conditional** is used in a *present* or *future* time period to express something more politely, i.e.:

- a **request**:
  - Mi **daresti** il numero di tua sorella, per favore? *(Would you give me your sister's phone number, please?)*

- a **wish**:
  - **Vorrei** tanto andare in vacanza! *(I would love to go on holiday!)*

In the two examples above do the actions take place in the present, the future or the past?
It is important to understand this in order to use the conditional correctly.

With a present or future time reference, it is also used to express:

- a **doubt**:
  - Non so se Giovanni **verrebbe** a cena da noi domani sera.
    (I don't know if Giovanni would come to dinner at our place tomorrow evening.)

- a **personal opinion**:
  - A mio parere il governo **dovrebbe** fare di più per combattere la disoccupazione.
    (In my opinion the Government should do more to fight unemployment)

- to report **unconfirmed news**:
  - Il Primo Ministro inglese **arriverebbe** in Italia il mese prossimo.
    (The English Prime Ministre should arrive in Italy next month)

- to politely express **orders, strong suggestions** or **advice**, often with the conditional of the verb *dovere*:
  - Ragazzi, **dovreste** studiare di più! *(You should study more, kids!)*
  - Sig. Santi, Lei **dovrebbe** smettere di fumare. *(Mr Santi, you ought to give up smoking)*

For the use of **vorrei**, see Unità 14.
For the use of the **conditional** in *hypothetical clauses*, see Unità 74.

1. Put the words into order and rewrite the sentences with the correct form of the verb.

1. Per/mi/un/di/bicchiere/vino/darebbe/bianco/favore?
Mi darebbe un bicchiere di vino bianco per favore?
2. Sera/ti/andare/domani/piacerebbe/cinema/al?
....
3. Penso/meglio/in/andare/discoteca/sarebbe/che.
....
4. L'/anno/l'/dovrebbe/inflazione/del/essere/2%/prossimo.
....
5. Non/se/capirebbe/la/scrittura/Barbara/mia/so.
....
6. Ci/a/la/pitturare/casa/aiutereste?
....

2. Complete the sentences with the correct form of the conditional. Use the verbs from the box below.

1. Giorgio, mi ....*passeresti*......... il sale?
2. Ti .... a traslocare, ma non ho tempo.
3. Mi .... andare al mare domani, ma non so se farà bel tempo.
4. .... tanto dormire un paio d'ore, ma chi pulisce la casa?
5. .... con me domani sera? .... andare al cinema.
6. Secondo *La Repubblica* la nave .... al porto di Genova domani con i superstiti dell'incidente.
7. .... smettere di fumare; fumi troppo e sei ormai vecchio.
8. Non so se .... quel libro. Non mi sembra molto interessante.

leggere	uscire	potere	aiutare	piacere	arrivare	passare	dovere	volere

3. Read the situations and give some advice using the conditional form, with *tu* or *voi*.

1. Pino ha il mal di testa.
Dovresti prendere un'aspirina
2. Tua sorella perde spesso l'autobus.
....
3. Il professore non è contento dei risultati di Franco.
....
4. Patrizia e Chiara sono ingrassate molto.
....
5. Tony ha problemi di grammatica in italiano.
....

4. Look at the situations and write a request using the conditional form.

1. Hai sete, sei a casa di un amico.
Mi daresti un po' d'acqua per favore?
2. Sei al ristorante, chiedi il conto.
....
3. Sei in una birreria. Ordini una birra.
....
4. Sei in una città che non conosci. Chiedi dov'è la stazione.
....
5. Conosci un ragazzo che ti piace. Gli chiedi il numero di telefono.
....

Study the following example.
Does it refer to the present or the past?

– L'anno scorso mi **sarebbe piaciuto** andare alla Fiera di Francoforte.
(I would have liked to go to the fair in Frankfurt last year.)

sarei **saresti** **sarebbe**	**partito/a**	**avrei** **avresti** **avrebbe**	**mangiato**
saremmo **sareste** **sarebbero**	**partiti/e**	**avremmo** **avreste** **avrebbero**	**mangiato**

The **perfect conditional** is formed with the *conditional* of the auxiliaries *essere* or *avere* and the *past participle* of the verb.

The **perfect conditional** is used to express in the *past:*

- an unfulfilled **wish**:
  – **Sarei andato** volentieri al mare domenica scorsa, ma purtroppo pioveva.
  (I would have loved to go to the sea last Sunday, but unfortunately it was raining)

- some **unconfirmed news**:
  – Secondo voci non ancora confermate, il terremoto **avrebbe causato** danni per oltre mille miliardi.
  (According to unconfirmed reports the earthquake is supposed to have caused over 1,000 billion worth of damage)

The **perfect conditional** is also used as **future in the past**, i.e. it is used to talk about an action which takes place in a future time with respect to a past action.

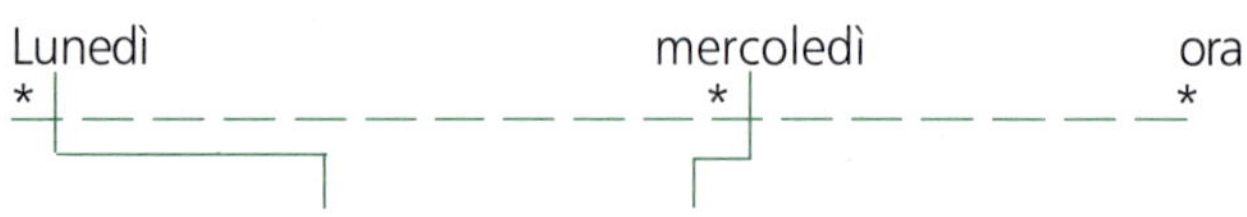

– Gregorio **disse** che **sarebbe arrivato** mercoledì. *(Gregorio said he would arrive on Wednesday)*

– Prima di arrivare in stazione non **sapevo** che il treno per Londra delle 10.30 **sarebbe partito** con 40 minuti di ritardo.
(Before getting to the station I didn't know the 10.30 train to London would be delayed 40 minutes)

For the use of the **perfect conditional** in *hypothetical clauses*, see Unità 74.

1. Rewrite the sentences using the perfect conditional.

1. Vorrei andare al mare domani.
Sarei voluto andare al mare .... ieri.
2. Ti piacerebbe andare al cinema domani sera?
.... ieri sera?
3. Penso che sarebbe meglio andare in discoteca.
.... ieri sera.
4. L'anno prossimo l'inflazione dovrebbe essere del 2%.
L'anno scorso ....
5. Non sappiamo se Barbara capirebbe la mia scrittura.
Non sapevo ....
6. Ci aiutereste a pitturare la casa?
Non sapevamo ....
7. Credo che Roberto ci presterebbe un po' di soldi.
Credevo..
8. Vorrei mangiare una buona pizza stasera.
Ieri sera ....

2. Put the verbs in brackets into the correct conditional form.

1. Paolo disse che *sarebbe partito* (partire) alle 8.
2. (Io)...................................... (volere) arrivare prima, ma c'era molto traffico.
3. Pensavo che la nazionale italiana .... (vincere) il campionato mondiale di calcio, e invece....
4. Mi ....(piacere) andare al mare domenica scorsa.
5. La madre sgridò il figlio che le promise che non lo .... (fare) più.
6. La ditta Savi .... (dovere) consegnare la merce richiesta entro lunedì prossimo.
7. .... (studiare) chitarra, ma non ho mai tempo libero.
8. Secondo una radio locale, l'incendio di ieri presso Nuoro .... (distruggere) vari ettari di bosco.
9. .... (desiderare) uscire un po', ma purtroppo sta nevicando.
10. Pensavo che questa mattina ci .... (essere) più caldo.

Study the picture.

The structure **stare + gerund** indicates an on-going action.

- Le vacanze **stanno trascorrendo** senza incidenti. *(The holidays are going well.)*
- Carlo **stava mangiando** quando bussarono alla porta.
  (Carlo was eating when someone knocked at the door.)

The structure **stare + gerund** is used almost exclusively with the *present* and l'*imperfect* forms, occasionally with the future simple, but **never** with compound tenses (passato prossimo, trapassati, future perfect, etc.).

- Ieri ~~**sono stato dormendo**~~ tutto il pomeriggio.
- Ieri **ho dormito** tutto il pomeriggio. *(I slept all afternoon yesterday)*

It is not necessary to use the structure **stare + gerund.** The present or imperfect are often used in its place.

- **Nevica** da questa mattina.
- **Sta nevicando** da questa mattina. *(It has been snowing since this morning)*

The structure **stare + gerund** is used almost exclusively with verbs which express an action, but it is generally *not* used with verbs of feeling or opinion; essere; avere; dovere; volere; potere; sapere; stare (*be, have, must/ have to, want, can/be able to, know, stay*), etc.

- Il bambino **stava giocando** con il suo gatto, quando arrivarono i genitori.
  (The little boy was playing with his cat when his parents arrived)
- ~~**Sto sapendo**~~ che Luisa torna il 30 agosto dalla montagna.
- **So** che Luisa torna il 30 agosto dalla montagna.
  (I know that Luisa is coming back from the mountains on 30th August)

For the gerund, see Unità 90.

1. Complete the sentences with *stare* + *gerund*. Use the verbs from the box below.

1. Guarda, ...sta nevicando...!
2. Non mi disturbare, ...
3. Non posso uscire adesso; ....
4. In questi giorni Luigi .... molto tempo con gli amici.
5. La situazione economica italiana ....
6. Quando mi hai chiamato .... la doccia, per questo non ho risposto.
7. .... l'autostrada A15 quando un camion lo ha tamponato.
8. Luca adesso ....; quando finirà, tornerà in ufficio.
9. .... la televisione quando c'è stato il terremoto.
10. Il tuo attore preferito .... un nuovo film che uscirà a Natale.

percorrere	nevicare	piovere	girare	guardare	trascorrere	studiare	peggiorare	mangiare	fare

2. Rewrite the sentences using the correct form of *stare* + *gerundio* where possible.

1. Fa molto freddo in questo periodo.
   Sta facendo molto freddo in questo periodo
2. Quando era in vacanza stava sempre a letto fino alle 12.
   ....
3. Parlava spesso con i suoi amici dei suoi problemi.
   ....
4. Penso che domani farà bello.
   ....
5. Fin da quando ero piccolo mi piace molto l'opera lirica.
   ....
6. Quel bimbo ha pianto tutto il giorno.
   ....
7. Guardi un programma interessante o hai voglia di aiutarmi a cucinare?
   ....
8. In questi giorni Lino beve molto.
   ....
9. Mia nonna ha problemi di pressione.
   ....
10. Aspettavo l'autobus quando è scoppiata una bomba nella stazione.
   ....

3. Complete the dialogue with the verbs in brackets using either *stare* + *gerundio* or other verb forms.

Ispettore: Cosa ...facevi/stavi facendo... (fare) ieri sera vicino alla Banca Popolare di Via Sauro?
Renato: Ispettore, Lei si ....2.................(sbagliare), non ....3................. (essere) io.
Ispettore: Non dire stupidate. Ti ....4................. (riconoscere) due testimoni oculari.
Renato: Le ....5................. (assicurare) che non ero io.
Ispettore: Chi ....6................. (essere) gli altri due che ....7................. (stare) con te?
Renato: Di chi ....8................. (parlare)? Che cosa ....9................. (volere) da me?
Ispettore: ....10................ (sapere) benissimo che io non mi ....11................ (sbagliare) mai.
Renato: Mi scusi, ma questa volta Lei si ....12................. (sbagliare).
Ispettore: E allora dimmi dov'...........13................ (essere) ieri sera alle 11.30?
Renato: Non ....14................ (potere) dirglielo; non le farebbe molto piacere.
Ispettore: Dimmelo o ti arresto subito.
Renato: E va bene; l'ha voluto lei. ....15................ (essere) al cinema con sua figlia. ....16................ (guardare) l'ultimo film di Sherlock Holmes. Sa, ...17................ (stare) con lei da tre mesi.

Study the picture.

The structure **stare per + infinitive** indicates an *imminent* action.

- **Stavo per fermarmi** al semaforo, quando un'auto mi ha tamponato.
  (I was about to stop at the traffic lights when a car ran into the back of me)

The structure **stare + infinitive** is used almost exclusively with the *present* and *imperfect* forms, occasionally with the future simple, but **never** with compound tenses (passato prossimo, trapassati, future perfect, etc.). See Unità 52.

- Il bambino **stava per uscire**, quando sua mamma lo ha chiamato.
  (The little boy was about to go out when his Mum called him)

- Mia sorella **sta per tornare** dalla Gran Bretagna.
  (My sister is coming back from Great Britain soon)

1. Write the sentences with the words below using *stare per + infinito*.

1. Che freddo!/Nevicare.
   Che freddo / Sta per nevicare
2. Il negozio/chiudere.
   ....
3. Claudio/fare/il bagno.
   ....
4. Lisa/andare/a letto.
   ....
5. Il treno/partire.
   ....
6. Donatella/laurearsi.
   ....
7. L'anno scolastico/finire.
   ....
8. Noi/andare/ a Norimberga.
   ....

2. Rewrite the sentences from exercise 1 using the past form.

1. Stava per nevicare
2. ....
3. ....
4. ....
5. ....
6. ....
7. ....
8. ....

3. Look at the situations below and make some appropriate predictions.

1. C'è una nuvola nera e densa sopra di te.
   Sta per piovere
2. Vedi due persone che stanno entrando in una chiesa, vestiti da sposi.
   ....
3. Vedi uno che ha rotto il finestrino di una macchina e sta aprendo la porta.
   ....
4. È un gran premio di Formula uno. Le auto sono ferme e aspettano il semaforo verde.
   ....
5. Sono le 7.30 di sera. Il fruttivendolo sta spegnendo le luci.
   ....
6. Ci sono due persone al ristorante, hanno finito di mangiare e stanno chiamando il cameriere.
   ....

There are:

- *indefinite adjectives only*
- *indefinite adjectives and pronouns*
- *indefinite pronouns only.*

Do you remember the difference between an adjective and a pronoun?
See Appendix 3.

Indefinite adjectives.

Ogni *(every, each)*
is invariable and is always used with a singular noun; it is a synonym of *tutti/e (all)*. It is placed before the noun.

- Domani **ogni** studente *(tutti gli studenti)* deve portare 20 euro per la gita a Firenze.
  (Every student must bring 20 euro for the trip to Florence tomorrow)

Qualche *(some, a few)*
is invariable and is always used with a singular noun; it is a synonym of *alcuni (some)*. It is placed before the noun.

- Rimarremo a Napoli **qualche** giorno *(alcuni giorni)*. *(We'll stay in Naples for a few days)*

Qualsiasi/qualunque *(any, whatever/whichever)*
are synonyms. They mean *tutto/i, non importa chi/quale (every, all, it doesn't matter who/which)*.
They are invariable. They are placed before the noun.

- **Qualunque/qualsiasi** città tu visiti in Italia, trovi sempre qualche opera d'arte interessante.
  (Whichever town you visit in Italy, you always find some interesting work of art.)

In **qualsìasi** the stress goes on the first **i**, not on the **a**.

1. Complete the sentences using *ogni, qualche* or *qualsiasi/qualunque* and a word from the box below.

1. Vado al cinema ....*ogni mattina*............ (ogni).
2. .... (qualche) vado a ballare il sabato sera.
3. Mi piace .... (qualsiasi) western.
4. .... (ogni) lavoro dalle 8 alle 13.
5. Silvia cambia macchina .... (ogni).
6. Questa mattina .... (qualche) non ricordava la regola di grammatica.
7. Puoi telefonarmi in .... (qualsiasi).
8. .... (qualsiasi) tu abbia, credo di potere aiutarti.

settimana	problema	film	studente	volta	giorno	anno	momento

2. Complete the sentences using *ogni* or *qualche*.

1. ......*Ogni*...... bambino deve andare a scuola a sei anni.
2. .... bambino italiano gioca a pallacanestro, molti giocano a calcio.
3. .... città italiana ha la metropolitana.
4. .... studente studia cinque ore al giorno, la maggior parte due o tre.
5. .... esame è un rischio.
6. .... lavoro è molto interessante, ma altri sono molto noiosi.

3. Answer the following questions about yourself using *qualche, ogni* or *qualsiasi/qualunque*.

1. Vai spesso al cinema?
....
2. Leggi molto?
....
3. Che film ti piacciono?
....
4. Quali sport pratichi?
....
5. Che piatti italiani preferisci?
....
6. Quali città italiane vorresti visitare?
....
7. Vai spesso in vacanza?
....
8. Quali lingue ti piacerebbe conoscere?
....

There are:

- *indefinite adjectives only*
- *indefinite adjectives and pronouns*
- *indefinite pronouns only.*

Indefinite adjectives and **pronouns**:

Alcuni/e *(some)*

is variable. When it means *qualche* it is used in the plural form.
It goes before the noun when it is an adjective.

- Ieri sera ho rivisto **alcuni** miei compagni *(qualche mio compagno)* del liceo. ➜ *adjective*
  (Yesterday I saw some of my friends from Grammar School again)

- **Alcuni** sono invecchiati moltissimo ➜ *pronoun*
  (Some have really aged a lot)

Ciascuno *(each, every, any)*

is only used in the singular form and only changes according to gender.
When it is an adjective it means *ogni* and goes before the noun.

- **Ciascun** lavoratore *(ogni lavoratore)* ha diritto a 5 settimane di ferie all'anno. ➜ *adjective*
  (Every worker has a right to five week's holiday a year)

When it is an adjective it follows the same rule as the indefinite article *un/uno/una*.

- Ciasc**un l**avorator**e** *(every worker)*
- ciasc**uno st**udent**e** *(every student)*
- ciasc**una m**aestr**a** *(every primary school teacher)*
- ciasc**un'i**nfermier**a** *(every nurse)*

When it is a pronoun it means *ognuno, ogni persona o cosa (everyone, everthing, each person/thing).*

- **Ciascuno** *(ogni persona)* pensi anche agli altri se vuole migliorare la società. ➜ *pronoun*
  (We should all think of other people)

Nessuno *(no, noboby, anyone)*

is only used in the singular form and only changes according to gender.

- **Nessun** essere umano ha mai messo piede su Marte. ➜ *adjective*
  (No human being has ever set foot on Mars)

When it follows the verb it needs the negative adverb *non (not.)*.

- Non c'è stato **nessun** problema allo stadio questa domenica. ➜ *adjective*
  (There were no problems at the stadium this Sunday)

- Ieri sono stato in casa tutto il giorno e non ho visto **nessuno**. ➜ *pronoun*
  (I stayed at home all day yesterday and I didn't see anyone)

When it is an adjective it follows the same rule as the indefinite article *un/uno/una*.
See above: ciascuno.

1. Put the words into order.

1. Mi/nessuno/ha/non/visto.
   Non mi ha visto nessuno
2. Ho/regali/per/tuo/comprato/il/compleanno/alcuni/ti.
   ....
3. Non/che/l'arabo/nessuno/conosco/sappia.
   ....
4. Di/dovrà/i/presentare/ciascuno/documenti/voi/necessari.
   ....
5. Ieri/c'è/non/incidente/strade/stato/sulle/nessun.
   ....
6. Le/alcune/non/leggi/persone/rispettano.
   ....

2. Answer the questions using *nessuno, alcuni* or *ciascuno*.

1. Quanti bicchieri di vino hai bevuto?
   Ne ho bevuti *alcuni* .
2. Chi c'era ieri all'assemblea?
   Non c'era ....
3. A chi bisogna dare l'omaggio?
   A .... studente.
4. Chi deve rispondere alle richieste della gente?
   .... amministratore pubblico deve assumersi le proprie responsabilità.
5. Chi ti ha detto cosa mi è successo?
   Me lo sono immaginato, non me l'ha detto ....
6. Quanto tempo occorre per finire la tua casa?
   Occorrono ancora .... mesi.

3. Correct the mistakes.

1. Ciascuna ha diritto a una casa.
   Ciascuno ha diritto a una casa
2. Nessuno giovane conosce il dialetto.
   ....
3. Ciascun studente deve presentare una relazione per il seminario.
   ....
4. Alcuni dicono che non ci sono nessuni problemi di razzismo in Italia.
   ....
5. Nessuno non può andare a letto molto tardi la sera prima dell'esame.
   ....
6. Alcuna volta mi sento un po' solo.
   ....

There are:

- *indefinite adjectives only*
- *indefinite adjectives and pronouns*
- *indefinite pronouns only.*

Indefinite pronouns.

Chiunque *(anyone)*

is invariable and is only used in the singular form. It means *qualunque persona*.

- **Chiunque** *(qualunque persona)* può collegare il proprio Pc a Internet.
  (Anyone can connect their Pc to Internet.)

Niente/nulla *(nothing, anything)*

are synonyms. They mean *nessuna cosa*. They are invariable.

- **Niente/nulla** *(nessuna cosa)* può far paura a quella donna. *(Nothing can scare that woman)*

When they follow the verb they need the negative adverb *non*.

- Hanno rubato in casa dei vicini, ma **non** mi sono reso conto di **niente/nulla**.
  (They broke into our neighbours'house, but I didn't notice anything)

Ognuno *(everyone)*

is only used in the singular form and changes according to gender. It means *ogni persona*, it is a synonym of *ciascuno*.

- **Ognuno** *(ogni persona)* deve sapere cosa fare in caso d'incendio.
  (Everyone should know what to do in case of fire)

Qualcosa *(something)*

is invariable and is always used in the singular form. It means *qualche cosa*.

- C'è **qualcosa** *(qualche cosa)* nell'aria che mi dà fastidio.
  (There is something in the air that's irritating me)

Qualcuno *(someone, anyone, some)*

is only used in the singular form and changes according to gender. It can also mean *qualche persona* or *qualche cosa*.

- **Qualcuno** di voi ha perso questi occhiali? *(Has anyone [of you] lost these glasses?)*

- Ho letto varie novelle di Hesse. **Qualcuna** mi piace, altre no.
  (I've read several short stories by Hesse. Some of them I like, others I don't.)

Uno

is only used in the singular form. It means *una persona (a person).*

- Cosa pensi di **uno** *(una persona)* che dice: "È giusto non pagare più tasse allo stato."?
  (What do you think of someone who says: "We shouldn't pay the State any more taxes"?)

1. Rewrite the sentences with the opposite meaning.

1. Chiunque può permettersi una macchina.
Nessuno può permettersi una macchina
2. Ho scoperto qualcosa.
....
3. Non c'era nessuno a casa.
....
4. Ognuno pensi per sé.
....
5. Ieri sera al bar c'era uno che conoscevo.
....

2. Answer the questions using *niente, qualcuno, qualcosa, uno*.

1. Cosa hai fatto domenica scorsa?
Niente di interessante. Mi sono molto annoiata.
2. Cosa vuoi mangiare?
..........di buono. Ho molta fame.
3. Ti ha visto qualcuno?
No, non mi ha visto..........
4. Sei tutto sporco. Cosa è successo?
Non ti preoccupare, non è successo.......... .
5. Chi è quel signore?
È .... che conosco, ma non mi ricordo il nome.
6. Cosa fai questo fine settimana?
Vorrei fare ....d'interessante, ma non so ancora cosa.

3. Read the answers and write the questions.

1. *Cos'hai fatto ieri sera*?
Niente.
2. ....?
Nessuno.
3. ....?
Chiunque voglia iscriversi può farlo.
4. ....?
Uno mi ha detto di sì, l'altro invece non ha tempo.
5. ....?
Ognuno deve fare la propria parte.
6. ....?
Nulla.

In this unit and in the following we go from *niente (nothing)* to *tutto (everything)*, i.e. the structures are presented in order of increasing quantity.

Niente/nulla: see Unità 56. **Nessuno:** see Unità 55.

Poco *(few, not many/much, little)*

is variable, it is used both as an adjective and as a pronoun. When it is used as an adjective it goes before the noun.

– Ci sono **poche** uova in casa.
(There aren't many eggs in the house) ➜ *adjective*
– Silvia ha molti amici inglesi, io ne ho **pochi.**
(Silvia has a lot of English friends, I don't have many) ➜ *pronoun*

It is also used as an adverb.
– Ieri mi sono allenato **poco**. *(I didn't do much training yesterday)*

Alcuni/e: see Unità 55. **Qualche**: see Unità 54.

Un po' *(some, a little, a few)*

is a synonym of *qualche* and *alcuni*. When it is placed before the noun it is followed by the preposition **di**.

– Ho **un po' di** soldi in banca, ma sono pochi per comprare una casa.
(I have some money in the bank, but it is too little to buy a house)

It is also used as an adverb.
– Ho mangiato **un po'**, ma non abbastanza; ho ancora fame.
(I have eaten a little, but not enough; I'm still hungry.)

Vari, diversi *(several, some)*

used in the plural form and placed before the noun mean *alcuni*. They change according to gender.
They can be both adjectives and pronouns.
– Ho visto **vari** film interessanti questa settimana.
(I've seen several interesting films this week) ➜ *adjective*
– Ci sono studentesse brave qui, però **diverse** non studiano abbastanza
(There are good female students here, but some of them don't study enough) ➜ *pronoun*

In the singular form **vario** means *multiforme (various)* and **diverso** *differente (different)*. In the plural form, if they come after the noun, they both mean *differente*.
– Sul giornale di oggi ho letto articoli che trattavano di argomenti **diversi/vari**.
(I've read articles about various topics in today's newspaper)

Abbastanza *(enough)*

is invariable. It is used both as an adjectives and as a pronoun. It means *a sufficienza*.
– Ho visitato **abbastanza** paesi di lingua inglese per poter riconoscere i diversi accenti. ➜ *adjective*
(I have visited enough English speaking countries to be able to recognize the different accent)
– Ho letto vari libri, ma non **abbastanza** per fare l'esame.
(I've read several books, but not enough to take the esam.) ➜ *pronoun*

It is also used as an adverb.
– Ieri mattina ero stanco, ma stanotte ho dormito **abbastanza**.
(I was tired yesterday morning, but I got enough sleep last night)

Abbastanza has a second meaning as synonym of *piuttosto (rather, quite)*.
– Questa mattina ti vedo **abbastanza/piuttosto** allegro. Cosa hai fatto ieri sera?
(I see you are quite cheerful this morning. What did you do yesterday evening?)

Parecchio *(quite a few, quite a lot)*

is variable. It indicates a quantity which is bigger than *abbastanza*, but smaller than *molto*. It is an adjectives and a pronoun.
– Ho **parecchie** possibilità di essere assunto da una agenzia pubblicitaria.
(I have quite a few chances of being employed by an advertising agency) ➜ *adjective*
– Sono molti i turisti tedeschi contenti dell'Italia, ma **parecchi** non vogliono tornarci.
(Many German tourists enjoy Italy, but quite a few don't want to come back) ➜ *pronoun*

1. Complete the sentences with the correct word.

1. Ieri ho mangiato due pizze. Avevo ...*molta*... fame!

Poco molta varie niente.

2. Sto leggendo .... libri interessanti in questo periodo.

Molto qualche vari nessun

3. C'è .... di nebbia. Fa' attenzione.

Diversa qualche abbastanza un po'

4. Sono stato in Belgio .... volte. Mi piace molto.

Diverse nessuna qualche alcuna

5. La birra mi piace ....; preferisco il vino.

Poco abbastanza varia nulla

6. Oggi ho lavorato .... Dovevo finire tante cose.

Parecchio qualche alcuno diverso

2. Match the sentences from the columns.

1. *Ti ho telefonato,*
2. È rimasto poco pane,
3. Quante sigarette hai fumato?
4. Conosci qualcuno a Mosca?
5. Vieni al cinema stasera?
6. Ti piace Bruce Springsteen?
7. Hai letto molti libri quest'estate?
8. Giochi spesso a tennis?

a Diverse.
b Mi spiace ho parecchie cose da fare.
c Abbastanza.
d *ma non c'era nessuno.*
e Alcuni.
f Qualche volta.
g scendo a comprarlo.
h Sì, ho alcuni amici che ci abitano.

3. Answer the questions about yourself.
Use *niente, nessuno, poco, alcuni, qualche, un po', vari/diversi, abbastanza, parecchio.*

1. Quante persone hai visto oggi? ....
2. Quante ore hai lavorato? ....
3. Ti sei stancato? ....
4. Quanto guadagni al mese? ....
5. Ti piace il tuo lavoro? ....
6. Ti piace studiare le lingue? ....
7. Quante lingue straniere conosci? ....
8. Leggi molti giornali stranieri? ....
9. Vedi molti film in italiano? ....
10. Ti piace ascoltare canzoni italiane? ....

Molto *(much, many, a lot of)*
is variable, it is used as an adjective and as a pronoun. It expresses a big quantity but not the whole.

- **Molti** vecchi hanno oggi bisogno di assistenza, ma non vogliono lasciare la propria casa. ➜ *adjective*
  (Nowadays many elderly people need assistance but they do not want to leave their homes)
- Ho visitato parecchi posti, ma ce ne sono ancora **molti** che vorrei conoscere. ➜ *pronoun*
  (I have visited quite a few places, but there are still many I would like to see.)

It is also used as an adverb.
- Ho camminato **molto** e mi sento stanchissimo. *(I have walked a lot and I feel really tired)*

Tanto *(many, a lot)*
is variable. It is a synonym of *molto* and is used in the same way.

- **Tanti** vecchi hanno oggi bisogno di assistenza, ma non vogliono lasciare la propria casa. ➜ *adjective*
- Ho visitato parecchi posti, ma ce ne sono ancora **tanti** che vorrei conoscere. ➜ *pronoun*
- Ho camminato **tanto** e mi sento stanchissimo ➜ *adverb*

Troppo *(too much, too many)*
is variable. It indicates excessive quantity. It is used both as an adjective and as a pronoun.

- Mio figlio di solito non ha molti compiti da fare, ma per domani ne ha **troppi**. ➜ *pronoun*
  (My son doesn't usually have a lot of homework to do, but he has too much for tomorrow)
- È **troppo** tempo che non vedo Sandro. Stasera gli telefono. ➜ *adjective*
  (I haven't seen Sandro for such a long time. I'm going to call him this evening)

It is also used as an adverb.

- Ho fumato **troppo** questa settimana. Devo cercare di smettere.
  (I have smoked too much this week. I must try to give up)

Tutto *(all)*
is variable. It indicates the whole. It is used as an adjective and as a pronoun.
- Non **tutto** è perduto. *(Not all is lost)* ➜ *pronoun*
- **Tutti** sono d'accordo con lui, ma nessuno lo ammette. ➜ *pronoun*
  (Everyone agrees with him, but no one will admit it)

When it is used as an adjective it is followed by the definite article.
- **Tutta la** città ha festeggiato la vittoria della sua squadra. ➜ *adjective*
  (The whole town celebrated its team's victory)
- **Tutti i** prodotti di quel supermercato sono scontati. ➜ *adjective*
  (There are discounts on all the products in that supermarket)

When **tutto** is followed by a number, there is an **e** (2) after **tutti/e** (1), followed by the number (3), the article (4) and then finally the noun (5).

- **Tutti** (1) **e** (2) **5** (3) **i** (4) **figli** (5) di Marta vanno all'università. ➜ *adjective*
  (Marta's five children all go to University)

1. Complete the sentences using con *molto/tanto*.

1. Oggi ho ....*molto/tanto*............ sonno.
2. Mi sento .... stanca a causa della differenza di fuso orario.
3. Sono appena tornato dalle vacanze. Ho speso ....
4. Però ho visto .... posti interessanti.
5. Ho conosciuto .... persone cordiali.
6. Il Guatemala è un paese .... bello.
7. Mi piacerebbe .... tornarci.
8. Ma so che ci sono .... altri paesi che vorrei visitare.
9. Bisognerebbe avere .... soldi e .... tempo.
10. Penso che viaggerei .... volte all'anno.

2. Complete the sentences as in the example, using *troppo* and a word form the box below.

1. Stasera non esco. *Sono troppo stanco*.........
2. In certe zone della città è meglio non uscire da soli di sera ....
3. In questa strada è difficile parcheggiare. ....
4. Oggi resto a letto tutto il giorno. ....
5. Simone non può ancora prendere la patente. ....
6. Filippo voleva continuare a giocare a calcio, ma ....
7. Questo quartiere non mi piace. .... e pochi alberi.
8. Roberto è sempre ubriaco. ....
9. Non so se riuscirò a darti il tuo libro domani. ....
10. Non riesco a capire l'articolo che mi hai detto di leggere. ....

stanco	pagine	macchine	difficile	case	birra	pericoloso	giovane	vecchio	freddo

3. Complete the sentences using *tutto.*

1. Quante sigarette ti sono rimaste?
Nessuna; le ho fumate ....*tutte*......... .
2. Ieri è piovuto .... il giorno.
3. Stasera vedo .... e tre i miei fratelli.
4. Giovanni ha finito di pitturare .... la casa.
5. .... le sere guardo la televisione.
6. .... conoscono Franz.
7. .... hanno bisogno degli amici.
8. Conoscete .... le persone in questa foto?

4. Correct the mistakes.

1. Tanti i bambini stanno giocando nel parco.
......*Tanti bambini stanno giocando nel parco*...................
2. Ho corso molto chilometri stamattina.
....
3. Ho pensato a tutti problemi di cui mi hai parlato.
....
4. Ho bevuto troppo tazze di caffè; stasera non dormirò.
....
5. Hai mangiato tutti due i cioccolatini?
....
6. Non tutti è perduto. Bisogna discutere il problema della tangenziale con il sindaco.
....

Study the picture.

The **comparativo di maggioranza** *(more/-er ... than)* (see Appendix 3) of adjectives is formed with the word **più** *(more)* followed by the *adjective*. The second term of comparison is introduced by **di** or **che** *(than)*.

– La Germania è **più** popolata **dell**'Italia. *(Germany has a bigger population than Italy.)*

Di is used when the world that follows is

- a **noun**
  – Carla è **più** bella **di** sua sorella. *(Carla is prettier than her sister.)*
- a **personal pronoun**
  – Giorgio è **più** vecchio **di me**. *(Giorgio is older than me.)*

Che is used when the word that follows is

- an **adjective**
  – Lino è **più** simpatico **che attraente**. *(Lino is nice rather than attractive.)*
- a **verb in the infinitive**
  – Stare in vacanza è **più** bello **che lavorare**. *(Being on holiday is better than working)*
- a **prepositional phrase**
  – Pavarotti è **più** bravo dal vivo **che su disco**. *(Pavarotti is better live than recorded.)*
- an **adverb**
  – Certi studenti rispondono alle domande **più** meccanicamente **che intelligentemente**. *(Some students answer questions more in a mechanical way than intelligently.)*

Che is also used when the comparison is between

- **two nouns** which *are not subjects*.
  – In televisione vedo **più film che programmi** di informazione. *(I see more films than documentaries on television)*

For the use of the subjunctive with the comparativo di maggioranza + a relative clause introduced by **di quanto** (than) see Unità 70.

– Flavio è **più** vecchio **di quanto credessi**. *(Flavio is older than I thought)*

The **comparativo di minoranza** *(less... than, not as... as)* (see Appendix 3) is formed in the same way as the *comparativo di maggioranza*, using the word **meno** *(less)* instead of *più*.
– Il tedesco è **meno** difficile del russo. *(German is less difficult than Russian.)*

The **comparativo di uguaglianza** *(as... as)* (see Appendix 3) is formed by using.

- **(tanto)** + adjective, **quanto** + adjective, when comparing two *adjectives*
  – Il mio barbiere è **(tanto)** bravo **quanto** simpatico. *(My barber is not only friendly but also very good)*
- **(tanto)... quanto** or **(così)...come** when comparing *nouns*, *pronouns* and *verbs in the infinitive*.
  – Il lago è **(tanto)** riposante **quanto** la montagna. *(Lakes are just as relaxing as mountains)*
  – Rossana è **(tanto)** alta **quanto** me. *(Rossana is just as tall as me)*
  – Leggere è **(così)** stimolante **come** andare al cinema. *(Reading is just as stimulating as going to the cinema)*

Tanto and **così** can often be left out.

1. Complete the sentences using one of the comparative forms.

1. Il mio appartamento è diventato troppo piccolo per noi. Ne stiamo cercando uno ...*più grande*... .
2. La ragazza di Sandro ha 23 anni; è di un anno .... di lui.
3. La macchina di Piero fa i duecento. E' molto .... della mia.
4. Oggi fa molto freddo. Ieri si stava meglio: faceva ....
5. Non condivido la soluzione del direttore. La mia era ....
6. Napoli è bella, ma Roma è ....
7. In questo esame ci sono molti errori, ma quello che hai corretto prima era addirittura ....
8. Quella segretaria risponde sempre in modo scortese. L'altra invece è ....

2. Complete the sentences with *di*, or *che*.

1. Gianni è più alto ....*di*.......... Francesco.
2. Una Mercedes è più cara .... una Fiat.
3. L'Italia è più ricca .... Cuba.
4. Davide è più simpatico .... intelligente.
5. Fare un po' di sport è più salutare .... restare sempre seduti a leggere.
6. Suly è più giovane .... me.
7. Vado più volentieri al mare .... in montagna.
8. Molte persone leggono più giornali .... libri.
9. Patrizia è meno fortunata .... te.
10. Il congiuntivo in italiano è meno difficile .... quanto credessi.

3. Complete the sentences using *tanto*/*quanto* and a word from the box below.

1. Silvia è ....*tanto*.......... simpatica ....*quanto sua sorella*....
2. Viaggiare è .... educativo ....
3. Francesco è .... bravo ....
4. Mia nonna è.. vecchia ....
5. La vita in Italia è .... cara ....

simpatico	stressante	suo marito	studiare	sua sorella

4. Rewrite the sentences without changing the meaning.

1. Luigi è più grasso di Fabrizio.
...*Fabrizio è più magro di Luigi*...
2. Per uno spagnolo l'italiano è più facile dell'arabo.
....
3. Paolo è meno interessante di sua moglie.
....
4. Le mele verdi sono più dolci delle rosse.
....
5. Andare a teatro costa più che andare al cinema.
....
6. Studiare è più produttivo che passare il tempo senza far niente.
....
7. Parigi è più vicina all'Italia di Londra.
....
8. Il Brasile è più grande della Svizzera.
....

Study the picture.

Is anyone taller than Nicola in his class? And in the world?

The **superlativo relativo** *(the most/-est, least)* is formed with the *definite article* and the *comparativo (di maggioranza* or *minoranza*).
It indicates the characteristic of a person or object by comparing it with other people or objects.

- Davide è **il** musicista **più esperto** dell'orchestra. *(Davide is the most experienced musician in the orchestra)*

- È **lo** studente **meno preparato** della scuola. *(He is the student who studies the least in the whole school)*

The noun can sometimes follow the adjective, however the article is always placed before the adjective.
- Roma è **la più grande** città d'Italia. *(Rome is the largest city in Italy)*

The second element can be introduced by **di** but also by **fra** or by **che + subjunctive**.
- È l'appartamento più ampio **dell'**edificio. *(It is the largest flat in the building.)*
- Lo Zio Camillo è il più ricco **fra** tutti i miei parenti. *(Uncle Camillo is the richest of all my relatives.)*
- È la macchina più veloce **che** io **abbia** (mai) **avuto**. *(It's the fastest car I've (ever) had.)*

Fra cannot be used when the word that follows is a *noun of place*.
- Londra è la più popolata città **d'**Europa. *(London is the most populated city in Europe)*

For the use of the sybjunctive with the superlativo relativo see Unità 70.

Study the picture.

Is there anyone better looking than this girl?
We do not know, as there are no comparisons in the sentence.

The **superlativo assoluto** *(very/really + adjective)* is formed by adding the suffix **-issimo** to the adjective.
It emphasizes the characteristic of a person or an object without making any comparison.

- Il film di ieri sera era noios**issimo**. *(The film yesterday evening was very boring)*
- La storia è una materia interessant**issima**. *(History is a really interesting subject)*

The sentences above could also be said in the following way:
- Il film di ieri sera era **molto** noioso.
- La storia è una materia **molto** interessante.

The structure with **-issimo** however is very common and is particularly expressive.

Adjectives ending in **-co** and **-go** add an **h**.
lungo ➜ lung**h**issimo *(long)*
bianco ➜ bianc**h**issimo *(white)*..

1. Make comparisons using the words below.

1. Leone/gatto.
   Il leone è più feroce del gatto
2. Ricchi/poveri.
   ....
3. Automobile/bicicletta.
   ....
4. Vecchi/giovani.
   ....
5. Bere vino/bere acqua
   ....
6. Appartamento/villa.
   ....

2. Use the words from exercise 1 to make sentences with the *superlativi relativi*.

1. Leone/gatto.
   Il leone è l'animale più feroce
2. Ricchi/poveri.
   ....
3. Automobile/bicicletta.
   ....
4. Vecchi/giovani.
   ....
5. Bere vino/bere acqua
   ....
6. Appartamento/villa.
   ....

3. Rewrite the sentences with the correct form of the *superlativi relativi* using the words in brackets.

1. Roma è una città molto grande.
   Roma è la più grande città italiana .... (italiana)
2. Il cinese è una lingua molto difficile.
   .... (Secondo me)
3. La Germania è molto grande.
   .... (d'Europa).
4. La nazionale italiana di pallavolo è molto forte.
   .... (del mondo).
5. Giove è un pianeta molto grande.
   .... (del sistema solare).
6. La *Divina Commedia* è un libro molto famoso.
   .... (della letteratura italiana).

4. Rewrite the sentences using the *superlativi assoluti*.

1. Questo monumento è molto importante. *Questo monumento è importantissimo*
2. Il mio appartamento è molto piccolo. ....
3. Il vino francese è molto buono. ....
4. La Russia è molto grande. ....
5. Questa valigia è molto pesante. ....
6. L'Avana è molto bella. ....

Irregular comparatives and superlatives

base form	*comparativo*	*superlativo relativo*	*superlativo assoluto*
buono *(good)*	**migliore** *(better)*	**il migliore** *(the best)*	**ottimo** *(excellent)*
cattivo *(bad)*	**peggiore** *(worse)*	**il peggiore** *(the worst)*	**pessimo** *(the absolute worst)*
grande *(big, old, great)*	**maggiore** *(bigger, elder, greater)*	**il maggiore** *(the biggest, the eldest, the greatest)*	**massimo** *(maximum)*
piccolo *(small, young)*	**minore** *(smaller, younger)*	**il minore** *(the smallest, the youngest)*	**minimo** *(ninimum)*

- È la pizza **peggiore** che abbia mai assaggiato. *(It's the worst pizza I've ever eaten.)*

In addition to the irregular forms there are also regular forms which are generally used to indicate human qualities.

- Mia mamma dice che sono **più cattivo** di mio fratello. *(My mum says I'm naughtier than my brother)*

When talking about sizes the adjectives **grande** and **piccolo** are used.

- La Fiat Punto è **più piccola** della Volvo 850. *(A Fiat Punto is smaller than a Volvo 850)*

When talking about age it is better to use **maggiore** and **minore**.

- Mio fratello **maggiore** lavora in una ditta edile. *(My elder brother works for a construction firm)*

In modern Italian the *superlativo assoluto* can also be expressed with prefixes, i.e. **arci-**, **iper**, **stra-**, **super-**, **ultra-**.

- È un apparecchio **ultraveloce**. *(It's an ultra.fast plane)*
- Quell'uomo è **straricco**. *(That man is really loaded)*
- È un'opera **arcinota**. *(It's a very famous opera)*
- Luigi è un lavoratore **superefficiente**. *(Luigi is a super-efficient worker)*
- Come mi stressi! Sei così **iperattivo**! *(You really stress me out! You're so hyperactive!)*

The *superlativo assoluto* can sometimes be expressed by repeating the adjective which indicates the quality.

- Vivo in un appartamento **piccolo piccolo**. *(I live in a really tiny flat)*

Different expressions can be used to emphasise comparative, i.e.:
molto, assai, notevolmente, estremamente, etc. *(much, far, a lot, etc.)*

These words go before **più**.

- Il tuo nuovo ragazzo è **molto più** interessante di Mauro.
  (Your new boyfriend is far more interesting than Mauro)
- La soluzione di questo problema risulta **estremamente più** complessa di quanto pensassi.
  (The solution to this problem appears to be much more complicated thain I thought)

1. Write the correct form of the comparative and *superlativo assoluto*.

1. Corto .... più corto .... cortissimo ....
2. Magro ....
3. Ricco ....
4. Lungo ....
5. Bello ....
6. Stanco ....
7. Antico ....
8. Grande ....
9. Cattivo ....
10. Piccolo ....

2. Write sentences with the *superlativo relativo.*

1. Il Nilo è un fiume molto grande.
....Il Nilo è il maggior fiume dell'Africa.. (dell'Africa).
2. La cucina italiana è molto buona.
(Secondo me)..
3. Paolo è uno studente molto bravo.
....(della classe).
4. Hai fatto un esame molto brutto.
....(della tua vita).
5. Questo risultato deve essere raggiunto con uno sforzo estremamente piccolo.
....
6. Francesco è il primo figlio di Maurizio.
....

3. Reinforce the comparative sentences using *molto, assai, notevolmente, estremamente.*

1. L'esame che hai fatto ieri è stato ......assai........ peggiore dell'ultimo.
2. Milano è .... più grande di Cremona.
3. Il tasso d'inflazione in Italia è .... più alto che in Germania.
4. La disoccupazione in Italia è .... maggiore che in Giappone.
5. Il fiume Po è .... più lungo del Taro.
6. Oggi ho lavorato .... di più di ieri.
7. La grammatica italiana è .... più complessa di quella inglese.
8. L'Italia è .... più ricca di tesori artistici dell'Argentina.

Adverbs of manner

base form	*comparativo di maggioranza e minoranza*	*superlativo relativo*	*superlativo assoluto*
giustamente *(rightly)*	**più/meno giustamente** *(more/less rightly)*	**nel modo più giusto** **nella maniera più giusta** *(in the best way)*	**giustissimamente** **molto giustamente** *(very rightly)*

– Ti farò arrivare il pacco **nel modo più veloce**. *(I'll send you the parcel the fastest way possible)*

– Ricordati di parlagli **più chiaramente** di quanto tu abbia fatto finora. *(Remember to speak to him more clearly than you have done so far)*

Irregular forms

base form	*comparativo di maggioranza e minoranza*	*superlativo relativo*	*superlativo assoluto*
bene *(good)*	**meglio** *(better)*	**nel modo migliore** **nella maniera migliore** *(in the best way)*	**benissimo** *(very well)*
male *(badly)*	**peggio** *(worse)*	**nel modo peggiore** **nella maniera peggiore** *(in the worst way)*	**malissimo** *(very badly)*
molto *(a lot)*	**più** *(more)*	**il più possibile** *(the most possible, as much as)*	**moltissimo** *(very much)*
poco *(little, few)*	**meno** *(less, fewer)*	**il meno possibile** *(the least possible, the fewest, as little as)*	**pochissimo** *(very little/few)*

– Mangia **il più possibile**! Sei così magra! *(Eat as much as you can! You're so thin!)*

– L'esame mi è andato **malissimo.** *(My esam went really badly)*

Other adverbs

base form	*comparativo di maggioranza e minoranza*	*superlativo relativo*	*superlativo assoluto*
presto *(soon, early)*	**più/meno presto** *(sooner, earlier, less soon/early)*	**il più presto possibile** *(as soon as possible)*	**prestissimo** *(very soon/early)*
spesso *(often)*	**più/meno spesso** *(more/less often)*	**il più spesso possibile** *(as often as possible)*	**spessissimo** *(very often)*

– Cerca di telefonare a tua madre **più spesso**. *(Try and phone your mother more often)*

– Questa mattina mi sono alzato **prestissimo.** *(I got up really early this morning)*

The **comparative** of adverbs can be modified by using **molto** or **assai.**

– In treno arrivo a casa **molto/assai più rapidamente** che in macchina. *(I get home much faster by train than by car)*

Apart from the structure **nel modo più** giusto, etc., the superlativo relativo can also be expressed with: **nel più** giusto **dei modi** *(in the best of ways)*, etc.

– Durante un colloquio di lavoro bisogna cercare di esprimersi **nel più corretto dei modi**. *(During an interview one must try to express oneself as correctly as possible)*

1. Rewrite the sentences with the opposite meaning.

1. Hai risolto il problema nel modo migliore.
Hai risolto il problema nel modo peggiore
2. Si è comportato in modo molto più corretto del solito.
...
3. Carlo reagisce sempre più lentamente.
...
4. Alfredo parla spagnolo sempre meglio.
...
5. Anita balla benissimo.
...
6. Raccontami cosa è successo in modo più esteso.
...

2. Put the words into order. Rewrite the adverb in the form of the *superlativo assoluto.*

1. Sento/oggi/male/mi.
Oggi mi sento malissimo
2. Storia/ho/esame/l'/bene/superato/di.
...
3. Mese/guadagnato/Lisa/poco/ha/questo.
...
4. Domani/devo/presto/svegliare/mi.
...
5. Ieri/molto/Gianni/studiato/ha.
...
6. Tornata/casa/Ilaria/rapidamente/è.
...

REVISION EXERCISE: COMPARATIVE AND SUPERLATIVE FORMS (ADJECTIVES AND ADVERBS)

3. Complete the sentences with the correct form of the comparative or superlative. Use the words from the box below.

1. Mi piace molto come suona Tom; suona *benissimo*
2. Adoro la Quinta sinfonia di Beethoven; mi piace...
3. Aldo ha 20 anni, Silvia 16. Aldo è ... di Silvia.
4. Il prosciutto di Parma è ... della mortadella.
5. Paolo è un genio. È ... della classe.
6. Sara è ... ...
7. Il Monte Everest è la montagna ... del mondo.
8. Gennaio è il mese ... dell'anno.
9. La cucina italiana è ... ...
10. La figlia di Patricia è ...; non piange mai.

attraente	intelligente	molto	bene	buona	tranquillissima	sana	caro	vecchio	alto	simpatica	freddo

Study the picture.

Affirmative form of the **imperative** for second person singular and first and second perosn plural.

Regular verbs

I - ARE: cantare *(sing)*	II - ERE: prendere *(take)*	III a - IRE: sentire *(hear)*	III b - IRE: finire *(finish)*
cant - **a!** cant - **iamo!** cant - **ate!**	prend - **i!** prend - **iamo!** prend - **ete!**	sent - **i!** sent - **iamo!** sent - **ite!**	fin - **isci!** fin - **iamo!** fin - **ite!**

Verbs *essere* and *avere*

AVERE	ESSERE
abbi! **abbiamo!** **abbiate!**	**sii!** **siamo!** **siate!**

– **Sii** più determinato e vedrai che otterrai maggiori successi!
(Be more determined and you'll see that you'll be more successful!)

Irregular verbs

Andare	**va'!** **andiamo!** **andate!**	*Dire*	**di'!** **diciamo!** **dite!**	*Sapere*	**sappi!** **sappiamo!** **sappiate!**
Dare	**da'!** **diamo!** **date!**	*Fare*	**fa'!** **facciamo!** **fate!**	*Stare*	**sta'!** **stiamo!** **state!**

– **Andate** a casa subito, sta per piovere! *(Go home right away, it's going to rain!)*

For the polite **affirmative form** of the **imperative** (Lei - Loro) the *present subjunctive* is used.

Regular verbs

I - ARE: cantare *(sing)*	II - ERE: prendere *(take)*	III a - IRE: sentire *(hear)*	III b - IRE: finire *(finish)*
(Lei) cant **- i!** (Loro) cant **- ino!**	(Lei) prend - **a!** (Loro) prend - **ano!**	(Lei) sent - **a!** (Loro) sent - **ano!**	(Lei) fin - **isca!** (Loro) fin - **iscano!**

– **Prenda** un caffè, Signora! Glielo offro con piacere. *(Please have a coffee! It's on me.)*

▶ The polite form with **Loro** is very rarely used in modern Italian. See Unità 38.
▶ For irregular verbs see Unità 66.

For the **negative structure** of the **imperative non** is placed before the forms used in the affirmative.
▶ For the second person singular **non + infinito** is used.

I - ARE: cantare	II - ERE: credere	III a - IRE: sentire	III b - IRE: finire
non cant - **are!** non cant - **i!** non cant - **iamo!** non cant - **ate!** non cant - **ino!**	non prend - **ere!** non prend - **a!** non prend - **iamo!** non prend - **ete!** non prend **- ano!**	non sent - **ire!** non sent - **a!** non sent - **iamo!** non sent - **ite!** non sent **- ano!**	non fin - **ire!** non fin - **isca!** non fin - **iamo!** non fin - **ite!** non fin - **iscano!**

– **Non aprire** la finestra, fa troppo freddo! *(Don't open the window, it's too cold!)*
– Per favore, **non urlate**, voglio riposare! *(Please don't shout, I want to have a rest!)*

1. **Write the verbs in the correct form of the imperative.**

infinito	*imperativo* tu	noi	voi
1. *Cantare*	*canta*	*cantiamo*	*cantate*
2. Giocare	....	....	....
3. Prendere	....	....	....
4. Leggere	....	....	....
5. Ascoltare	....	....	....
6. Andare	....	....	....
7. Avere	....	....	....
8. Finire	....	....	....
9. Partire	....	....	....
10. Dare	....	....	....
11. Dire	....	....	....
12. Scrivere	....	....	....
13. Pulire	....	....	....
14. Venire	....	....	....

2. **Rewrite the opposite of the following sentences using either the negative or affirmative form of the imperative.**

1. Non parlare a voce alta!
Parla a voce alta!
2. Telefona a Fausto!
....
3. Apri la finestra!
....
4. Non accendere la televisione!
....
5. Bevi una birra!
....
6. Non scendere le scale!
....
7. Attraversa la strada lentamente!
....
8. Non cantare!
....
9. Prendi una mela!
....
10. Raccogli quel fiore!
....

3. **Rewrite the sentences with the correct form of the third person singular Lei.**

1. Prendi una pasta! *Prenda una pasta!*
2. Scrivi a macchina la relazione! ....
3. Rispondi meglio! ....
4. Ascolta con più attenzione! ....
5. Va più piano in macchina! ....
6. Vieni a trovarmi presto! ....

Study the picture.

Unstressed object pronouns, ne and **ci** follow the second person singular and the first and second person plural.

- Ricordiamo**ci** di chiudere la finestra quando usciamo!
  (We must remember to close the window when we go out!)
- Passa**mi** l'acqua per favore! *(Pass me the water, please!)*
- Togliete**vi** le scarpe prima di entrare in casa! *(Take your shoes off before you come into the house!)*
- Se vedi Giovanna, non parlar**le** della festa per il suo compleanno!
  (If you see Giovanna, don't tell her about her birthday party!)

Unstressed object pronouns, ne and **ci** are placed before the polite forms Lei and Loro.

- **Lo** guardi bene e **mi** dica se lo riconosce! *(Take a good look and tell me if you recognize him!)*

Some irregular verbs in the second person singular, when followed by **unstressed object pronouns, ne** or **ci** double the consonant of the pronoun, e.g.:

Andare ➜ Va**cci** piano con quel vino! *(Go steady on that wine!)*

Dare ➜ Da**lle** una mano, non riesce a sollevare la valigia! *(Give her a hand, she can't lift her suitcase!)*

Dire ➜ Di**mmi** come ti chiami! *(Tell me your name!)*

Fare ➜ Fa**mmi** un favore, spegni la luce! *(Do me a favour, switch off the light!)*

Stare ➜ Sta**cci** attento, è uno sport pericoloso! *(Be careful, it's a dangerous sport!)*

Exception: there is no double **g** with **gli**.

- Da**gli** il mio numero di telefono e di**gli** di chiamarmi presto!
  (Give him my phone number and tell him to call me soon!)

1. Rewrite the verbs using the imperative with pronouns.

	tu	voi	Lei
1.	Fermati!	fermatevi	si fermi
2.	Deciditi!	....	....
3.	Sbrigati!	....	....
4.	Alzati!	....	....
5.	Siediti!	....	....
6.	Parlagliene!	....	....
7.	Vacci!	....	....
8.	Dalle una mano!	....	....
9.	Fammi vedere!	....	....
10.	Vergognati!	....	....

2. Complete the sentences with the correct form of the imperative. Use the verbs from the box below.

1. Che scarpe sporche! Puliscile!
2. Stasera andiamo da Sandra. .... di comprarle un mazzo di fiori.
3. Sta facendo molto freddo. .... una sciarpa.
4. Hai ancora problemi con la tua collega? .... con il tuo direttore!
5. ...., hai già pensato dove andare in vacanza per Natale?
6. Fulvio, o andiamo a mangiare una pizza o andiamo al cinema. ....!
7. Guarda che dobbiamo andare al matrimonio di Teo. .... più elegantemente!
8. Sono appena tornato da Cordoba. .... anche tu perché è bellissima!

vestirsi	ricordarsi	parlarne	pulirle	decidersi	andarci	mettersi	dirmi

3. Answer the questions using the correct form of the imperative.

1. Posso dare a Giancarlo il tuo indirizzo?
Sì, daglielo!
2. Posso chiamarti più tardi?
....quando vuoi!
3. Posso andare in discoteca stasera?
...., ma non tornare tardi!
4. Posso andare in vacanza a New York con Patty?
...., ma fate attenzione!
5. Posso parlare a Stefano del tuo nuovo libro?
No,...; è un segreto!
6. Stasera Lucia ed io diremo ai miei genitori che ci vogliamo sposare!
No, ...; gli darà un infarto!
7. Possiamo prendere la tua macchina?
No, ...; è senza benzina e frena malissimo!
8. Mamma, possiamo iscriverci al corso di aerobica?
Sì, ... pure; ma quest'anno niente vacanze!

- The **imperative** only has one tense, the present.
- It is used to express

orders

(Come back here right away!)

prohibitions

(Do not speak to the driver.)

invitations

(Come on, let's do something, let's go to the cinema!)

suggestions

(Give up smoking, believe me, it's better for us all!)

request/appeals

(Please don't leave me!)

1. Rewrite the following sentences using the imperative with *tu*.

1. Vietato fumare.
Non fumare!
2. Vietato sporgersi dal finestrino.
....
3. Vietato gettare oggetti dal finestrino.
....
4. Stop a 150 metri.
....
5. Divieto di sosta.
....
6. Film vietato ai minori di 14 anni.
....
7. Silenzio!
....
8. Vietato l'accesso ai non addetti ai lavori.
....

2. Look at the situations below. Give an order or make a request using the imperative.

1. Vuoi la bottiglia dell'acqua.
Passami l'acqua, per favore!
2. Hai bisogno di un maglione in prestito. Lo chiedi a tuo fratello.
....
3. I tuoi compagni continuano a parlare, non senti l'insegnante.
....
4. Suona il telefono; tu stai facendo la doccia. Chiedi a tua sorella Sonia di rispondere.
....
5. Un poliziotto ti ordina di mostrargli i documenti.
....
6. Il professore vi dice di studiare di più.
....

3. Look at the situations below. Give an order or make a request using the imperative.

1. Hai voglia di andare al cinema. Lo proponi ai tuoi amici.
Andiamo al cinema!
2. Sei in discoteca. Inviti a ballare i tuoi amici
....
3. Tommaso ti dice che ha il mal di testa.
....
4. Silvia ti dice che ha litigato con il suo ragazzo e che vuole parlargli, ma lui abita lontano.
....
5. Carlo non sa cosa fare stasera. Invitalo a casa tua.
....
6. Tua madre ha il colesterolo alto.
....
7. Sei medico. Un tuo paziente fuma molto e soffre di cuore.
....
8. Tua cugina sta piangendo. Vuoi sapere cosa succede.
....

Verbi regolari

I - ARE: cantare *(sing)*	II - ERE: vedere *(see)*	III a - IRE: sentire *(hear)*	III b - IRE: finire *(finish)*
che (io) cant - **i**	che (io) ved **- a**	che (io) sent **- a**	che (io) fin **- isc- a**
che (tu) cant **- i**	che (tu) ved **- a**	che (tu) sent **- a**	che (tu) fin **- isc- a**
che (lui, lei, Lei) cant **- i**	che (lui, lei, Lei) ved **- a**	che (lui, lei, Lei) sent **- a**	che (lui, lei, Lei) fin **- isc-a**
che (noi) cant **- iamo**	che (noi) ved **- iamo**	che (noi) sent **- iamo**	che (noi) fin **- iamo**
che (voi) cant **- iate**	che (voi) ved **- iate**	che (voi) sent **- iate**	che (voi) fin **- iate**
che (loro) cant **- ino**	che (loro) ved **- ano**	che (loro) sent **- ano**	che (loro) fin **- isc- ano**

- Desidero che mia sorella **finisca** bene gli esami. *(I hope my sister does well in her final exams)*
- Non credo che il cantante del gruppo musicale di Gianluca **canti** nel modo migliore.
  (I don't think the vocalist in Gianluca's band sings particularly well)

For the **verbs *essere*** and ***avere***: see Unità 68.

Irregular verbs

potere *(can)*	**volere** *(want)*	**dovere** *(must)*	**sapere** *(kenow)*
che (io) **possa**	che (io) **voglia**	che (io) **debba**	che (io) **sappia**
che (tu) **possa**	che (tu) **voglia**	che (tu) **debba**	che (tu) **sappia**
che (lui, lei, Lei) **possa**	che (lui, lei, Lei) **voglia**	che (lui, lei, Lei) **debba**	che (lui, lei, Lei) **sappia**
che (noi) **possiamo**	che (noi) **vogliamo**	che (noi) **dobbiamo**	che (noi) **sappiamo**
che (voi) **possiate**	che (voi) **vogliate**	che (voi) **dobbiate**	che (voi) **sappiate**
che (loro) **possano**	che (loro) **vogliano**	che (loro) **debbano**	che (loro) **sappiano**
piacere *(like)*	**bere** *(drink)*	**andare** *(go)*	**stare** *(be, staiy)*
che (io) **piaccia**	che (io) **beva**	che (io) **vada**	che (io) **stia**
che (tu) **piaccia**	che (tu) **beva**	che (tu) **vada**	che (tu) **stia**
che (lui, lei, Lei) **piaccia**	che (lui, lei, Lei) **beva**	che (lui, lei, Lei) **vada**	che (lui, lei, Lei) **stia**
che (noi) **piacciamo**	che (noi) **beviamo**	che (noi) **andiamo**	che (noi) **stiamo**
che (voi) **piacciate**	che (voi) **beviate**	che (voi) **andiate**	che (voi) **stiate**
che (loro) **piacciano**	che (loro) **bevano**	che (loro) **vadano**	che (loro) **stiano**
fare *(do, make)*	**dare** *(give)*	**dire** *(say)*	**uscire** *(go out)*
che (io) **faccia**	che (io) **dia**	che (io) **dica**	che (io) **esca**
che (tu) **faccia**	che (tu) **dia**	che (tu) **dica**	che (tu) **esca**
che (lui, lei, Lei) **faccia**	che (lui, lei, Lei) **dia**	che (lui, lei, Lei) **dica**	che (lui, lei, Lei) **esca**
che (noi) **facciamo**	che (noi) **diamo**	che (noi) **diciamo**	che (noi) **usciamo**
che (voi) **facciate**	che (voi) **diate**	che (voi) **diciate**	che (voi) **usciate**
che (loro) **facciano**	che (loro) **diano**	che (loro) **dicano**	che (loro) **escano**

tenere *(keep, hold)*	**porre** *(put, place)*	**trarre** *(pull, draw)*	**venire** *(come)*
che (io) **tenga**	che (io) **ponga**	che (io) **tragga**	che (io) **venga**
che (tu) **tenga**	che (tu) **ponga**	che (tu) **tragga**	che (tu) **venga**
che (lui, lei, Lei) **tenga**	che (lui, lei, Lei) **ponga**	che (lui, lei, Lei) **tragga**	che (lui, lei, Lei) **venga**
che (noi) **teniamo**	che (noi) **poniamo**	che (noi) **traiamo**	che (noi) **veniamo**
che (voi) **teniate che**	che (voi) **poniate**	che (voi) **traiate**	che (voi) **veniate**
che (loro) **tengano**	che (loro) **pongano**	che (loro) **traggano**	che (loro) **vengano**

- Spero che **possiate** venire presto a trovarci.
  (I hope you'll able to visit us soon)
- Tua madre vuole che i tuoi cugini **escano** con noi domani sera.
  (Your mother wants your cousins to come out with us tomorrow evening)

▸ The **present subjunctive** is based on the form of the present indicative.

1. Rewrite the verbs in the present subjunctive.

1. Io sento ....*che io senta*........
2. Lui parla ....
3. Tu canti ....
4. Tu leggi ....
5. Io dormo ....
6. Lui finisce ....
7. Tu scrivi ....
8. Lei mangia ....
9. Io ascolto ....
10. Tu prendi ....

2. Rewrite the verbs from exercise 1 in the plural form.

1. ......*Noi sentiamo*...... ......*che noi sentiamo*......
2. ....
3. ....
4. ....
5. ....
6. ....
7. ....
8. ....
9. ....
10. ....

3. Rewrite the verbs in the present subjunctive.

1. Io posso ......*che io possa*......
2. Tu vuoi ....
3. Lui deve ....
4. Io vengo ....
5. Lei piace ....
6. Tu sai ....
7. Io do ....
8. Lui esce ....
9. Tu stai ....
10. Lei va ....
11. Tu fai ....
12. Lei tiene ....

4. Rewrite the verbs from exercise 3 in the plural form.

1. ......*Noi possiamo*...... ......*che noi possiamo*......
2. ....
3. ....
4. ....
5. ....
6. ....
7. ....
8. ....
9. ....
10. ....
11. ....

Regular verbs

I - ARE: cantare *(sing)*		II - ERE: vedere *(see)*		III a - IRE: sentire *(hear)*		III b - IRE: finire *(finish)*	
che (io)	cant - **assi**	che (io)	ved - **essi**	che (io)	sent - **issi**	che (io)	fin - **issi**
che (tu)	cant - **assi**	che (tu)	ved - **essi**	che (tu)	sent - **issi**	che (tu)	fin - **issi**
che (lui, lei, Lei)	cant - **asse**	che (lui, lei, Lei)	ved - **esse**	che (lui, lei, Lei)	sent - **isse**	che (lui, lei, Lei)	fin - **isse**
che (noi)	cant - **assimo**	che (noi)	ved - **essimo**	che (noi)	sent - **issimo**	che (noi)	fin - **issimo**
che (voi)	cant - **aste**	che (voi)	ved - **este**	che (voi)	sent - **iste**	che (voi)	fin - **iste**
che (loro)	cant - **assero**	che (loro)	ved - **essero**	che (loro)	sent - **issero**	che (loro)	fin - **issero**

– Pensavo che i tuoi amici **giocassero** in una squadra di pallavolo.
(I thought your friends played in a volleyball team)

– Alcuni anni fa volevo che i miei genitori **andassero** in vacanza sulle Dolomiti.
(A few years ago I wanted my parents to go to the Dolomites for their holidays)

For the **verbs *essere*** and ***avere***: see Unità 68.

Some verbs which are irregular in the *imperfect indicative* maintain the same characteristics in the *imperfect subjunctive*.

DIRE *(say)*	che (io)	**dicessi**	FARE *(do, make)*	che (io)	**facessi**	PORRE *(put, place)*	che (io)	**ponessi**
	che (tu)	**dicessi**		che (tu)	**facessi**		che (tu)	**ponessi**
	che (lui, lei, Lei)	**dicesse**		che (lui, lei, Lei)	**facesse**		che (lui, lei, Lei)	**ponesse**
	che (noi)	**dicessimo**		che (noi)	**facessimo**		che (noi)	**ponessimo**
	che (voi)	**diceste**		che (voi)	**faceste**		che (voi)	**poneste**
	che (loro)	**dicessero**		che (loro)	**facessero**		che (loro)	**ponessero**
TRADURRE *(translate)*	che (io)	**traducessi**	TRARRE *(pull, draw)*	che (io)	**traessi**			
	che (tu)	**traducessi**		che (tu)	**traessi**			
	che (lui, lei, Lei)	**traducesse**		che (lui, lei, Lei)	**traesse**			
	(noi)	**traducessimo**		che (noi)	**traessimo**			
	che (voi)	**traduceste**		che (voi)	**traeste**			
	che (loro)	**traducessero**		che (loro)	**traessero**			

Also: che io **bevessi**.

Dare and **stare**

DARE *(give)*	che (io)	**dessi**	STARE *(be, stay)*	che (io)	**stessi**
	che (tu)	**dessi**		che (tu)	**stessi**
	che (lui, lei, Lei)	**desse**		che (lui, lei, Lei)	**stesse**
	che (noi)	**dessimo**		che (noi)	**stessimo**
	che (voi)	**deste**		che (voi)	**steste**
	che (loro)	**dessero**		che (loro)	**stessero**

The forms for the *first* and *second person singular* are the same in the *imperfect subjunctive*. It is therefore necessary to express the subject of the sentence.

– Michela non sapeva come **io potessi** lavorare tanto.
(Michela couldn't understand how I could work so hard)

1. Rewrite the verb in the imperfect subjunctive.

1. Io salivo ......*che io salissi*......
2. Lui ascoltava ....
3. Tu cantavi ....
4. Tu perdevi ....
5. Io partivo ....
6. Lui finiva ....
7. Tu dormivi ....
8. Lei pensava ....
9. Io giocavo ....
10. Tu vedevi ....

2. Rewrite the verb from exercise 1 in the plural form.

1. ......*Noi salivamo*...... ......*che noi salissimo*......
2. ....
3. ....
4. ....
5. ....
6. ....
7. ....
8. ....
9. ....
10. ....

3. Rewrite the verb in the imperfect subjunctive.

1. Io dicevo ......*che io dicessi*......
2. Lui faceva ....
3. Tu proponevi ....
4. Io traducevo ....
5. Lei protraeva ....
6. Tu dicevi ....
7. Io davo ....
8. Lui stava ....

4. Rewrite the verb from exercise 3 in the plural form.

1. ......*Noi dicevamo*...... ......*che noi dicessimo*......
2. ....
3. ....
4. ....
5. ....
6. ....
7. ....
8. ....

Study these examples.

– Spero che tu **sia stata** bene in vacanza e che non **abbia avuto** problemi.
(I hope you had a good time on holiday and didn't have any problems)

– Gli esperti pensano che l'inflazione non **sia cresciuta** molto il mese scorso.
(Experts think inflation did not go up much last month)

The **past subjunctive** is formed with the *present subjunctive* of *essere* and *avere* plus the *past participle* of the verb.

Present subjunctive of the verbs ***essere*** and ***avere***

AVERE		ESSERE	
che (io)	**abbia**	che (io)	**sia**
che (tu)	**abbia**	che (tu)	**sia**
che (lui, lei, Lei)	**abbia**	che (lui, lei, Lei)	**sia**
che (noi)	**abbiamo**	che (noi)	**siamo**
che (voi)	**abbiate**	che (voi)	**siate**
che (loro)	**abbiano**	che (loro)	**siano**

Study these examples.

– Credevo che **fossi** già **arrivata** a casa, per questo ti ho chiamato.
(I thought you were already home, that's why I called you)

– Mi sarebbe piaciuto che Rossana **avesse preso** il lavoro che gli avevano offerto.
(I would have liked Rossana to take the job they offered her)

The **past perfect subjunctive** is formed with the *imperfect subjunctive* of *essere* and *avere* plus the *past participle* of the verb.

Imperfect subjunctive of the verbs ***essere*** and ***avere***

AVERE		ESSERE	
che (io)	**avessi**	che (io)	**fossi**
che (tu)	**avessi**	che (tu)	**fossi**
che (lui, lei, Lei)	**avesse**	che (lui, lei, Lei)	**fosse**
che (noi)	**avessimo**	che (noi)	**fossimo**
che (voi)	**aveste**	che (voi)	**foste**
che (loro)	**avessero**	che (loro)	**fossero**

1. Rewrite the verbs using the past and past perfect subjunctive.

1. Che io vada ....*che io sia andato*........ ....*che io fossi andato*........
2. Che tu esca ....
3. Che lui parta ....
4. Che lei nasca ....
5. Che tu sia ....
6. Che io venga ....

2. Rewrite the verbs from exercise 1 in the plural form.

1. ......*che noi andiamo*........ ......*che noi siamo andati*...... ......*che noi fossimo andati*......
2. ....
3. ....
4. ....
5. ....
6. ....

3. Rewrite the verbs using the past and past perfect subjunctive.

1. Che lei mangi ......*che lei abbia mangiato*...... ......*che lei avesse mangiato*......
2. Che io prenda ....
3. Che tu apra ....
4. Che lui chieda ....
5. Che lei pianga ....
6. Che tu dica ....

4. Rewrite the verbs form exercise 3 in the plural form.

1. ......*che loro mangino*........ *che loro abbiano mangiato* *che loro avessero mangiato*
2. ....
3. ....
4. ....
5. ....
6. ....

REVISION EXERCISE: SUBJUNCTIVE

5. Complete with the correct ending of the verb.

1. Che io veng.....*a*.......
2. Che lei foss...............
3. Che tu mang.............
4. Che voi poss............
5. Che noi av............... dovuto.
6. Che loro ascolt..........
7. Che io foss........ andato.
8. Che lei legg........

The **subjunctive** is used after

- verbs and phrases which express **feelings**:
temere, avere paura, piacere/dispiacere, sperare, essere contento/felice, vergognarsi, ecc.
(fear, be afraid, be pleased/sorry, hope, be glad/happy, be ashamed, etc.*)*

  – **Temo** che Mauro **arrivi** in ritardo. *(I'm afraid Mauro will be late)*
  – **Sono contento** che il tuo libro **abbia** successo. *(I'm pleased your book is successful)*
  – Mi **dispiace** che tu non **possa** venire in vacanza con noi. *(I'm sorry you can't come on holiday with us)*

- verbs and phrases which express **opinion**:
credere, pensare, ritenere, supporre, avere l'impressione, ecc.
(believe, think, consider, suppose, have the impression, etc.*)*

  – **Penso** che Marcello Mastroianni **sia** il miglior attore italiano.
  (I think Marcello Mastroianni is the best Italian actor)
  – **Ho l'impressione** che Matteo non **conosca** molto bene lo spagnolo.
  (I have the impression that Matteo doesn't know Spanish very well)

- In spoken Italian the indicative is often used instead of the subjunctive, even though it is not correct:

  – **Credo** che **va** bene così. *(I think that's fine as it is)*

- verbs which express **volition**:
volere, desiderare, preferire, pretendere, ordinare, vietare, permettere, ecc.
(want, would like, prefer, expect, order, forbid, allow, etc.*)*

  – **Desidero** che tu mi **dica** la verità! *(I want you to tell me the truth!)*
  – Il professore **pretende** che tutti gli studenti **siano** sempre pronti.
  (The teacher expects her students always to be ready for a test.)
  – **Non permetto** che qualcuno **parli** male del mio paese, senza conoscerlo.
  (I won't let anyone speak badly of my country when they don't know anything about it)

- verbs and phrases which express **doubt**:
dubitare, non essere sicuro/certo, ecc. *(doubt, be unsure/uncertain,* etc.*)*

  – **Non sono sicuro** che la Nazionale italiana di calcio **possa** vincere contro il Brasile.
  (I'm not sure if the Italian football team can beat Brazil)

- **impersonal verbs**:
basta, bisogna, conviene, occorre, pare, può darsi, sembra, ecc.
(be enough, need, be better, have to, seem, may, look like, etc.*)*

  – **Sembra** che ci **siano** molti nuovi iscritti ai corsi d'italiano.
  (There seems to be a lot of new enrolments for the Italian courses)
  – **Bisogna** che l'Italia **risolva** i problemi del Meridione. *(Italy needs to solve the problems in the South)*

- the verb **essere** in the **impersonal form** (è, era. etc.) **+ adjective, adverb** or **noun.**

  – **È meglio** che tu **venga** in Italia, se vuoi imparare l'italiano veramente bene.
  (You had better come to Italy if you want to learn Italian really well)
  – **È giusto** che ogni bambino **possa** frequentare la scuola gratuitamente.
  (It is right that every child should attend school free of charge)
  – **È importante** che un giovane **impari** diverse lingue straniere.
  (It is important for a young person to learn several foreign languages)

- The verb **sapere** is followed by the subjunctive only when it is used in the negative form.

  – **Non so** se Jean **sia** francese o belga. *(I don't know whether Jean is French or Belgian)*

- When the verb **dire** is used in the impersonal form **si dice/dicono** it is always followed by the subjunctive.

  – **Si dice/dicono** che in Italia si **viva** meglio che in molti altri paesi.
  (They say/It is said that the way of life in Italy is better than in many other countries)

1. Complete the sentences with the correct form of the subjunctive. Use the verbs from the box below.

1. Penso che Franco ....*abiti*........ a Genova.
2. Temo che in montagna .... troppo freddo.
3. Ho la sensazione che il treno .... in ritardo.
4. Mi dispiace che voi non .... venire al cinema domani.
5. Ogni professore desidera che i propri studenti .... a casa.
6. Non sono sicuro che Luigi .... partecipare alla conferenza.
7. Spero che noi .... passare un buon ultimo dell'anno insieme.
8. Temo che lei .... farsi operare presto.
9. Spero che il regalo di Sara le ....
10. Bisogna che tu .... tutta la verità ai tuoi genitori.

dire	abitare	fare	potere	studiare	potere	dovere	piacere	arrivare	volere

2. Match the sentences from the columns.

1. *Pretendo*
2. Temiamo
3. Bisogna
4. Spero
5. Mi auguro
6. Sono contento
7. Ho l'impressione
8. Mi sembra

a che il governo riduca le tasse.
b che il parlamento approvi una legge giusta sull'immigrazione.
c che tu voglia continuare a studiare.
d che mi diciate dove siete stati ieri serra.
e che Cristiano e Sabrina non stiano più insieme.
f che Giordano non sappia guidare molto bene.
g che i prezzi aumentino più dei salari.
h che la polizia trovi i ladri.

3. Answer the questions by butting the words into order. Rewrite the verbs in italics in the correct form of the verb.

1. Cosa pensi che si debba fare per risolvere il problema del debito pubblico?
Stato/bisogna/e/meglio/meno/lo/*spendere*.
Bisogna che lo stato spenda meno e meglio..

2. Cosa desideri di più per il 1996.
Desidero/gli/*cominciare*/italiani/ripensare/il/loro/modo di vita/a.
....

3. Cosa pretendi da uno studente d'italiano di livello elementare.
Pretendo/che/le/cose/sa/che/poche/*usare*/per/parlare.
....

4. Cosa pensi dell'Italia?
Credo/un/*essere*/paese/ma/disorganizzato/bello/che.
....

5. Cosa pensi che debba fare per dimagrire?
Soprattutto/che/*mangiare*/meno/occorre.
....

6. Cosa hanno detto sulle elezioni politiche?
Pare/che/l'opposizione/vincere/*potere*.
....

4. Answer the questions with your own opinion.

1. Cosa pensi dell'Italia?
Credo che sia un paese molto bello..
2. Cosa pensi della cultura italiana, letteratura, musica, cinema, arte, ecc.?
....
3. Ti piace il calcio?
....
4. Cosa pensi della cucina italiana?
....
5. Cosa bisogna fare per diffondere meglio la lingua italiana nel tuo paese?
È necessario che ....

The **subjunctive** is used after

Affinché *(so that)*

- L'idraulico ha finito la riparazione velocemente, **affinché** gli inquilini **possano** nuovamente aprire l'acqua. *(The plumber has finished the repair quickly so that the tenants can turn the water on again)*

Benché, malgrado, nonostante, sebbene *(although, even though)*, which have basically the same meaning an use.

- **Benché** non **sappia** nuotare, Carlo si è tuffato dove l'acqua è profonda. *(Although he can't swim, Carlo dived in where the water is deep)*
- **Nonostante** non **conosca** una parola di turco, sono andato in vacanza in Turchia. *(Even though I don't know a word in Turkish, I went to Turkey on holiday)*

Purché, a patto che, a condizione che *(as long as, provided, on condition that)*, which have basically the same meaning and use.

- Vengo a trovarti, **a condizione che** tu non **prepari** niente di speciale. *(I'll come to see you as long as you don't prepare anything special)*
- Compreremo una nuova macchina a fine anno, **purché riusciamo** a risparmiare tutti i soldi necessari. *(We'll buy a new car at the end of the year, provided we can save up enough money)*

A meno che non *(unless)*

- **A meno che non decidiamo** di andare al mare, rimarremo in città. *(Unless we decide to go to the seaside, we'll stay in town)*

Senza che *(without)*

- Donatella incontra spesso Adriano, **senza che** suo marito lo **sappia**. *(Donatella often sees Adriano without her husband knowing)*

Prima che *(before)*

- **Prima che nasca** il figlio di Patricia, gli prenderò un regalino. *(Before Patricia's baby is born, I'll buy him a little present)*

Nel caso che *(in case)*

- **Nel caso che** nessuno ve lo **abbia detto,** vi avverto che le lezioni ricominceranno il primo novembre. *(In case nobody has told you, I just want to tell that you the lessons will start again on Novembre 1)*

The subjunctive is used in a **relative clause**

- when there is a **superlativo relativo** in the main clause:
  - È il libro **più** bello che io **abbia** letto. *(It's the best book I've ever read)*
- with **di quanto** and a **comparative** in the main clause:
  - Questo film è **più** interessante **di quanto pensassi**. *(This film is more interesting than I thought)*
- to express a requirement. In the main clause there often is a verb like cercare, desiderare, aspettare, volere, avere bisogno, ecc.: *(look for, would like, expect, want, need, etc.):*
  - Stefano **ha bisogno** di una compagna **che** gli **dedichi** molto tempo. *(Stefano needs a partner who will devote a lot of time to him)*
  - **Cerco** un computer più veloce del mio, **che mi faccia** risparmiare tempo. *(I'm looking for a faster computer than mine, that will save me time)*
- with some **indefinite** adjectives and pronouns: *chiunque*, *comunque*, *dovunque*, *qualunque (anyone, anyhow, anywhere, anything):*
  - **Chiunque** ti **conosca**, sa che sei un bugiardo. *(Anyone that knows you knows you're a liar)*
  - In Italia **dovunque** uno **vada**, occorrono sempre molti soldi. *(Wherever you go in Italy, you always need a lot of money)*

1. Correct the verbs in the sentences below with the correct form of the subjunctive where necessary.

1. Compro queste scarpe purché posso cambiarle se non mi vanno bene.
   Compro queste scarpe purché possa cambiarle se non mi vanno bene
2. Benché chiamo spesso casa tua, non ti trovo mai.
   ....
3. Nonostante la tua collega è molto interessante, c'è qualcosa in lei che non mi convince.
   ....
4. Ti do le chiavi del mio appartamento al mare affinché tu puoi passarvi alcuni giorni di vacanza.
   ....
5. Prima che Gianni si laurei, faremo un viaggio insieme.
   ....
6. Ti invito a cena al ristorante, purché tu riesci a sistemarmi il computer.
   ....
7. Il governo sta lavorando affinché le tasse vengono ridotte.
   ....
8. Non si stanca mai benché lavora molto.
   ....

2. Complete the sentences with a suitable word or expression.

1. *Nonostante* non ne abbia molta voglia, mi metterò a fare gli esercizi.
2. Vi chiamerò .... possiate raccontarmi quello che vi è successo.
3. .... non spieghi quello che ti ha detto il medico, non posso aiutarti.
4. .... giochi spesso a tennis, dopo la partita di ieri ho le gambe a pezzi.
5. .... il professore ti chiami, digli che non hai potuto fare i compiti.
6. .... a Chicago faccia molto freddo d'inverno, vi ho passato mesi indimenticabili.
7. .... tu non voglia rispondere all'annuncio del giornale, lo farò io.
8. Prendi un po' di cioccolato .... tua mamma se ne accorga.
9. .... inizino le vacanze dovremo presentare tre ricerche sulla storia d'Italia.
10. .... sappia cucinare, Silvana è riuscita a preparare un risotto squisito.

3. Join the sentences using *affinché, nonostante, purché, senza che, prima che*, etc.

1. L'università potrà accettare la tua iscrizione. Ma devi mandare una richiesta scritta.
   L'università potrà accettare la tua iscrizione, purché tu mandi una richesta scritta
2. Jo conosce molto bene l'italiano. Tuttavia in questi giorni fa degli errori banali.
   ....
3. Oggi vado a casa di mia zia. Voglio che mi mostri le foto di quando era giovane.
   ....
4. Oggi vado in libreria. Ma mi sembra che i negozi siano chiusi.
   ....
5. La questura può rilasciarti il permesso di soggiorno entro lunedì. Ma devi presentare i documenti necessari oggi.
   ....
6. Pete studia molto. Tuttavia non riesce a raggiungere i risultati sperati.
   ....

If the verb in the main clause is in the **present indicative** and

- the subordinate clause expresses a *future time,* i.e. the action in the subordinate clause happens after the action in the main clause, then the **present** or **future indicative** is used;.

– **Sono certo** che domani **vado/andrò** al mare. *(I'm sure I'm going to the seaside tomorrow)*

- the subordinate clause expresses *contemporary time*, i.e. the two actions happen *at the same time,* then the **present indicative** is used;

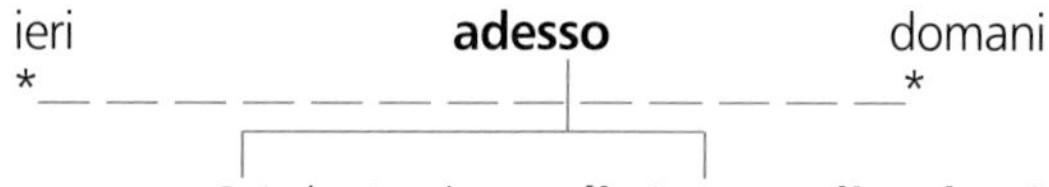

– **So** che Lucia **studia/sta studiando** pianoforte. *(I know that Lucia is learning to play the piano)*

- the subordinate clause expresses an *earlier time,* i.e. the action in the subordinate clause happened *first,* then the **passato prossimo/remoto** or **imperfect indicative** is used.

– **Ti dico** che ieri Gloria si **è laureata**. Non mi credi?
(I'm telling you that Gloria graduated yesterday. Don't you believe me?)

If the verb in the main clause is in the **passato prossimo/remoto, imperfect** or **past perfect indicative** and

- the subordinate expresses a *future time*, i.e. the action in the subordinate clause happens *after* the action in the main clause, then the **perfect conditional** is used;

– Nell'aprile del 1989 **ero sicuro** che **avrei iniziato** a lavorare in una scuola di montagna in novembre.
(In April 1989 I knew I would start working in a school in the mountains in November)

- the subordinate clause expresses *contemporary* time, i.e. the two actions happen *at the same time*, then the **passato prossimo/remoto, imperfect** or **past perfect indicative** is used;

– Anni fa mia madre mi **diceva** spesso che mio padre **ballava** molto bene.
(Years ago my mother often used to tell me that my father danced really well)

- the subordinate clause expresses an *earlier time,* i.e. the action in the subordinate clause happened *first*, then the **past perfect indicative** is used.

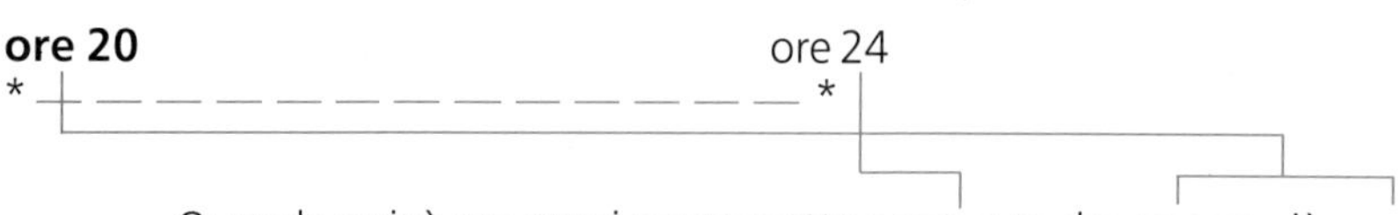

– Quando arrivò era quasi mezzanotte e **sapevo** che **aveva** già **cenato**.
(When he arrived it was almost midnight and I knew he had already had dinner)

1. Complete the sentences with the correct verb forms. Use the verbs from the box below.

1. Luca, ti ripeto che domani non ..... *potrò/posso* .... venire da te.
2. Sono sicuro che non .... problemi con il tuo esame.
3. Siamo certi che un nostro rappresentante .... da voi nel pomeriggio.
4. Sai che ieri .... Ramona che non vedevo da anni?
5. È venuta la polizia. Ditemi che non .... voi la bicicletta di Martino!
6. È evidente che ieri sera Sergio non .... per Pistoia. È ancora a Napoli.

potere	partire	rubare	venire	vedere	avere

2. Complete the sentences with the correct verb forms. Use the verbs from the box below.

1. Ti ho detto che adesso non ...... *ho* .... voglia di andare a far spesa. Forse più tardi.
2. Sei sempre così puntuale. Ero sicuro che .... in tempo. Ma ora dobbiamo sbrigarci!
3. Mio nonno mi diceva spesso che da giovane .... in campagna.
4. Al commissario ho risposto che non lo .... Ma lui non mi ha creduto.
5. Ho sentito che Franco non .... molto bene. Che cosa ha?
6. Sapevo che non .... mai in Germania, ma pensavo che ti sarebbe interessato conoscerla.

avere	stare	arrivare	sapere	essere	vivere

3. Match the sentences from the columns.

1. *So che*
2. Mia madre mi diceva che non
3. Ero certo che
4. Ho sentito che
5. Ti ripeto che
6. Avevo capito che
7. Sapevamo che
8. Vedo che

a non dovevo mangiare e bere molto, purtroppo....
b hai finito gli esami. Complimenti!
c nessuno mi ha baciato. È il mio profumo!
d in Norvegia avremmo avuto problemi a causa del freddo.
e *non parli l'italiano, ma vedrai imparerai presto!*
f sei dimagrita. Brava! Così stai molto meglio.
g tu avevi lavorato in Inghilterra. Forse mi sono sbagliato.
h un giorno ti saresti sposata.

4. Answer the following questions.

1. Quando pensi di andare in vacanza quest'anno?
Sono sicuro che..
2. Che tempo farà domani?
Ho sentito che...
3. Cosa hai detto a Giorgio quando ti ha chiesto se lo inviti alla tua festa?
Gli ho risposto che..
4. Hai parlato con il tuo professore per farti spostare la data dell'esame?
Sì, mi ha detto che..
5. Quali sono i maggiori problemi del tuo paese?
È evidente che...
6. Come sono cambiate le tue idee sull'Italia da quando studi italiano?
Ho capito che..

■ If the verb in the main clause is in the **present indicative** and

● the subordinate clause expresses a *future time,* i.e. the action in the subordinate clause happens *after* the action in the main clause, then the **present subjunctive** or **future indicative** is used;

adesso **domani**

– **Spero** che domani Suly non **vada/andrà** a lavorare. *(I hope Suly won't go to work tomorrow)*

● the subordinate clause expresses *contemporary time,* i.e. the two actions happen *at the same time*, then the **present subjunctive** is used;

ieri **adesso** domani

– Non **so** che cosa **faccia/stia facendo** Giovanni in questo momento.
(I don't know what Giovanni is doing now)

● the subordinate clause expresses a *earlier time,* i.e. the action in the subordinate clause happens *first,* then **the past** subjunctive is used.

ieri adesso

– **Penso** che ieri Fausto **abbia fatto** un giro nei boschi con i suoi figli.
(I think Fausto went for a walk in the woods with his children yesterday)

■ If the verb in the main clause is in the **conditional** and

● the subordinate clause expresses a *future time,* i.e. the action in the subordinate clause happens *after* the action in the main clause, then the **imperfect subjunctive** is used;

adesso **domani**

– Mi **piacerebbe** che tu **smettessi** di lavorare presto domani per andare al ristorante insieme.
(I'd be really pleased if you could finish work early tomorrow so we can go to the restaurant together)

● the subordinate clause expresses *contemporary time,* i.e. the two action happen *at the same time*, then the **imperfect subjunctive** is used;

ieri **adesso** domani

– **Vorrei** che qualcuno mi **aiutasse** a correggere gli esami.
(I wish someone would help me correct the exams)

● the subordinate clause expresses an *earlier time*, i.e. the action in the subordinate clause happened *first*, then the **past perfect subjunctive** is used;

l'anno scorso adesso

– **Vorrei** che l'anno scorso vi **foste iscritti** all'università.
(I wish you had enrolled at University last year)

1. Complete the sentences with the correct verb form. Use the verbs from the box below.

1. Credo che l'aereo ...*atterri*... alle 12.35.
2. Spero che lo spettacolo .... La prima parte è stata noiosissima.
3. Penso che .... molto difficile studiare chimica.
4. Mi sembra che .... più freddo di ieri.
5. Non so cosa .... a Martin; non si fa più vedere.
6. Credo che ieri sera la riunione .... molto tardi.
7. Penso che Pierre .... mezz'ora fa; ma non ha ancora chiamato.
8. Non mi pare che la tua squadra .... molto bene ieri sera.
9. Mi sembra che il film di Bertolucci che sta per uscire .... molto successo.
10. Non credo che la festa di ieri ti .... molto.

arrivare	finire	migliorare	atterrare	piacere	giocare	essere	fare	succedere	avere

2. Complete the sentences with the correct verb form. Use the verbs from the box below.

1. Desidererei che tu ...*venissi*... con me a visitare Napoli.
2. Mi piacerebbe che voi ci .... più spesso.
3. Vorrei che il treno non .... in orario. Non l'avrei perso.
4. Vorrei che tu non .... così triste.
5. Desidererei che i miei studenti .... molto di più.
6. Vorrei che non .... mai .... il 1992.
7. Mi piacerebbe che la lingua italiana .... più conosciuta nel mondo.
8. Vorrei che domani noi .... andare a sciare.
9. Desidererei che con l'anno nuovo tutti .... di essere più solidali.
10. Vorrei che non ci .... mai .... la Guerra Fredda.

essere	cercare	potere	venire	arrivare	essere	essere	finire	studiare	scrivere

3. Match the sentences from the columns.

1. *Mi dispiace che*
2. Temo che domani
3. Che cielo nero! Penso che
4. Mi sembra che tu
5. Vorrei che
6. Salvatore vorrebbe che
7. Lina vorrebbe che
8. La vita è cara e mia nonna desidererebbe che
9. Voglio che
10. Ci piacerebbe che voi
11. Credo che i Pasquini
12. Credo che Luigi

a stia per piovere.
b esca subito dal mio ufficio!
c sua moglie non fosse fuggita con un altro.
d le aumentassero la pensione.
e nessuno sia venuto a trovarti all'ospedale.
f si perda molto tempo in discussioni inutili.
g ci mandaste una cartolina dai Caraibi.
h tu mi telefonassi più spesso.
i vogliano vendere la loro casa.
l sia andato a parlare con il suo avvocato.
m non abbia capito molto della lezione di oggi.
n sua sorella tornasse in Italia a vivere.

■ If the verb in the main clause is in the **passato prossimo/remoto, imperfect** o **past perfect indicative** and

- the subordinate clause expresses a *future* time, i.e. the action in the subordinate clause happens *after* the action in the main clause, then the **perfect conditional** is used;

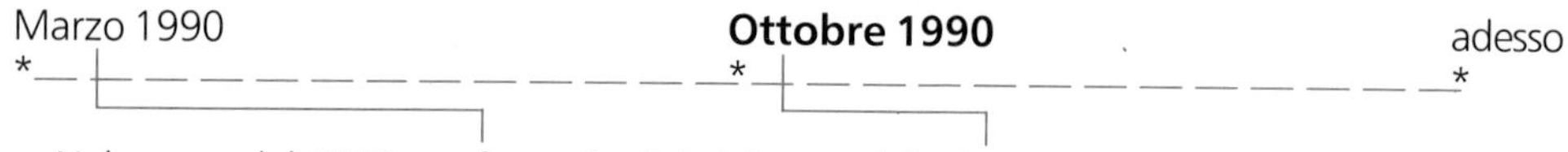

– Nel marzo del 1990 **credevo** che Fabrizio **avrebbe iniziato** il servizio militare agli inizi di ottobre.
(In March 1990 I thought Fabrizio would start his military service at the beginning of October)

- the subordinate clause expresses a *contemporary* time, i.e. the two action happen *same time*, then the **imperfect subjunctive** is used;

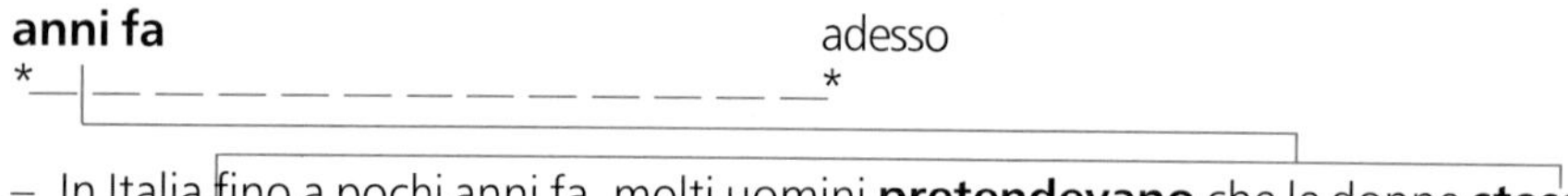

– In Italia fino a pochi anni fa, molti uomini **pretendevano** che le donne **stessero** in casa con i figli e non **lavorassero**.
(Up to a few years ago many men in Italy expected women to stay home with the children and not go out to work)

- the subordinate clause expresses *an earlier* time, i.e. the action in the subordinate clause happened *first,* then the **past perfect subjunctive** is used.

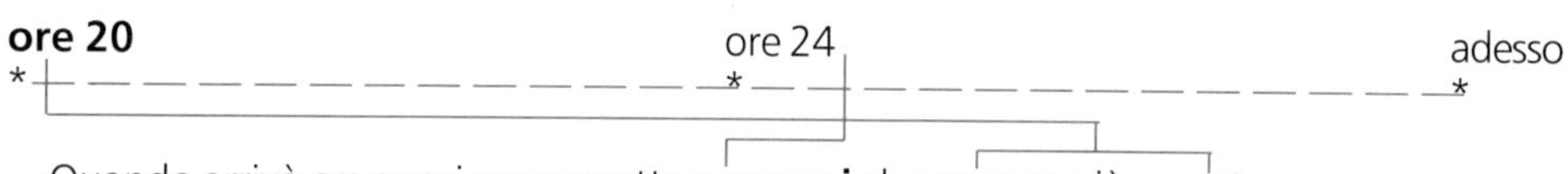

– Quando arrivò era quasi mezzanotte e **pensai** che **avesse** già **cenato**.
(When he got home it was almost midnight and I thought he had already eaten)

■ If the verb in the main clause is in the **perfect conditional** and

- the subordinate clause expresses a *future time*, i.e. the action in the subordinate clause happens *after* the action in the main clause, then the **imperfect subjunctive** or **future indicative** is used;

– Una settimana fa **avrei voluto** che il giorno dopo Rita **prendesse** un appuntamento con lo specialista.
(A week ago I would have liked Rita to make an appointment with the specialist)

- the subordinate clause expresses contemporary time, i.e. the two actions happen at the *same time*, then the **imperfect subjunctive** is used;

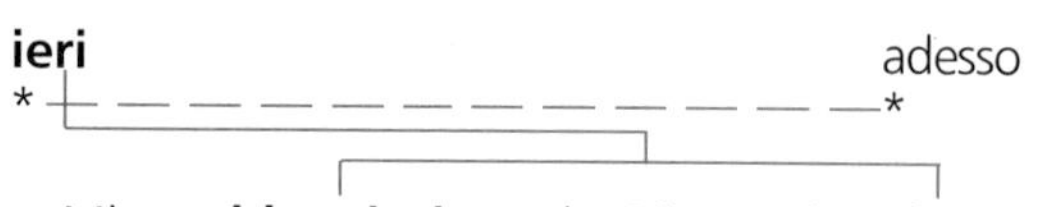

– Mi **sarebbe piaciuto** che Diego mi **parlasse** del suo progetto di ricerca.
(I would have liked Diego to tell me about his research project)

- the subordinate clause expresses an *earlier* time, i.e. the action in the subordinate clause happened *first,* then the **past perfect subjunctive** is used.

– **Avrei voluto** che l'anno precedente vi **foste iscritti** all'università.
(I would have liked you to have enrolled at University the previous year)

1. Complete the sentences with the correct verb forms. Use the verbs from the box below.

1. Speravo che oggi non ......*piovesse*.......... e invece....
2. Credevo che tuo padre .... il meccanico.
3. Non pensavo che la settimana scorsa Anila .... per l'Inghilterra.
4. Non sapevo che Fabrizio e Cristina .... già .... dalle vacanze.
5. Mirta voleva che sua figlia .... lavoro.
6. Credevo che l'esperto in filologia non .... In realtà il treno aveva solo dieci minuti di ritardo.
7. Mia mamma mi faceva leggere ad alta voce affinché .... a pronunciare correttamente.
8. Mio nonno riteneva che l'Italia del 2000 .... un paese industrializzato, ma con molta ingiustizia.

piovere essere fare ritornare andare imparare arrivare cambiare

2. Put the verbs in brackets into the perfect conditional or the imperfect subjunctive.

1. ...*Avrei voluto*...(volere) che Francesca mi ...*dedicasse*....... (dedicare) più tempo.
2. .... (preferire) che tu .... (comprare) a tuo padre una cravatta.
3. Mi .... (piacere) che Fiorenza mi .... (invitare) a cena a casa sua.
4. .... (pensare) che Juan .... (essere) cileno e invece è venezuelano.
5. .... (preferire) che mia figlia .... (prendere) un volo di linea e non un charter.
6. .... (volere) che Carlo e Antonella .... (tornare) insieme.

REVISION EXERCISE: SEQUENCE OF TENSES.

3. Put the verbs in brackets into the correct verb forms.

1. Pensavo che Giovanni non ....*finisse*.............. (finire) più di fare trasloco.
2. Spero che la tua nuova macchina da scrivere .... (durare) più a lungo.
3. Paola comprò un giochino alla sua nipotina affinché non .... (piangere) più.
4. Nonostante non ci .... (essere) il sole, oggi non fa tanto freddo.
5. Quando ho finito l'università, pensavo che .... (andare) a vivere all'estero.
6. Credo che Fabrizia .... (essere) una brava libraia.
7. Mi sembra che Clive .... (partire) ieri per Cuba.
8. Mi piacerebbe che voi .... (leggere) l'ultimo libro di G. Garcìa Marquez.
9. Vorrei che il tempo .... (tornare) bello.
10. Ho paura che .... (formarsi) un ingorgo sull'autostrada a causa della neve.
11. Bisognerebbe che tu .... (parlare) al tuo amico di quell'appartamento da affittare.
12. È importante che la Russia .... (risolvere) al più presto i problemi etnici interni.
13. Senza che tu me ne .... (parlare), ho capito che c'era qualche problema.
14. Il concerto è stato più bello di quanto .... (aspettarsi)
15. A chiunque mi .... (chiedere) di te, dirò che non vivi più a Napoli.
16. Sembrava che Roberto .... (partire) per la Tunisia, invece era ancora a Milano.
17. Dovunque lui .... (andare), trovava qualcuno che conosceva.
18. Pensai che lei non mi .... (riconoscere) perché mi guardò senza salutarmi.
19. Pensavo che .... (ricevere) più soldi di tredcisima e invece, tante tasse!
20. Credevo che tuo zio .... (lavorare) per una ditta farmaceutica già da molto tempo.

Study the examples. Which sentences express a probable hypothesis? Which one expresses an improbable hypothesis, which cannot be fulfilled because it refers to the past?

- Se mia madre mi **inviterà, andrò** da lei a pranzo domenica.
  (If my mother invites me, I'll go there for lunch on Sunday)
- Se **avessi** più tempo libero, **andrei** a trovare tutti i miei vecchi amici.
  (If I had more free time, I would go and see all my old friends)
- Se **fossi stato** meno pigro e avessi imparato qualche sport, non **sarei diventato** così grasso.
  (If I hadn't been so lazy and had learnt to do some sport, I wouldn't have got so fat)

The hypothetical clause of **reality**

Probable condition: **se *(if)* + present or future indicative**	*Consequence:* **present or future indicative, or imperative**
Se avrò abbastanza soldi, *(If I have enough money,*	andrò in vacanza alle Maldive. *I'll go to the Maldives on holiday)*
Se vieni a teatro stasera, *(If you come to the theatre this evening,*	dopo lo spettacolo ti invito a bere qualcosa. *I'll buy you a drink after the show)*
Se chiami tua nonna *(If you call your Grandmonther,*	salutamela! *give her my regards!)*

The hypothetical clause of **possibility**

Improbable condition, although theoretically possible in the present or future: **se + imperfect subjunctive**	*Consequence in the present or future:* **conditional**
Se avessi abbastanza soldi, *(If I had enough money,*	andrei in vacanza alle Maldive. *I would go to the Maldives on holiday)*
Se venissi a teatro stasera, *(If you came to the theatre this evening,*	dopo lo spettacolo ti inviterei a bere qualcosa. *I would buy you a drink after the show)*

The hypothetical clause of **impossiblllty**

Condition which was not fulfilled in the past: **se + past perfect subjunctive**	*Consequence in the past:* **perfect conditional**
Se avessi avuto abbastanza soldi, *(If I had had enough money,*	sarei andato in vacanza alle Maldive. *I would have gone to the Maldives on holiday)*
Se fossi venuta a teatro ieri sera, *(If you had come to the theatre yesterday evening,*	dopo lo spettacolo ti avrei invitata a bere qualcosa. *I would have bought you a drink after the show)*

Condition which was not fulfilled in the past: **se + past perfect subjunctive**	*Consequence in the present:* **conditional**
Se avessi guadagnato abbastanza soldi, *(If I had earned enough money,*	ora anrei in vacanza alle Maldive. *I would go to the Maldives on holiday now)*
Se avessi preso qualche antibiotico, *(If I had taken antibiotics,*	ora non avrei più febbre. *(I wouldn't have a temperature now)*

In spoken Italian the structure **se + imperfect indicative** + **imperfect indicative** is often used instead of **se + past perfect subjunctive** + **perfect conditional**.

Se **avevo** abbastanza soldi,	**andavo** in vacanza alle Maldive.
Se **venivi** a teatro ieri sera,	dopo lo spettacolo ti **invitavo** a bere qualcosa.

the order of clauses can be inverted, with the if-clause coming after the main clause.

Avrei fatto un po' di ginnastica ieri sera, *(I would have done some exercise yesterday evening,*	se non avesse fatto tanto freddo. *if it hadn't been so cold)*
Ti inviterò a cena, *(I'll ask you to dinner,*	se mi farai vedere le tue diapositive del Portogallo. *if you show me your slides of Portugal)*

1. Match the sentences from the columns.

1. *Se studierai di più,*
2. Se trovassi un'altra casa,
3. Se non fossi tornata a casa così tardi,
4. Se non avessi perso le chiavi,
5. Se mi telefonerai,
6. Se hai fame,
7. Se non avvessi la macchina,
8. Se tu non ci fossi,

a ora non dovresti andare all'ufficio oggetti smarriti.
b ti racconterò le ultime novità.
c dovrei prendere sempre l'autobus.
d non vivrei più con Federica.
e dovrebbero inventarti.
f i miei genitori non si sarebbero preoccupati tanto.
g non avrai problemi all'esame.
h serviti pure; nel frigorifero c'è di tutto.

2. Underline the correct form of the verb.

1. Se l'Italia vincerebbe/*vincerà* contro la Germania, mi tufferei/*tufferò* in piscina vestito.
2. Se riuscirò/riuscissi a trovare i biglietti, andrebbe/andrò all'opera.
3. Se Sara dimagrirà/dimagrisse, si sentirebbe/sentisse meglio.
4. Se avvessi avuto/avrei avuto tempo, ieri sera andrei/sarei andato al cinema.
5. Se ti avessi conosciuto/conoscessi dieci anni fa, mi sarei innamorato/innamorassi perdutamente di te.
6. Se torni/torneresti a casa tardi, per favore non fare/non faresti rumore.
7. Se parlassi/parli più piano, ti capisco/avrò capito meglio.
8. Se quei due si sposassero/sposerebbero, mi stupirei/stupirò molto.

3. Put the verbs in brackets into the correct verb forms.

1. Fabio, se *vedi/vedrai* Cristina stasera, *puoi* dirle di restituirmi il mio libro? (vedere, potere)
2. Laura, se .... freddo, ... il riscaldamento. (avere, accendere)
3. Se Michele .... l'esame, ... un vero miracolo. (superare, essere)
4. Ieri sera .... alla tua festa, se mi .... (venire, invitare)
5. Se domani non mi .... bene, non .... a lavorare. (sentire, andare)
6. Ti ...., se .... un po' di musica? (dispiacere, mettere)
7. Se .... in te, non mi .... Pensaci, sei ancora in tempo! (essere, sposare)
8. Mi dispiace, non glielo ...., se .... che era un segreto. (dire, sapere)
9. Se ieri sera mi .... il suo numero di telefono, ora la .... subito. (dare, chiamare)
10. Se .... meno tempo con i tuoi amici, non .... problemi di studio. (stare, avere)

4. Complete the sentences about yourself.

1. Se domani facesse bello, *andrei al mare*
2. Se non avesse fatto così freddo la settimana scorsa ....
3. Se imparerò bene l'italiano ....
4. Troverò un buon posto di lavoro ....
5. Mi trasferirei definitivamente all'estero ....
6. Se vincessi alla lotteria ....
7. Se mio nonno fosse stato milionario ....
8. Avrei provato i tuoi spaghetti alle vongole ....

Study the example.

– Questa mattina l'agenzia 7 della Cassa di Risparmio **è *stata rapinata da*** *tre uomini armati e mascherati.*
(This morning the number 7 branch of the Cassa di Risparmio was robbed by three armed men wearing masks)

The **passive** is formed with the auxiliary *essere* in the various tenses plus the *past participle* of the verb.

Indicative

	ACTIVE	*PASSIVE*
present	ascolto	**sono ascoltato**
passato prossimo	ho ascoltato	**sono stato ascoltato**
imperfect	ascoltavo	**ero ascoltato**
passato remoto	ascoltai	**fui ascoltato**
past perfect	avevo ascoltato	**ero stato ascoltato**
trapassato remoto	ebbi ascoltato	***non si usa***
simple future	ascolterò	**sarò ascoltato**
future perfect	avrò ascoltato	**sarò stato ascoltato**

Subjunctive

	ACTIVE	*PASSIVE*
present	che io ascolti	che io **sia ascoltato**
past	che io abbia ascoltato	*che io* **sia stato ascoltato**
imperfect	che io ascoltassi	*che io* **fossi ascoltato**
past perfect	che io avessi ascoltato	*che io* **fossi stato ascoltato**

Conditional

	ACTIVE	*PASSIVE*
present	ascolterei	**sarei ascoltato**
perfect	avrei ascoltato	**sarei stato ascoltato**

The **passive** can only be formed with **transitive** verbs.

– Il bimbo **è stato morso** da un cane randagio. *(The little boy was bitten by a stray dog)*

Do you remember what *transitive verb* means? See Appendix 3.

The person or thing that performs the action (i.e. agent or instrument) is introduced by the preposition **da** *(by)*.

– Parma **fu fondata dai** Romani. *(Parma was founded by the Romans)*

For the agreement of the past participle with the verb **essere** see, Unità 31.

1. Rewrite the following sentences using the correct form of the passive, without changing the meaning.

1. Hanno invitato Giorgio alla festa?
...*Giorgio è stato invitato alla festa?*...
2. Hanno sgridato gli studenti che sono arrivati in ritardo?
....?
3. La polizia ha arrestato i ladri.
....
4. Un guasto alla pompa ha causato la rottura del riscaldamento.
....
5. Stamattina hanno pulito le finestre.
....
6. Rinvieranno la partita di stasera a causa del maltempo.
....
7. Costruiranno due nuove case in Via Savani.
....
8. A causa della nebbia avevano sospeso tutti i voli.
....
9. Fino alla fine del secolo scorso la gente non usava l'elettricità.
....

2. Complete the sentences with the correct form of the passive. Use the verbs from the box below.

1. Durante la riunione di oggi ...*sarà decisa*... la fusione delle due società.
2. Questa pagina Internet .... da 1200 persone negli ultimi 10 giorni.
3. L'edificio scolastico .... dal maltempo.
4. La mia casa .... 5 anni fa.
5. Un quadro di Leonardo .... all'asta la settimana prossima.
6. Questo tasto non deve mai ....
7. Il trattato di pace .... a Parigi il prossimo 20 gennaio.
8. Questo diamante potrebbe .... due anni fa a Stoccolma.

decidere	vendere	rubare	visitare	costruire	danneggiare	premere	firmare

3. Put the verbs in brackets into the active or passive voice.

Il portavoce del governo ...*ha comunicato*... (comunicare) questa mattina che la legge finanziaria per il prossimo anno ....2.................. (presentare) in Parlamento entro la fine della settimana. Il Senato ne ....3.................. (esaminare) il testo che ....4.................. (portare) poi alla Camera dei Deputati, la quale ....5.................. (dovere) approvarlo entro la fine del mese.
Nella legge ....6................. (contenere) tagli alle spese sanitarie, ma ....7................. (prevedere) anche misure per aiutare le fasce più deboli della società.
Il progetto ....8................ (sostenere) dai partiti della maggioranza, ma l'opposizione ....9................ (promettere) una dura battaglia in Parlamento. "Se ....10.................... (occorrere) trovare nuove entrate, le tasse devono ....11.................... (pagare) da chi i soldi ce li ha e non dai soliti lavoratori e dai più deboli."
...........12.................. (dichiarare) questa mattina un leader dell'opposizione.

Changing a verb from **active** to **passive**.

active:	Molti lettori *(Many readers*	**hanno apprezzato** *appreciated*	*Il Nome della Rosa.* *Il Nome della Rosa.)*
passive:	*Il Nome della Rosa* *(Il Nome della Rosa*	**è stato apprezzato** *was appreciated*	**da** molti lettori. *by many readers.)*

When the subject in the active is not defined (loro as in the following example, or qualcuno, etc.), the agent is **not** expressed il complemento d'agente (da loro, da qualcuno, ecc.).

- Hanno perso un mazzo di chiavi *(They have lost a bunch of keys.)* ➜ È stato perso un mazzo di chiavi. *(A bunch of keys has been lost)*

Questions with **chi** *(who)?*

ACTIVE: **Chi** ha scritto *Il Nome della Rosa*? *(Who wrote Il Nome della Rosa?)* ➜ *Il Nome della Rosa* is the object.

PASSIVE: **Da chi** è stato scritto *Il Nome della Rosa*? *(Who was Il Nome della Rosa written by?)* ➜ *Il Nome della Rosa* is the subject.

The passive with the **gerund**.

- La ricerca sul cancro sta facendo enormi progressi, **essendo** ora **finanziata** con nuovi fondi.
  (Cancer Research is making great progress, now being financed with new funds)

The passive with the **infinitive**.

- Non piace a nessuno **essere deriso**. *(No one likes being mocked)*

Apart from the verb *essere*, the passive can also be formed with the verbs **venire** and **andare**, but only in the simple tenses, not in the perfect ones.

The passive with **venire**.

- La squadra argentina di calcio **veniva indicata** come la favorita del torneo.
- La squadra argentina di calcio **era indicata** come la favorita del torneo.
  (The Argentinian team was considered favourite in the tournament)
- L'inglese **viene** oggi **studiato** nella maggior parte dei paesi.
- L'inglese **è** oggi **studiato** nella maggior parte dei paesi.
  (English is studied in most countries nowadays)

The forms with **essere** and **venire** normally have the same meaning.

The passive with **andare**.
The passive with **andare** in most cases means **dovere** *(must, have to).*

- L'ultimo film di Bernardo Bertolucci **va visto** appena esce; dicono che sia un capolavoro.
- L'ultimo film di Bernardo Bertolucci **deve essere visto** appena esce; dicono che sia un capolavoro.
  (It's a must to go and see Bernardo Bertolucci's latest film as soon as it comes out; they say it's a masterpiece)
- Il divieto di fumare **andrebbe esteso** a tutti i locali pubblici.
- Il divieto di fumare **dovrebbe essere esteso** a tutti i locali pubblici.
  (The no-smoking law should be extended to all public places)

In some cases **andare** does not express obligation..

- Nei roghi dell'Inquisizione **andarono perduti** libri di inestimabile valore.
  (Invaluable books were lost in the fires of the Inquisition)

When it does not express obligation **andare** can also be used in perfect tenses.

- Durante la notte alcune case **sono andate** parzialmente **distrutte** a causa di un'improvvisa tromba d'aria.
  (Some houses were partially destroyed during the night by an unexpected tornado)

1. Rewrite the sentences using the verb *venire* instead of *venire*.

1. Alcuni anni fa l'italiano era insegnato solamente in pochi paesi.
   Alcuni anni fa l'italiano veniva insegnato solamente in pochi
2. Tutti gli anni in Italia a Babbo Natale sono scritte migliaia di lettere.
3. Ogni anno a mezzanotte della Vigilia del Natale è celebrata la Santa Messa.
4. Il conto corrente della ditta fu chiuso l'anno scorso.
5. Quello scrittore è ricordato più per il suo stile di vita che per le sue opere.
6. L'ultimo modello della Fiat è prodotto in uno stabilimento del Sud Italia.
7. Il cinema fu evacuato a causa di un incendio.
8. Al mondo ogni anno sarebbero uccisi migliaia di detenuti.
9. I consoli romani dopo le vittorie militari erano portati in trionfo.

2. Rewrite the sentences using the verb *andare*.

1. Questa porta non deve essere mai aperta.
   Questa porta non va mai aperta
2. Dopo una partita di calcio, le scarpe dovrebbero essere ingrassate.
3. Il problema della fame nel mondo deve essere risolto con il contributo di tutti i paesi ricchi.
4. Quello studente doveva essere promosso con voti migliori.
5. Per alcuni ambientalisti il divieto di caccia dovrebbe essere esteso a tutte le specie animali.
6. Il vino bianco di solito deve essere bevuto fresco.
7. Per ottenere un buon brasato, la carne deve essere cotta a lungo.
8. Bisogna pagare la tassa sulla casa entro il venti dicembre.
9. Il bilancio annuale della ditta dovrebbe essere rivisto.
10. I libri più belli dovrebbero essere riletti a distanza di tempo.

Study the picture.

Do you remember what a transitive verb is? See Appendix 3.

Instead of using the passive structures with *essere, venire* or *andare,* it is possible to use the structure with **si** + the active voice of the verb, but only with transitive verbs where the object is expressed.

- A Firenze **si insegna** l'italiano a stranieri in molte scuole.
- (A Firenze l'italiano a stranieri **è/viene insegnato** in molte scuole.)
  (Italian is taught to foreigners in many schools in Florence)

- Sull'Appennino **si trovano** molti funghi in autunno.
- (Sull'Appennino **vengono trovati** molti funghi in autunno.)
  (You can find a lot of mushrooms on the Apennines in autumn)

In the passive structure with **si** the verb is in the third person singular if the noun it refers to is singular (1), or in the third person plural if the noun it refers to plural (2).
The verb is in the tense required by the meaning of the sentence.

- (1) Fino a pochi decenni fa in Italia **si parlava** soprattutto **il dialetto**.
- (Fino a pochi decenni fa in Italia **era parlato** soprattutto **il dialetto**.)
  (Up to a few decades ago mostly dialect was spoken in Italy)

- (2) In Italia **si spendono molti soldi** per costruire nuove autostrade.
- (In Italia **vengono spesi molti soldi** per costruire nuove autostrade.)
  (In Italy a lot of money is spent on building new motorways)

In the perfect tenses the auxiliary is *essere* and the past participle agrees in gender and number with the noun it refers to.

- L'anno scorso **si sono registrat*i* tassi** d'interesse in leggero calo.
  (A slight drop in interest rates was registered last year)

- **Si sono viste cose** interessantissime durante l'ultimo Festival di Spoleto.
  (There were some very interesting things to see during the last Festival in Spoleto)

For the use of the **impersonal si**, see Unità 78.

1. Rewrite the sentences using the passive *si* in the singular form.

1. Nelle scuole italiane oggi viene insegnato poco latino.
   ......*Nelle scuole italiane oggi si insegna poco latino*..........
2. Durante le feste natalizie viene consumata una notevole quantità di vino spumante.
   ....
3. Nei libri di storia è spesso citato il nome di Garibaldi.
   ....
4. In Italia viene guardata troppo la televisione.
   ....
5. Il Presidente della Repubblica Italiana viene eletto ogni sette anni.
   ....
6. La storia deve essere studiata con attenzione.
   ....
7. La poesia è spesso considerata difficile.
   ....
8. La notizia del matrimonio della principessa verrà pubblicata su tutti i giornali.
   ....

2. Rewrite the sentences using the passive *si* in the plural form.

1. Nelle scuole italiane oggi vengono insegnate molte materie.
   ......*Nelle scuole italiane oggi si insegnano molte materie*..........
2. Durante le feste natalizie vengono spesi molti soldi.
   ....
3. Le partite di calcio vengono spesso seguite alla radio.
   ....
4. In questi anni sono stati fatti molti progressi nella ricerca sul cancro.
   ....
5. Nei prossimi anni saranno costruite molte nuove case.
   ....
6. Le malattie come l'influenza non vengono normalmente curate con gli antibiotici.
   ....
7. Alcune vecchie canzoni italiane sono conosciute in tutto il mondo.
   ....
8. In Italia non vengono venduti molti libri.
   ....

Impersonal si.
Study the following sentences and consider the differences:

- In Toscana **si beve** del buon vino.
  (You can drink good wine in Tuscany)
- In Italia **si beve** molto a tavola.
  (People drink a lot at meal times in Italy)

In the first case there is a **passive structure with si,** because the verb is transitive *(beve)* and the object is expressed *(buon vino)*.
In the second case it is an **impersonal si;** the verb is transitive (*beve*), but the object is not expressed.

With the **impersonal si** the verb is always in the **third person singular**.

- In Spagna **si mangia** bene e non **si spende** molto. *(You eat well and don't spend much in Spain)*

The verb can be *transitive*, with no object expressed, or *intransitive*.

- In estate **si va** spesso in piscina per rinfrescarsi un po' ➜ *intransitive*
  (People often go to the swimming pool in summer to cool down a little)
- Se **si desidera** comunicare, **si parla**, ma **si deve** anche **ascoltare**. ➜ *all transitive*
  (If you want to communicate you need to speak, but must also listen)

The **impersonal si** is sometimes used instead of the subject **noi** *(we)*.

- **Si è pensato** di andare in montagna domani. *(We were thinking about going to the mountains tomorrow)* ➜ – **(Noi) abbiamo pensato** di andare in montagna domani.

Study the following sentences and consider the differences:

- **Si è partit*i*** tardi e si è perso il traghetto per la Sardegna.
- (**Noi siamo partit*i*** tardi e abbiamo perso il traghetto per la Sardegna).
  (We left late and missed our connection for Sardinia)

- **Si è mangiato** molto bene nella trattoria che ci hai consigliato.
- (**Abbiamo mangiato** molto bene nella trattoria che ci hai consigliato).
  (We ate really well in the trattoria you recommended)

The auxiliary in the compound tenses in *essere*, but only the past participle of verbs which have *essere* as an auxiliary in the active form agrees with the subject.

The **impersonal si** with *reflexive* or *pronominal* verbs.
In impersonal sentences with **si**, the **si** particle of the reflexive verb becomes **ci**.

- **Ci si alza** più tardi quando si è in vacanza. *(People get up later when they are on holiday)*
- **Ci si incontra** spesso in birreria al sabato sera. *(We often meet up in the pub on Saturday evenings)*

The *past participle* in compound tenses is in the *plural masculine* form.

- **Ci si è vist*i*** varie volte e ci si saluta, ma non conosco il suo nome.
  (We have often seen and said hello to each other, but I don't know his/her name)

The **impersonal si** with the verb *essere + adjective*.
In sentences with the verb **essere + si**, the adjective is always in the plural masculine form.

- Quando **si è stanchi**, sarebbe meglio non uscire di sera.
  (When you are tired, it would be better not to go out in the evening)

- **Si è felici** quando si ama. *(People are happy when they are in love)*

1. Make sentences about Italy using the information below.

	mangiare	*molto*
	giocare al Totocalcio	*spesso*
	bere al bar con gli amici	*spesso*
	lavorare	*molto*
In Italia	leggere	*non abbastanza*
	risparmiare	*poco*
	andare in bicicletta	*raramente*
	giocare a carte	*a volte*

1. ....
2. ....
3. ....
4. ....
5. ....
6. ....
7. ....
8. ....

2. Rewrite the sentences using the passato prossimo.

1. Si mangia molto bene in quel ristorante.
   Si è mangiato molto bene in quel ristorante..........
2. Si va spesso al mare.
   ....
3. Si nuota volentieri in quella piscina.
   ....
4. Si sta bene in quel parco.
   ....
5. Si chiacchiera volentieri con i tuoi amici.
   ....
6. Si parte alle 9.
   ....
7. Ci si alza tardi per Natale.
   ....
8. Si beve vino bianco in Toscana.
   ....

Loro *(they)*
The structure with the third person plural **loro** *(they)* is often used instead of the structure with the impersonal **si**. The subject **loro** is often not expressed.

- **Hanno** cambiato il nome della via in cui abito.
  (They have changed the name of the street where I live)
- **Dicono** che in centro aprirà presto una nuova gelateria.
  (They say a new ice-cream shop will soon open in the centre)

Uno *(one)*
The pronoun **uno** *(one)* can also be used for the impersonal form. The verb is in the third person singular.

- **Uno** può viaggiare moltissimo, ma se non impara le lingue, si troverà sempre in difficoltà.
  (You can travel a lot, but if you don't learn languages you will always have difficulty)
- Se **uno** prende una multa, cosa deve fare?
  (What do you have to do if you get a fine?)

Tu *(you)*
The impersonal form is sometimes expressed with the pronoun **tu** *(you)*. The verb is therefore in the second person singular.
The subject **tu** is often not expressed.

- Se **vai** a Perugia, **trovi** sempre tanti giovani di paesi lontani.
  (If you go to Perugia you always meet lots of young people from foreign countries.)
- In montagna **devi** fare attenzione alle vipere.
  (In the mountains you must watch out for snakes.)

In these examples the subject **tu** indicates anyone.

For the **impersonal si** see Unità 78.

1. Rewrite the sentences using the impersonal form with *loro.*

1. È stato rapito il figlio dello sceicco arabo.
...*Hanno rapito il figlio dello sceicco arabo*...
2. Il problema del traffico è stato affrontato con serietà.
....
3. Sarà cambiato l'orario dei treni.
....
4. Sono stati sospesi gli scioperi.
....
5. La casa non è ancora stata pulita.
....
6. Quando fu costruito il Duomo di Firenze?
....
7. Come è stato concluso l'affare?
....
8. Dove sarà girato il nuovo film sulla guerra civile spagnola?
....
9. Si dice che ci sarà un aumento dei salari per i lavoratori del settore chimico.
....
10. Un tempo si pensava che la terra fosse piatta.
....

2. Complete the sentences using the impersonal form with *uno* or *tu.*

1. ......*Uno*...... pensa che dopo la laurea sia finito tutto e invece...
2. .... non può mai stare tranquillo. C'è sempre qualche imprevisto.
3. Essere insegnanti a volte è deprimente: .... parli, parli, parli, ma chi ti ascolta?
4. Mi hanno detto che se .... arrivi tardi a teatro, non puoi entrare.
5. In Italia un tempo .... viveva meglio.
6. Quando la strada è ghiacciata, ... deve guidare con molta attenzione.

3. Put the words into order using the present impersonal form with: *si, uno, tu*.

1. Viaggiare/con/male/nebbia/la.
...*Si viaggia male con la nebbia*...
2. Bene/ferie/stare/in.
....
3. Quando/dal/ritornare/lavoro/amare/il/pronto/trovare/pranzo.
....
4. Finire/imparare/mai/di/non.
....
5. In/mangiare/ristorante/bene/questo.
....
6. A/volte/sapere/fare/in/cosa/inverno/non.
....
7. Se/nuotare/volere/imparare/a/dovere/paura/avere/non/dell'/acqua.
....
8. Quando/del/economia/paese/migliorare/l'/meglio/vivere.
....

fui **fosti** **fu**	**partito/a**	**ebbi** **avesti** **ebbe**	**mangiato**
fummo **foste** **furono**	**partiti/e**	**avemmo** **aveste** **ebbero**	**mangiato**

The **trapassato remoto** is formed with the *passato remoto* of the auxiliaries *essere* or *avere* and the *past participle* of the verb.

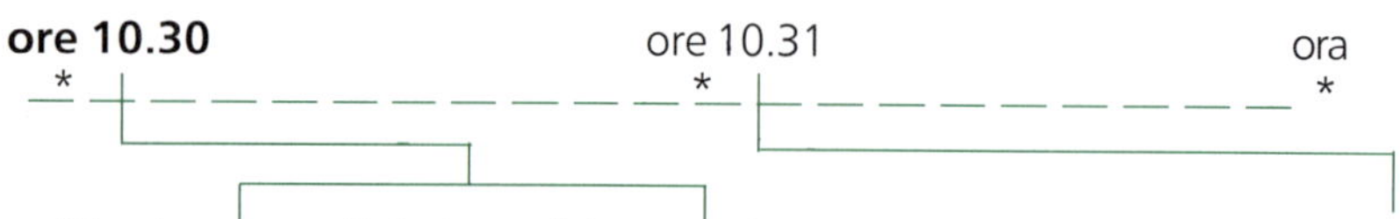

– (**Non**) **appena** il sindaco **ebbe terminato** il suo comizio, la gente **cominciò** a lasciare la piazza.
(As soon as the mayor had finished his speech the people started to leave the square)

The **trapassato remoto** is used to talk about an action which took place *immediately before* another event expressed in the un *passato remoto.*

It is only used in subordinate time clauses and it follows conjunctions like **dopo che** *(after),* **quando** *(when),* **(non) appena** *(no sooner than as soon as).*

– **Dopo che** Lisa **ebbe appreso** la notizia della partenza di Tommaso, **corse** a casa di Giuseppe.
(After she had heard about Tommaso leaving, Lisa ran to Giuseppe's house)

The *trapassato prossimo* is rarely used.

See also Unità 48 - The past perfect.

1. Complete the table with the correct form of the *passato remoto* and *trapassato remoto.*

Infinito	Passato remoto	Trapassato remoto
conoscere	*conobbi*	*ebbi conosciuto*
avere		
mettere		
fare		
dare		
nascere		
vivere		
andare		
venire		
cadere		
tenere		
partire		
vedere		

2. Put the verbs in brackets into the correct form of the *passato remoto* and *trapassato remoto*.

1. Dopo che il film ...*fu finito*... (finire), il produttore ...*decise*... (decidere) di non farlo uscire.
2. Non appena ....(consegnare) la tesi di laurea, Luigi ....(fare) una festa.
3. Dopo che i Franchi .... (ricevere) le chiavi della nuova casa, ... (fare) trasloco.
4. Non appena la polizia .... (andarsene), i ladri .... (uscire) dal loro nascondiglio.
5. Poco dopo che Flavio .... (cominciato) il nuovo lavoro, la sua ditta............................ (fallire).
6. Dopo che l'aereo .... (toccare) la pista d'atterraggio, i passeggeri .... (applaudire).
7. Non appena gli studenti .... (ritornare) dalle vacanze, il professore .... (assegnare) un esame.
8. Dopo che il governo .... (firmare) il nuovo decreto, i lavoratori .... (smettere) lo sciopero.

3. Finish the sentences.

1. Mi alzai dopo che ...*il telefono ebbe finito di suonare*...
2. Non appena ebbi finito di fare gli esercizi ....
3. Tornai a casa dopo che ....
4. Mi preparai un caffè non appena ....
5. Dopo che ebbi parlato con Sandro ....
6. Provai la nuova macchina non appena ....

Study the picture.

There are two ways of telling someone something. Directly: *"Ci vediamo a casa sua alle 8".*
Or with reported/indirect speech, i.e. reporting what someone else raid: *Anna dice che vi vedete a casa tua alle 8.*

When transforming direct speech into reported speech it is necessary to change different elements in the sentence, for example subject, verb (sense and form), personal pronouns, possessive adjectives, time and place expression, etc.

Changes in tenses starting from the past.

When reporting something that was said/thought/believed, etc. in the past, the verb in the main clause is in the *passato prossimo/remoto* or *imperfect*: *disse, ha detto, diceva*, etc.

DIRECT SPEECH	→	REPORTED SPEECH
Present Grazia **disse**: "**Devo** andare a casa" *(Grazia said: "I have to go home")*	→	*Imperfect* *Grazia* **disse** che **doveva** andare a casa. *(Grazia said that she had to go home.)*
Passato prossimo Grazia **disse**: "**Sono arrivata** a casa tardi." *(Grazia said: "I got home late.")*	→	*Past perfect* Grazia **disse** che **era arrivata** a casa tardi. *(Grazia said that she had got home late.)*
Passato remoto *Grazia* **disse**: "Da piccola **volli** imparare a giocare a tennis". *(Grazia said: "When I was a child I wanted to learn to play tennis.")*	→	*Past perfect* Grazia **disse** che da piccola **aveva voluto** imparare a giocare a tennis. *(Grazia said that when she was a child she had wanted to learn to play tennis.)*
Future Quando aveva 10 anni Grazia **disse**: "Da grande **imparerò** a giocare a tennis." *(When she was 10 Grazia said: "When I'm big I'll learn to play tennis.")*	→	*Perfect conditional* Quando aveva 10 anni Grazia **disse** che da grande **avrebbe imparato** a giocare a tennis. *(When she was 10 Grazia said that when she was big she would learn to play tennis.)*

Study the time line and the example:

stamattina **ora** domani
*— — — — — — — — — — * — — — — — — — — *

– Sonia stamattina mi **ha detto**: "**Tornerò** domani."
– Sonia stamattina mi **ha detto** che **tornerà** domani.

If the action expressed in reported speech has not taken place yet, i.e. it is still a future event, the verb remains in the future.

Changes in tenses starting from the present.

When reporting something that is said/thought/believed, etc. in the present or future, the verb in the main clause is in the present or future: *dice, dirà*, etc.
When transforming direct speech into reported speech, tenses do not change.

DIRECT SPEECH	→	REPORTED SPEECH
Presente *Grazia* **dice**: "Gli Stati Uniti **sono** lontani." *(Grazia says: "The U.S.A. is far away".)*	→	*Presente* *Grazia* **dice** che gli Stati Uniti **sono** lontani. *(Grazia says that the U.S.A. is far away.)*
Passato prossimo Quando la vedrò Grazia mi **dirà**: "**Sono stata** in pizzeria ieri sera." *(When I see Grazia, she'll say: "I went to a pizzeria yesterday evening.")*	→	*Passato prossimo* Quando la vedrò Grazia mi **dirà** che **è stata** in pizzeria ieri sera." *(When I see Grazia, she'll tell me that she went to a pizzeria yesterday evening.)*

1. Rewrite the sentences using reported speech.

1. "Ho fame!"
Grazia disse che......aveva fame..........
2. "Presto partirò per il Brasile."
Grazia disse che..........
3. "Sto lavorando molto."
Grazia disse che..........
4. "Non vedo mia madre da alcuni giorni."
Grazia disse che..........
5. "Ti chiamerò non appena tornerò dalle vacanze."
Grazia disse che..........
6. "Ho trovato subito un lavoro dopo aver finito di studiare."
Grazia disse che..........
7. "Ho deciso all'ultimo momento di telefonare a Gigi."
Grazia disse che..........
8. "Ho già fatto gli auguri di buon anno alla nonna."
Grazia disse che..........

2. Complete the telephone conversation.

Anna:	Pronto, sono Anna; c'è Lia?
Mamma:	Ciao Anna, Lia sta facendo la doccia.
Anna:	Ho bisogno di chiederle alcune informazioni.
Mamma:	Dimmi, gliele chiedo io.
Anna:	Domani c'è l'esame?
Mamma:	Lia, Anna chiede se domani.......c'è l'esame..........
Lia:	Sì.
Mamma:	Lia dice che..........2..........
Anna:	A che ora?
Mamma	Anna chiede..........3..........
Lia:	Alle 9.
Mamma:	Lia dice che..........4..........
Anna:	Va all'università in autobus?
Mamma:	Anna chiede se..........5..........
Lia:	No, in macchina.
Mamma:	Dice che..........6..........
Anna:	Può passarmi a prendere?
Mamma:	Anna chiede se..........7..........
Lia:	Va bene. Non c'è nessun problema.
Mamma:	Lia dice he..........8..........
	Ascolta Anna non è che potresti chiamare fra 5 minuti?!

Changes in form: from the indicative to the subjunctive.

Osserva e analizza gli esempi.

Giovanni **chiese**: "Paul **è** inglese?" → Giovanni **chiese** se Paul **fosse** inglese.
(Giovanni asked: "Is Paul English?" *Giovanni asked if Paul was were English.)*
Paola **chiede**: "Tua sorella si **chiama** Alba?" → Paola **chiede** se sua sorella si **chiami** Alba.
(Paola asks: "Is your sister's name Alba?" *Paola is asking if your sister's name is Alba.)*

If the verb in the main clause takes the subjunctive, then the verb in the subordinate clauses is in the subjunctive and the tense changes are as shown in the table below.

Changes in form and tense starting from the past.

DIRECT SPEECH	→	REPORTED SPEECH
Present Grazia **chiese**: "Luca **deve** andare a casa?" *(Grazia asked: "Does Luca have to go home?")*	→	*Imperfect* Grazia **chiese** se Luca **dovesse** andare a casa. *(Grazia asked if Luca had to go home.)*
Passato prossimo *Grazia* **chiese**: "Cristina, **sei arrivata** a casa tardi sabato sera?" *(Grazia asked: "Cristina, did you get home late Saturday evening?")*	→	*Past Perfect* *Grazia* **chiese** se Cristina **fosse arrivata** a casa tardi sabato sera. *(Grazia asked if Cristina had got home late Saturday evening.)*
Passato remoto *Grazia* **disse**: " Quante volte Colombo **arrivò** in America?" *(Grazia asked: "How many times did Columbus reach America?")*	→	*Past Perfect* *Grazia* **chiese** quante volte Colombo **fosse arrivato** in America. *(Grazia asked how many times Columbus (had) reached America.)*
Future *Quando aveva 10 anni Grazia* **chiese**: "Da grande mi **insegnerete** a giocare a tennis?" *(When she was 10, Grazia asked: "When I'm older, will you teach me how to play tennis?")*	→	*Perfect conditional* *Quando aveva 10 anni Grazia* **chiese** se da grande le **avrebbero insegnato** a giocare a tennis. *(When she was 10, Grazia asked if they would teach her how to play tennis when she was older.)*

Tense changes are the same as for the indicative. Only the form changes, because in this case the subjunctive is used.

Study the example.

– Karl **dice**: "L'italiano **è** difficile." → Karl **crede** che l'italiano **sia** difficile.
(Karl says: "Italian is difficult.") *(Karl thinks that Italian is difficult.)*

When changing from direct speech to reported speech other verbs can be used instead of *dire (say)*, for example: *credere, pensare, ritenere (believe, think, consider)*, which take the subjunctive.

▶ *Chiedere (ask)* can be followed either by the subjunctive or the indicative.

Changes in form an tense starting from the present.

Sometimes when transforming direct speech into reported speech the tenses do not change, but the form does.

DIRECT SPEECH	→	REPORTED SPEECH
Present *Grazia* **chiede**: "Venezia **è** vicino a Padova?" *(Grazia asks: "Is Venice near Padua?")*	→	*Present* *Grazia* **chiede** se Venezia **sia** vicino a Padova. *(Grazia asks if Venice is near Padua.)*

Changes in form: from the imperative to the subjunctive.

DIRECT SPEECH	→	REPORTED SPEECH
Starting from the past *Imperative* Grazia **disse**: "**Andatevene**!" *(Grazia said: "Go away!")*	→	*Imperfect subjunctive* Grazia **ordinò** che se ne **andassero**. *(Grazia ordered them to leave.)*
Starting from the present *Imperative* Grazia **dice**: "**Andatevene**!" *(Grazia says: "Go away!")*	→	*Present subjunctive* Grazia **ordina** che se ne **vadano**. *(Grazia tells them to leave.)*

▶ In the two examples above the structure (**di + infinitive**) can be used instead of the subjunctive.
Grazia disse: "Andatevene!" → Grazia ordinò loro **di andarsene**.
Grazia dice: "Andatevene!" → Grazia ordina loro **di andarsene**.

1. Rewrite the sentences using reported speech.

1. Luc chiede: "L'Italia è un paese caro?"
Luc chiede se *l'Italia sia un paese caro*
2. Luc chiede: "Roma è la città più bella del mondo?"
Luc chiede se...
3. Luc chiede: "L'italiano e il francese sono lingue complesse?"
Luc chiede se...
4. Luc chiede: "I treni in Italia arrivano spesso in ritardo?"
Luc chiede se...
5. Luc chiede: " Agli Italiani piace parlare di politica?"
Luc chiede se...
6. Luc chiede: "Gli Italiani un tempo vivevano meglio?"
Luc chiede se...
7. Luc chiede: "L'economia italiana tornerà presto a crescere?"
Luc chiede se...
8. Luc chiede: "L'Italia è stata tra i fondatori dell'Unione Europea?"
Luc chiede se...

2. Rewrite the sentences using reported speech.

1. "Lara, smetti di piangere!"
Franca ordinò a Lara che... *smettesse di piangere*
2. "Uscite dalla mia casa!"
Lara volle che...
3. "Non chiacchierate!"
L'insegnante ordinò che...
4. "Studiate di più!
L'insegnante ordinò che...
5. "Cristiano, vattene!"
Lorenza vuole che...
6. "Finite tutta la pasta!"
La mamma vuole che i figli...

3. Add a comment expressing a different opinion to the statements below.

1. Il Chianti è un vino toscano.
Pensavo che.... *fosse umbro*
2. Juan è venezuelano.
Pensavo che...
3. *I Malavoglia* è stato scritto da G. Verga.
Pensavo che...
4. Ieri sono andato a Brescia e poi al Lago di Garda.
Credevo che...
5. Ho finito di lavorare alle 5.
Credevo che...
6. Ingrid parla tre lingue straniere.
Pensavo che...

Changes in subjects, personal pronouns and possessives.

Study the following examples.

- "Ciao, ragazzi. **Vi** telefon**o** più tardi!" *("Bye. I'll ring you later.")* → Sandro saluta gli amici, dicendo che telefon**a** **loro** più tardi. *Sandro is saying goodbye to his friends and promising to ring them later.*
- "Lucia, **vai** da **tua** madre stasera?" *("Lucia, are you going to your mother's this evening?")* → Sandro chiede a Lucia se **va** da **sua** madre stasera. *Sandro is asking Lucia if she is going to her mother's this evening.)*

When transforming direct speech into reported speech, subject and object personal pronouns, possessives and verbs all change. If the subject in the main clause is in the third person singular or plural (lui, lei, loro), as in the examples above (*Sandro dice…, Sandro chiede…*), pronouns, adjectives and verbs in the first and second person singular (io, tu) and plural (noi, voi) change to the third person (singular and plural).

- "Lucia, **dobbiamo** andare al mercato domattina o **ti sei** messa d'accordo con i **nostri** amici?" *("Lucia, do we have to go to the market tomorrow morning or have you arranged something with our friends?")*

→ – Sandro chiede a Lucia se domattina **devono** andare al mercato o se **si è** messa d'accordo con i **loro** amici. *(Sandro is asking Lucia if they have to go to the market tomorrow morning or if she has arranged something with their friends.)*

Il cambiamento delle espressioni di tempo.

Study the examples.

- **Oggi** sono contento perché ho superato l'esame di filologia. *(I'm happy today because I've passed my philology exam)*

→ Davide disse che **quel giorno** era contento perché aveva superato l'esame di filologia. *(Davide said he was happy that day because he had passed his philology exam)*

- **Domani** farò una festa con tutti i miei amici. *(I'll have a party with all my friends tomorrow)*

→ Davide disse che **il giorno dopo** avrebbe fatto una festa con tutti i suoi amici. *(Davide said he would have a party with all his friends the following day)*

DIRECT SPEECH	→	REPORTED SPEECH
oggi *(today)*	→	quel giorno *(that day)*
domani *(tomorrow)*	→	il giorno seguente/successivo, il giorno dopo *(the following/next day)*
fra una settimana *(in a week)*	→	la settimana dopo/la settimana seguente/successiva *(the following week)*
stamattina, questo pomeriggio, (ecc.) *(this, morning, this afternoon*, etc.)	→	quella mattina, quel pomeriggio (ecc.) *(that morning, that afternoon*, etc.)
ieri, ieri sera *(yesterday, yesterday evening)*	→	il giorno precedente, il giorno prima, la sera prima *(the previous day, the previous evening)*
un'ora fa, tre giorni fa un mese fa, il mese scorso, ora/adesso *(an hour ago, three days ago, a month ago, now)*	→	un'ora prima, tre giorni prima, un mese prima, il mese prima/precedente, allora/in quel momento *(an hour earlier, three days before, a month before, the previous month, then/at the time)*

Changes in expressions of place.

Qui, **qua** *(here)* → **lì**, **là** *(there)*

- "Non muoverti da **qui**!" *("Don't move from here!")* → Sandro ordinò a suo figlio di non muoversi da **lì**. *Sandro ordered his son not to move from there.)*

Changes in demonstratives.

Questo/a/i/e *(this/these)* → **quel/quella/**ecc. *(that/those)*

- "Non ho mai letto **questo** libro." *("I have never read this book.")* → Sandro disse che non aveva mai letto **quel** libro. *Sandro said he had never read that book)*

Andare → venire *(go → come)*

- Sandro mi disse: "vuoi **venire** al cinema con me?". *(Sandro said: do you want to come to the cinema with me?")*
- Sandro mi disse se volevo **andare** al cinema con lui. *(Sandro asked me if I wanted to go to the cinema with him)*

1. Rewrite the sentences using reported speech.

1. "Quanti anni ha tuo fratello, Sonia?
Patrizia chiese a Sonia. *quanti anni avesse/aveva suo fratello*
2. "Sonia, ti ricordi il numero di telefono del nostro professore?"
Patrizia chiese a Sonia se...
3. "Sonia, mi presti il tuo dizionario d'italiano?"
Patrizia chiese a Sonia se...
4. "Sonia, dove hai messo la mia penna stilografica?"
Patrizia chiese a Sonia...
5. "Sonia, hai voglia di andare a casa di tua madre?"
Patrizia chiese a Sonia se...
6. "Sonia, a che ora siete arrivati a casa tu e Gianni?"
Patrizia chiese a Sonia...

2. Rewrite the sentences using reported speech.

1. "Oggi pomeriggio vado a teatro."
Lucia disse che... *quel pomeriggio andava a teatro*
2. "Domani finiranno le lezioni."
Lucia disse che...
3. "Ieri sono stato da Paolo fino alle 2 di notte."
Lucia disse che...
4. "Il treno da Milano è arrivato pochi minuti fa."
Lucia disse che...
5. "Mi sento bene ora."
Lucia disse che...
6. "Secondo l'oroscopo il mese prossimo conoscerò il mio Principe azzurro."
Lucia disse che...

3. Rewrite the sentences using reported speech.

1. "Qui c'è molto inquinamento."
Renzo disse che... *lì c'era molto inquinamento*
2. "È in questa casa che vivremo dopo il matrimonio."
Renzo disse che...
3. "Questa città sarà la nostra città."
Renzo disse che...
4. "Con tutti i suoi problemi di lavoro questa regione è in profonda crisi."
Renzo disse che...
5. "È meglio rimanere qui, piuttosto che andare a vivere in un altro paese."
Renzo disse che...
6. "Sono sicuro che questa volta vincerà la mia squadra."
Renzo disse che...

Present infinitive: form.

PRESENT	PAST
andare *(to go)*	**essere andato** *(to have gone)*

Present infinitive: use.
Study the examples.

- **Fare** ginnastica fa bene alla salute. *(Doing gymnastics is good for your health)*
- Devi **dire** a tuo fratello di **venirmi** a **trovare**. *(You must tell your brother to come and see me)*

In the examples above there are various infinitives. In the first example the infinitive acts as a noun; it is also possible to say: la ginnastica fa bene alla salute, (Gymnastics is good for your health); in the second example, the three infinitives act as verbs.

When it acts as a **noun** the **infinitive** is the **subject** of the clause:

- Abitare in campagna è bello.
  (Living in the country is nice)

Sometimes the article **il, lo, l'** can be placed before the infinitive.

- **Il parlare** male di una persona in sua assenza non è corretto.
  (It is not nice to talk about a person behind his back)

When it acts like a verb it can be independent (especially as an imperative, both negative and affirmative):

- Non **gettare** oggetti dal finestrino.
  (Don't throw things out of the window.)

Or it can depend on another verb (with or without a preposition before it):

- Mi piace **nuotare**. *(I like swimming.)*

Verbs with the infinitive without preposition.

Dovere, potere, sapere, volere *(must, can, know, want)*	Devi **andare** a letto presto, se vuoi **stare** bene al mattino. *(You have to go to bed early if you want to feel good in the morning.)*
lasciare, fare *(let, make)*	Lascia **perdere**, è meglio! *(Forget it, it's better!)*
ascoltare, guardare, sentire, vedere, osservare, ecc. *(listen, look, hear, see, watch, etc.)*	Ti ascolto **suonare** la chitarra e mi ricordo quando ero giovane. *(Listening to you playing the guitar, reminds me of when I was young.)*
piacere, desiderare, preferire *(like, would like, prefer)*	Desidero **finire** questo lavoro al più presto. *(I'd like to finish this job as soon as possible)*
basta, bisogna, occorre *(be enough, need, be necessary)*	Bisogna **aspettare** un momento. *(We have to wait a bit.)*
essere + aggettivo, avverbio *(be + adjective, adverb)*	Spesso è inutile **piangere**, è meglio **affrontare** i problemi. *(Crying is often useless, it's better to face up to problems)*
osare *(dare)*	Non oso **disturbarla** quando dorme. *(I wouldn't dare disturb her when she's asleep)*

With *volere*, *desiderare*, *piacere* and *preferire (want, would like, like* and *prefer)* the structure with the infinitive cannot be used if the subject of the subordinate clause is different from the one in the main clause.

- (**Io**) **Preferisco** che **tu** venga da me domani.
  (I'd rather you came to see me tomorrow)
- (**Io**) **Vorrei** che **lei** fosse sempre con me.
  (I wish she was always with me)

The *unstressed personal pronouns, ne* and *ci* follow the infinitive and the final vowel of the verb is dropped. See Unità 40.

parlar**e** + **gli** ➜ parlar**gli** discuter**e** + **ne** discuter**ne**

The verb **sapere** *(know)* is used without the preposition **di** when it means *essere capace (be able to)*.

- So **nuotare** but So **di** non essere un bravo cuoco.
  = =
- Sono capace di nuotare Mi rendo conto di non essere un bravo cuoco.
  (I can swim) *(I know I'm not a good cook)*

1. Complete the sentences with the infinitive form. Use the verbs from the box below.

1. ....*Mangiare*.......... salume non fa molto bene alla salute.
2. .... agli amici buon anno è un gesto di cortesia.
3. .... gli anni dell'università fa spesso piacere.
4. .... molte sigarette fa male.
5. "... prima dell'uso": è spesso scritto sui medicinali.
6. "... le istruzioni prima dell'uso": è un'altra scritta che si trova spesso sui medicinali.

mangiare	agitare	augurare	fumare	ricordare	leggere

2. Match the clues with the instructions.

1. *È una scritta che si trova sui treni.*
2. È una scritta che si trova sugli aerei.
3. È una scritta che si trova ai caselli dell'autostrada.
4. È una scritta che si trova spesso sui pacchi.
5. È una scritta che si trova nelle biblioteche
6. È una scritta che si trova sugli autobus.
7. È una scritta che si trova spesso nei parchi.
8. È una scritta che si trova nelle stazioni di servizio.

a Maneggiare con cura.
b Non calpestare le aiuole.
c Spegnere i motori.
d Fare silenzio.
e Non gettare alcun oggetto dai finestrini.
f Rallentare.
g Non parlare al conducente.
h Allacciare le cinture.

3. Complete the sentences with the infinitive form. Use the verbs from the box below.

1. I bambini devono ....*andare*.......... a letto presto durante la settimana.
2. Se vuoi ...., devi .... di più.
3. Bisogna .... puntuali al lavoro.
4. Ho sentito .... il segretario del tuo partito. E' molto intelligente.
5. Mi piacerebbe .... un bel regalo il giorno della Befana.
6. Non oso .... al professore di rispiegarmi la lezione di ieri.
7. Preferisco .... le vacanze al mare, non in montagna.
8. Non fare .... i tuoi genitori! Sposati!

soffrire	mangiare	parlare	trascorrere	ingrassare	ricevere	chiedere	arrivare	andare

The most frequent verbs followed by preposition **di + infinitive** listed in alphabetical order.

affermare * *(maintain)*	L'imputato afferma di essere innocente.
ammettere * *(admit)*	L'imputato ha ammesso di essere colpevole.
avere bisogno *(need)*	I Rossi hanno bisogno di trovare un nuovo appartamento.
avere il diritto/dovere *(be one's right/duty)*	Ogni italiano ha il dovere di rispettare le leggi.
avere paura *(be afraid of)*	Ho paura di fare un incidente in moto.
avere tempo *(have time)*	Silvia non ha tempo di fare la traduzione.
avere voglia *(to feel like)*	Ho sempre voglia di dormire.
cercare *(try)*	Cerco sempre di fare del mio meglio.
chiedere *(ask)*	Gli ho chiesto di farmi un favore.
credere * *(believe, think)*	Credo di essere abbastanza fortunato nella vita.
decidere * *(decide)*	Abbiamo deciso di tornare in Francia.
dimenticare/si * *(forget)*	Mi sono dimenticato di fare la spesa.
dire *(say, tell)*	Ho detto alla donna di servizio di non cucinare più.
dubitare * *(doubt)*	Dubito di arrivare in tempo.
evitare * *(avoid)*	Bisogna evitare di mettersi nei guai.
finire *(finish)*	Ho finito di lavorare in tempo per prendere l'autobus
immaginare * *(imagine)*	Immagino spesso di essere su una spiaggia deserta.
impedire *(prevent, forbid)*	Ti impedisco di entrare in casa mia.
lamentarsi * *(complain)*	Ci lamentiamo sempre di vivere dove c'è nebbia.
negare * */deny)*	Nego di essere io il colpevole.
ordinare *(order)*	Gli ho ordinato di finire il lavoro prima di sera.
pensare * *(think)*	Penso di essere un calciatore molto mediocre.
permettere *(allow, let)*	Il dottore non mi permette di bere alcolici.
pregare *(pray)*	Prega di non incontrarlo per strada.
proibire *(forbid, not allow)*	Mi hanno proibito di fumare.
ricordarsi * *(remember)*	Non mi ricordo mai di telefonare a Carlo.
ritenere * *(think)*	Ritengo di poter andare in Cina presto.
sforzarsi *(try hard)*	Lui si sforza di essere simpatico, ma non ci riesce.
smettere *(give up)*	Ho smesso di fumare.
sognare * (dream)	Sogno di diventare un grande ballerino.
sperare * *(hope)*	Spero di andare in pensione presto.
supporre * *(suppose)*	Supponiamo di poter partire subito. Dove andresti?
temere * *(to be afraid)*	Teme di non poter aver figli.
tentare *(try)*	Ha tentato di battere il proprio record nei 100 metri.
terminare *(finish, stop)*	Terminiamo spesso di lavorare alle 8.
tollerare * (can't stand)	Non tollero di dovere svegliarmi sempre alle 7.
vergognarsi * *(be ashamed of)*	Mi vergogno di non sapere una parola di arabo.
vietare *(forbid)*	Mia moglie mi ha vietato di parlare con la mia ex.

The verbs marked with the asterisk * are followed by the preposition **di** if the subject of the main clause is the same as the subject in the subordinate clause.

– Penso **di** essere felice. *(I think I'm happy.)*

– Penso **che tu** sia felice. *(I think you're happy.)*

Some adjectives are followed by the preposition **di + infinitive**

capace *(able)*	Non sono capace di cantare.
contento *(pleased)*	Sono contento di fare il bagno nel mare di Capri.
convinto *(sure)*	Sei convinta di essere una brava attrice?
curioso *(curious)*	Sono curioso di leggere il tuo nuovo libro.
felice *(happy)*	Sono felice di stare in vacanza.
libero *(free)*	Sono libero di andare dove voglio.
orgoglioso *(proud)*	È orgoglioso di essere italiano.
sicuro *(sure)*	Sei sicuro di dire la verità?
stanco *(tired)*	Lino è stanco di lavorare.

1. Complete the sentences with a verb from the box below.

1. Ho ....*deciso*........ di emigrare.
2. Ho fretta. Non .... d'ascoltarti.
3. .... di mangiarmi un bel piatto di spaghetti.
4. .... di non sapere più parlare tedesco.
5. .... spesso di essere su una bella spiaggia nei Caraibi.
6. .... di studiare di più. Vedrai che ce la farai.
7. Ti .... di fumare qui! Ci sono dei bambini piccoli.
8. Vi .... di smettere di chiacchierare!
9. Mi .... spesso di non avere tempo di fare ciò che voglio.
10. Da qualche tempo .... di bere alcool: ho problemi di fegato.
11. .... di passare un buon ultimo dell'anno.
12. Dario non .... d'avere sbagliato.
13. Mario, ... di chiamare tua madre. È Natale.
14. Non ti .... di parlare male di mia cugina!

sognare	decidere	proibire	lamentare	sperare	ammettere	avere voglia
avere tempo	pregare	cercare	ricordarsi	credere	permettere	smettere

2. Make sentences with the words below using *di* + verb in the infinitive form or *che* + subject and verb.

1. Penso/il francese/essere/una lingua interessante.
Penso che il francese sia una lingua interessante..
2. Credo/non uscire/questa sera.
....
3. Ho deciso/studiare/l'arabo.
....
4. Mi dimentico/sempre/tu/essere/straniero.
....
5. Dubito/il treno/arrivare/in orario.
....
6. A volte/m'immagino/essere/su un'isola deserta.
....
7. Non tollero/qualcuno/maltrattare/gli animali.
....
8. Ritengo/la Svezia/essere/uno dei paesi più civili.
....

3. Complete the sentences with an adjective.

1. Sono .*contento/felice*.... di avere ricevuto un aumento di salario.
2. Sei .... di avere perso le chiavi?
3. Ogni essere umano deve essere .... di esprimere le proprie opinioni.
4. Non sempre sono .... di essere italiano.
5. Non sei .... di lavorare tanto?
6. Sei proprio .... di poter mangiare tre chili di cocomero in cinque minuti?

Study the pictures.

The most frequent verbs followed by the preposition **a + infinitive** listed in alphabetical order.

abituarsi *(get used to)*	È difficile abituarsi a mangiare sempre pasta.
accompagnare *(accompany, go with)*	Mi accompagni a far spesa?
andare *(go)*	Elena va a prendere la bimba all'asilo.
annoiarsi *(get bored)*	Teresa, l'ascensorista, non si annoia a far sempre gli stessi movimenti.
arrivare *(arrive, get to)*	Siamo arrivati a comprare il latte quando il negozio stava chiudendo.
aiutare *(help)*	Ti aiuto a finire i compiti?
cominciare *(start, take up)*	Ho cominciato a correre ogni giorno.
continuare *(continue, keep on)*	Voglio continuare a fare ginnastica con costanza.
convincere *(convince)*	Ho convinto mia moglie a correre con me.
correre *(run)*	Dopo due ore di ginnastica sono corso a dormire; ero stanco morto.
divertirsi *(enjoy oneself)*	I giovani si divertono a stare in discoteca fino alle 5 del mattino.
entrare *(go in)*	Il giovane è entrato nell'ufficio a parlare con il direttore.
fare in tempo *(make it/do something in time)*	Non ho fatto in tempo a scrivere una lettera a Andrea.
imparare *(learn)*	Non ho ancora imparato a giocare a tennis.
incoraggiare *(encourage)*	Sua moglie lo incoraggia spesso a ballare, ma lui non ne vuole sapere.
iniziare *(start)*	Ho iniziato a studiare l'inglese a 14 anni.
insegnare *(teach)*	Mi hanno insegnato a pronunciare l'inglese con un metodo efficace.
invitare *(invite)*	Ti invito a bere una birra; ci vieni?
mandare *(send)*	Ho mandato mio fratello in posta a spedire una raccomandata.
mettersi *(get down to)*	Se mi mettessi a studiare con questo caldo, non capirei niente.
portare *(lead to)*	Il troppo esercizio fisico mi ha condotto a mangiare il triplo.
prepararsi *(get ready)*	La signora si preparò a ricevere gli ospiti.
provare *(try)*	Ho provato a telefonarti ma non eri a casa.
restare *(stay)*	Stasera resto a giocare a carte con gli amici fino alle 11.
rinunciare *(give up)*	Ho rinunciato a imparare a ballare, dopo inutili tentativi.
riuscire *(manage)*	Sono riuscito a trovare il tuo numero di telefono sull'elenco.
spingere *(push)*	La tragedia che lo ha colpito lo ha spinto a suicidarsi.
stare (stay)	Devo stare in ufficio fino a tardi a finire un lavoro.
tornare *(go back)*	Torno a prenderti alle 10.
venire *(come)*	Vengo a trovarti domenica pomeriggio.
volerci *(take)*	Ci vogliono 3 ore a finire questo lavoro.

Some adjectives are followed by the preposition **a + infinitive.**

abile *(clever, good)*	Luca è molto abile a vendere cose inutili.
abituato *(used to)*	Sono abituato a svegliarmi presto.
attento *(careful)*	Stai attento a non sporcarti troppo.
interessato *(interested)*	Sono interessato a tutto quanto riguarda il Sud America.
lento *(slow)* veloce *(fast)*	Mio nonno non era lento a capire le cose, anzi era molto veloce a cogliere quanto poteva interessarlo.
occupato *(busy)*	Il direttore è occupato a controllare il lavoro degli operai.
pronto *(prepared/ready)*	Sono pronto a seguirti fino in capo al mondo.

1. Complete the sentences with a verb from the box below.

1. Non mi sono ancora ...*abituato*........ a vivere in Italia.
2. Io .... spesso a far spesa nel nuovo ipermercato.
3. Ti .... davvero a prendere in giro tutti?
4. .... a credere che avere dei figli non sia poi tanto negativo.
5. I bambini .... velocemente a parlare una lingua straniera.
6. Non mi .... a spendere tutta la tredicesima!
7. .... a prendere l'autobus, ma sono arrivato tardi.
8. Ieri mi .... a rileggere *La morte a Venezia*.
9. Non ho .... a salutare tua madre. Era già partita quando sono tornato a casa.
10. Lela, ... a mangiare da noi stasera?
11. .... a fare l'esercizio, ma era troppo difficile.
12. Aspetti, Signora; l'....................................... a portare la valigia!
13. .... a fare ginnastica, ma sono ancora fuori forma.
14. .... a sperare che il mondo possa cambiare, ma a volte penso di essere solo un idealista.

abituar(si)	correre	fare in tempo	provare	cominciare	andare	iniziare
metter(si)	venire	divertir(si)	imparare	continuare	aiutare	convincere

2. Complete the sentences with an adjective.

1. Quel cartomante è molto ....*abile*........ a imbrogliare la gente.
2. La segretaria di tuo marito è molto .... a battere a macchina. In un momento mi ha finito la lettera.
3. Non sono .... a mangiare molto di sera.
4. I ragazzi sono sempre molto .... a giocare con i videogiochi.
5. Poche persone sono .... ad aiutare gli altri.
6. Mia moglie è sempre .... a scoprire ciò che succede nel mondo.

Da indicates purpose

with **c'è/ci sono** *(there is/are)*:

- A Firenze **ci sono** molte cose **da** vedere. ➜ *(...cose che devono essere viste/che vale la pena vedere.)*
  There are many things to see in Florence
- **C'è** ancora molto **da** fare per uscire dalla crisi economica. ➜ *(Devono essere fatte molte cose/bisogna fare.)*
  There is still a lot to do to come out of the economic crisis
- Devono essere fatte molte cose/bisogna fare.
  Many things must/have to/need to be done

- with **avere**, meaning *dovere (must/have to)*:
  - **Ho** molto **da** lavorare oggi. ➜ *(Devo lavorare molto oggi.)*
    I have to do a lot of work today
- with a **noun**, in expressions such as:
  - Un appartamento **da** affittare. ➜ *(Un appartamento libero che si può affittare.)*
    A flat to let
  - Una macchina **da** cucire. ➜ *(Una macchina che si usa per cucire.)*
    A sewing machine
- with **qualcosa** *(somethings)*:
  - Vuoi **qualcosa da** leggere? ➜ *Do you want something to read?*
  - Mio zio ha sempre **qualcosa da** fare. ➜ *My uncle always has something to do*

Study the examples with **da** again. Is there a preposition with the same function in your language too?

Per + infinitive is used in clauses of purpose, i.e. it means **al fine di/allo scopo di** *(in order to)*.

- Mi sono alzato presto **per andare** in montagna. ➜ (...*al fine di*...)
  (I got up early to go to the mountains)
- L'ho chiamato **per sapere** cosa è successo ieri sera. ➜ (...*al fine di*...)
  (I called him to find out what happened yesterday evening)

▶ This construction can only be used when the subject in the main clause is the same as the subject in the subordinate clause.

IO ***IO***
- Le ho parlato **per spiegarle** cosa doveva fare.
  (I spoke to her to explain to her what she had to do.)

IO ***LEI***
- Le ho parlato **affinché lei mi spiegasse** cosa doveva fare.
  (I spoke to her so that she would tell me what she had to do)

For the use of *affinché (so that)*, see Unità 70.

▶ For the construction *stare per*, see Unità 53.

1. Complete the sentences with *da* + the infinitive.

1. *Il Gattopardo* è un film ......*da vedere*......
2. Pisa è una città ....
3. Ho già letto *I Malavoglia*, ma è un libro ....
4. La ribollita è un piatto toscano ....
5. La *Traviata* è un'opera ....
6. Il cinese deve essere una lingua difficile, ... con molta pazienza.

2. Guess the objects or expressions with *da.*

1. Si usa per creare vestiti o per rammendare.
   ...*Macchina da cucire*...
2. È un oggetto in metallo che si usa per stirare.
   ....
3. È un oggetto in legno o metallo che si usa per stirare.
   ....
4. Li usa chi non vede bene.
   ....
5. Li usa chi cammina molto in montagna.
   ....
6. La usa chi fa ginnastica.
   ....
7. È la stanza dove si dorme.
   ....
8. È un'espressione che si usa quando fa molto freddo, nevica e tira vento. Contiene un animale.
   ....
9. Vi si gioca a calcio.
   ....
10. Con quest'oggetto si evita di scrivere a mano.
    ....

ricordare	compilare	ritirare	prepararmi	risolvere	tornare

3. Complete the sentences with a verb from the box below.

1. Ti ho chiamato per ...*ricordarti*..... di riportarmi il mio libro.
2. Studio molto per .... a un lavoro.
3. È troppo tardi per .... a casa in autobus.
4. Ho bisogno di parlare con il direttore per .... il problema.
5. Devo passare dal fotografo per .... le foto di Siena.
6. Sto aspettando da un'ora per .... il modulo per l'iscrizione.

4. Make sentences using per + the infinitive or affinché + subject and verb.

1. Mi sono tolto le scarpe/asciugarmi i piedi.
   ...*Mi sono tolto le scarpe per asciugarmi i peli*...
2. Ho parlato con tua madre/lei dirmi come stai veramente.
   ....
3. Ti presto un po' di soldi/tu finire di pagare il mutuo per la casa.
   ....
4. Ho pensato di chiedere un mese di ferie/ripensare alla mia vita.
   ....
5. Ho un appuntamento con il dentista/curare una carie.
   ....

Perfect infinitive: form

PRESENT	PERFECT
essere	essere stato/a/i/e
avere	avere avuto
mangiare	aver mangiato
andare	essere andato/a/i/e
potere	aver potuto

The perfect infinitive is formed with the *present infinitive* of the verbs *essere* or *avere* + the *past participle* of the verb.

In the perfect infinitive *aver* is used instead of the full word *avere*.

Perfect infinitive: use.

Study the examples.

- **Dopo aver speso** tutti i soldi, sono tornato a casa.
  (After having spent all my money I went back home)
- Quando sono arrivato a casa, mi sono arrabbiato con me stesso **per** non **aver comprato** il latte.
  (When I got home I was really annoyed with myself for not having bought the milk)

In the two examples above the perfect infinitive is used because the action in the subordinate clause took place before the event in the main clause.

The **perfect infinitive** is used with

dopo *(after)*.

Study the examples.

- **Dopo aver dormito** dodici ore ero ancora stanco.
  (I was still tired even after having slept for twelve hours)
- **Dopo** che Luca **era arrivato** a casa, sua madre gli diede la buona notizia.
  (When Luca got home, his mother gave him the good news)

What are the subjects of two sentences above?

The phrase **dopo** + infinitive can only be used when the subject of the main clause is the same as the subject of the subordinate clause.

per, which introduces the cause of the event in the main clause.

- La conosco **per aver studiato** insieme all'università ➜ *(implicit)*
- La conosco **perché abbiamo** studiato insieme all'università. ➜ *(explicit)*
  (I know her because we studied together at University)

Even with **per**, the structure with the infinitive can only be used when the subject of the main clause in the same as the subject of the subordinate clause.

1. Match the sentences from the columns.

1. *Dopo aver fatto spesa,*
2. Dopo essermi laureato,
3. Dopo essere stato trasportato in ospedale,
4. Dopo essere stata sposata per quattro anni,
5. Dopo essermi arrabbiato tanto,
6. Dopo essere tornato dalle vacanze,
7. Dopo aver letto l'ultimo giallo,
8. Dopo aver rotto i vetri a sassate,

a ho trovato un lavoro da insegnante in una scuola privata.
b Evelina capì com'era suo marito.
c decisi di cambiare genere di libri.
d la Zia Giulia si è fermata dal parrucchiere.
e i ragazzi scapparono via.
f non avevo più voglia di lavorare.
g capii che non avevo ragione.
h Antonio è stato operato.

2. Make sentences using dopo + the infinitive or the subject and verb construction.

1. Luigi è andato a vivere da solo dopo/i suoi genitori cacciarlo via.
Luigi è andato a vivere da solo dopo che i suoi genitori lo hanno cacciato via
2. Che cosa ha fatto Detlev dopo/tornare in Germania?
....
3. Il suo libro è stato tradotto in inglese dopo/l'editore presentarlo alla fiera del libro.
....
4. Sono uscito dopo/telefonare a Maria.
....
5. Appena dopo andare a letto/Costanza fu svegliata dai ladri.
....
6. Dopo vincere la corsa/Roberto si sentì male.
....

3. Rewrite the sentences using *per* + the perfect infinitive where possible.

1. Ruba è stata premiata perché ha scritto una tesi importante sulle donne palestinesi.
Ruba è stata premiata per aver scritto una tesi importante sulle donne palestinesi
2. L'ortolano ha dovuto chiudere il negozio perché il padrone gli ha aumentato troppo l'affitto.
....
3. Ernesto è stato rimproverato perché ha picchiato un compagno di classe.
....
4. L'imputato è stato assolto perché non aveva commesso il fatto.
....
5. L'imputato è stato condannato perché aveva rapinato una banca.
....
6. Era arrabbiato con me perché gli avevo preso la bicicletta senza dirglielo.
....

The infinitive is used in expressions, such as

prima di *(before)*

- **Prima di salire** sul treno abbracciai mia madre.
  (I hugged my mother before getting on the train)

The phrase **prima** + infinitive can only be used when the subject of the main clause is the same as the subject in the subordinate.

- Prima di mangiare mi sono lavato le mani. *(I washed my hands before eating)*
- Prima che mia moglie tornasse ho passato l'aspirapolvere.
  (Before my wife came back I took the hoover over the room)

senza *(without)*

- Sono partito per la Svezia **senza cambiare** i soldi. *(I left for Sweden without changing any money)*

The phrase **senza** + infinitive can only be used when the subject of the main clause is the same as the subject in the subordinate.

- Senza fumare sto molto meglio. *(I feel much better now that I dont't smoke.)*
- Le ho preso 10 euro senza che se ne accorgesse. *(I took 10 euro from her without her noticing.)*

invece di *(instead of)*

- **Invece di lamentarti**, cerca di risolvere il problema! *(Instead of complaining, try and solve the problem!)*

Invece di is a synonym of *al posto di*, *anziché*.

The phrase **invece di +** infinitive can only be used when the subject of the main clause is the same as the subject in the subordinate clause.

a costo di *(even if)*

- **A costo di inventarmi** tutto, gli dirò che va tutto bene.
- Anche se dovrò inventarmi tutto, gli dirò che va tutto bene.
  (I'll tell him everything is going well even if I have to make it all up)

The phrase **a costo di +** infinitive can only be used when the subject of the main clause is the same as the subject in the subordinate clause.

a forza di *(by keeping on)*

- **A forza di ripetere** che in Italia si vive bene, se ne sta convincendo.
- Continuando a ripetere che in Italia si vive bene, se ne sta convincendo.
  (By keeping on repeating that life in Italy is good, he is convincing himself)

He's managing to convince himself that life is good in Italy by repeating it over and over again.

The phrase **a forza di +** infinitive can only be used when the subject of the main clause is the same as the subject in the subordinate clause.

in modo da *(so as to, in order to)*

- Ho scritto a mio fratello **in modo da raccontargli** ciò che è accaduto.
- Ho scritto a mio fratello, così posso raccontargli ciò che è accaduto.
  (I have written to my brother, in order to tell him what has happened)

The phrase **in modo da +** infinitive can only be used when the subject of the main clause is the same as the subject in the subordinate.

- Ho comprato una piccola barca in modo da poter visitare alcune spiaggette tranquille.
  (I have bought a little boat in order to visit some nice quiet beaches)
- Roberto ha detto tutta la verità a Stefania in modo che lei possa decidere liberamente che cosa fare.
  (Roberto told Stefania the whole truth so that she can decide what to do)

1. Match the sentences from the columns.

1. *Senza aver superato l'esame di guida,*
2. Scriviti un promemoria,
3. A costo di perdere molto tempo,
4. A forza di lavorare in una cella frigorifera,
5. Prima di sposarmi,
6. A forza di invitarci a cena,
7. Sabato sono rimasto a casa a riposarmi,
8. Senza saperlo,

a in modo da ricordare l'appuntamento col medico.
b a Costantino sono venuti i reumatismi.
c invece di uscire con la mia ragazza.
d non è possibile guidare la macchina.
e ho capito che Lucia e Filippo stanno insieme.
f sono riusciti a farci accettare l'invito.
g farò una festa con tutti i miei amici.
h voglio capire come funziona questo apparecchio.

2. Complete the sentences using *prima di, senza, invece di*.

1. Metti via i tuoi vestiti *prima di* andare a letto.
2. .... disperarti, affronta la situazione.
3. .... possedere l'attrezzatura necessaria è impossibile andare a sciare.
4. .... imparare da soli a sciare, è meglio prendere qualche lezione.
5. Ho corso sei chilometri .... mai fermarmi.
6. .... fare il bagno bisogna aspettare 3 ore da quando si è mangiato.
7. Non si può andare in India .... aver fatto il passaporto.
8. .... stare sempre in casa, perché non ti iscrivi a un corso di ballo?

3. Join the sentences.

1. Dino è uscito di casa. Non ha finito la cena.
Dino è uscito di casa senza finire la cena
2. Daniela ha lasciato il teatro. Lo spettacolo non era terminato.
....
3. Ha fatto gli esercizi. Non ha usato il dizionario.
....
4. Si sono divorziati. I loro genitori non lo sapevano.
....
5. Mi hanno cambiato il numero di telefono. Non mi hanno avvisato.
....
6. Volevo andare via. Sono rimasto in Italia.
....
7. Ho comprato il biglietto. Sono salito sull'autobus.
....
8. Sono tornato a vivere in Italia. Ho vissuto in vari paesi.
....

The **gerund** has two forms: *present gerund* and *past gerund*.

PRESENT	GERUND
cant - **are**	cant - **ando**
cred - **ere**	cred - **endo**
sent - **ire**	sent - **endo**
fin - **ire**	fin - **endo**

PAST GERUND
avendo cantato
avendo creduto
essendo andato/a/i/e
essendo partito/a/i/e

Some irregular forms.

bere	bev - **endo**
condurre	conduc - **endo**
dire	dic - **endo**
fare	fac - **endo**
porre	pon - **endo**
trarre	tra - **endo**

The **past gerund** is formed with the *present gerund* of the verbs *essere* or *avere* + the *past participle* of the verb.

The **gerund** can have different functions, indicating:

time

- **Giocando** a calcio bisogna osservare la posizione dei compagni.
- **Quando si gioca** a calcio bisogna osservare la posizione dei compagni.
  (When playing football you must watch where the other team members are positioned)

means

- **Leggendo** si imparano tante cose. /**Con la lettura** si imparano tante cose.
  (You learn lots of things by reading)

cause

- **Essendomi divertito** molto alcuni anni fa, quest'anno sono tornato in Sardegna.
- **Poiché/dato che mi sono divertito** molto alcuni anni fa, quest'anno sono tornato in Sardegna.
  (As I enjoyed myself so much a few years ago, I went back to Sardinia this year)

hypothesis

- **Risparmiando** molto riusciresti a comprarti un appartamento.
- **Se risparmiassi** molto, riusciresti a comprarti un appartamento.
  (If you saved hard you would be able to buy yourself a flat)

concession, used with **pur** *(although)*

- **Pur** non **avendo sonno** è andata a letto con il suo bimbo.
- **Anche se** non **aveva sonno**, è andata a letto con il suo bimbo.
  (Although she wasn't tired, she went to bed with her son)

The **present gerund** is used when the action in the main clause takes place at the same time as the event in the subordinate clause.

ore 17 — ora

- **Correndo** sono caduto *(I fell while I was running)*

The **past gerund** is used when the action in the main clause follows the event in the subordinate clause, i.e. the action expressed by the past gerund took place first.

ore 20 — ore 23

- **Avendo mangiato** troppo, ho dovuto prendere un bicchiere d'acqua con un po' di bicarbonato.
  (Having eaten too much, I had to have a glass of water with some baking soda)

The **gerund** is generally used when the subject in the main clause is the same as the subject is the subordinate clause (i.e. the sentence with the gerund).

▷ For the use of the **present gerund** with the verb *stare*, see Unità 52.
▷ The *unstressed personal pronouns*, *ci* and *ne* follow the **gerund**; see Unità 40.

1. Underline the correct form of the verb.

1. *Correndo/avendo corso,* sono caduto.
2. *Avendo lavorato/lavorando* molto, ieri sera sono andato a letto alle 10.
3. *Rimanendo/essendo rimasto* spesso in casa, ho la possibilità di leggere molto.
4. *Avendo fatto/facendo* molti errori, ho preso un brutto voto.
5. *Guarendo/essendo guarito* dall'influenza, sono tornato a lavorare.
6. *Avendo finito/finendo* il corso, mi sento molto perso.
7. *Essendo andato/andando* spesso al mare, ho deciso di comprarmi un camper.
8. *Raccontandomi/avendomi raccontato* la sua vita, piangeva.

2. Rewrite the sentences using the correct form of the gerund.

1. Quando piangono, i bambini non riescono a respirare.
Piangendo, i bambini non riescono a respirare
2. Quando arriverà la primavera, farò molte passeggiate.
......
3. Visto che non avevo tempo per andare da mia madre, le ho telefonato.
......
4. Se le proponessi un viaggio ai tropici, forse riusciresti a conquistarla.
......
5. Con l'ascolto di musica classica ci si rilassa.
......
6. Poiché mi era molto simpatico invitai Silvio a cena.
......
7. Quando si vive lontano da casa, ci si sente spesso soli.
......
8. Quando andrò al mare, mi fermerò a mangiare i funghi sull'Appennino.
......
9. Mentre fa i compiti, Piero ascolta musica.
......
10. Anche se non avevo fame, mi sono comprato una pizza.
......
11. Se vincessi al totocalcio, non so cosa farei.
......
12. Nonostante non ci sia molto freddo, mi sono messo la giacca a vento.
......

3. Rewrite the sentences without changing the meaning.

1. Avendo finito di mangiare, i commensali di alzarono da tavola.
Poiché *avevano finito di mangiare i commensali si alzarono da tavola*
Mentre ......
Se ......
2. Andando a casa, incontrai un vecchio compagno di scuola.
Anche se ......
Dato che ......
Mentre ......
3. Pur essendo rimasto più a lungo in ufficio, ieri sera non sono riuscito a finire tutto il lavoro.
Dato che ......
Nonostante ......
Quando ......
4. Avendo ascoltato il telegiornale, sappiamo cosa è successo in Burundi.
Quando ......
Anche se ......
Visto che ......

Present participle: form.

PRESENT PARTICIPLE	
cant - **are**	cant - **ante**
cred - **ere**	cred - **ente**
segu - **ire**	segu - **ente**

Some irregular forms.

PRESENT PARTICIPLE	
bere	bev - **ente**
condurre	conduc - **ente**
dire	dic - **ente**
fare	fac - **ente**
porre	pon - **ente**
trarre	tra - **ente**

Several verbs in -ire form the present participle in -**iente**.

ubbid**ire** ➜ ubbid**iente** *(obedient)*
conven**ire** ➜ conven**iente** *(convenient)*

Present participle: use.
The **present participle** can be used as an *adjective,* a *noun* or a *verb*.
It is most frequently used as an adjective and as a noun.

Adjectives Some examples.

Una casa **accogliente**. *(A welcoming house)* Una donna **affascinante**. *(A fascinating woman)*
Un incidente **terrificante**. *(A terrible accident)* Una borsa **pesante**. *(A heavy bag)*

Nouns Some examples

Il presidente, il/la commerciante, il/la partecipante, l'insegnante, il/la dipendente, il/la cantante, la corrente
(the president, the shopkeeper, the participant, the teacher, the employee, the singer, the current)

As adjective and as noun the present participle ends in **e** in the *singular* form and in **i** in the *plural* form.

Verbs

When it is used as a verb the present participle acts as a **relative clause** (che....).
In modern Italian this use is limited to bureaucratic language.

– I cittadini **residenti** in questo quartiere dovranno recarsi a votare al seggio 209.
– I cittadini **che risiedono** in questo quartiere dovranno recarsi a votare al seggio 209.
(Residents in this area must vote at polling station 209)

Past participle.
For the *forms* of the past participle see Unità 31.

Other uses of the **past participle:**

As an **adjective**

– Con il segnale luminoso **acceso** non si può utilizzare la macchina.
(The machine cannot be used when the light is on)

As a **noun**

– Gli **ammalati** gravi devono essere ricoverati in ospedale. *(Seriously ill people must be admitted to hospital)*

As a **verb**. For the use of the past participle in the *perfect tenses*, see the relevant units.

When it is used without an auxiliary, the past participle of transitive verbs has a *passive* meaning. It can replace a whole **relative** clause.

– La casa, **distrutta** dal terremoto, non fu ricostruita. = – La casa, **che era stata distrutta** dal terremoto non fu ricostruita.
(The house, destroyed by the earthquake, was not re-built)

1. Put the verbs in the present participle to form adjectives.

Infinito	*Participio presente*
ubbidire	*ubbidiente*....................
precedere	....
interessare	....
appartenere	....
affascinare	....
umiliare	....
permanere	....
impressionare	....

2. Put the verbs in the present participle to form nouns.

Infinito	*Participio presente*
commerciare	*commerciante*...............
aiutare	....
amare	....
presiedere	....
cantare	....
assistere	....
pagare	....
partorire	....

3. Rewrite the sentences using expressions with *che* or other words instead of the past participle.

1. Finito il film, uscirono dal cinema.
.....*Dopo che il film fu terminato, uscirono dal cinema*........................
2. Ritrovata la borsetta, la signora tirò un sospiro di sollievo.
....
3. Tornata a casa, la mamma si mise a cucinare.
....
4. Partiti i genitori, Paolo organizzò una grande festa.
....
5. Lette alcune pagine dell'ultimo libro di Umberto Eco, mi addormentai.
....
6. Interrogato dal Commissario Chiossi, il ladro sta dicendo chi sono i suoi complici.
....
7. Il quadro, acquistato a un'asta a Venezia, risultò essere un falso.
....
8. La pillola, presa a stomaco vuoto, può dare dolori di stomaco.
....
9. L'impiegato, assunto da pochi giorni, non conosce bene il lavoro.
....
10. La carta di credito, accettata in tutto il mondo, è uno dei mezzi di pagamento più comodi.
....

Coordinate conjunctions are used to join two main clauses in a single sentence.
The two sentences become two main *coordinate* clauses.

E *(and)*.

– La mia scuola è moderna **e** vi funzionano parecchi corsi. *(My school is modern and many course are run there)*

When it is followed by a word beginning in **e**, it normally becomes **ed**.

– La mia scuola è moderna **ed** efficiente. *(My school is modern and efficient)*

O *(or)*.

– In estate si può rimanere in città **o** si può evitare il caldo andando in montagna.
(In the summer you can stay in the town or you can get away from the heat by going to the mountains)

O introduces an alternative to what is said in the first clause.

Do you know any synonyms of **o**? See Unità 93.

Ma *(but)*.

– Quando andavo a scuola sapevo che la fisica era importante, **ma** non mi piaceva.
(When I went to school I knew physics was important, but I didn't like it)

Do you know any synonyms of **ma**? See Unità 93.

Anche *(also, too)*.

It is used in *affirmative* sentences. It can occupy different positions in the sentence.
It is usually placed before the word(s) it refers to.

– **Anche** in Italia c'è bisogno di operai specializzati come in Germania.
(In Italy, as in Germany, there is a demand for specialized workers)
– Mia sorella si diverte ad andare in bicicletta e **anche** a suo marito piace molto.
(My sister enjoys cycling and her husband really likes it too)

Neanche *(neither, not... either)*.

It is used in *negative* sentence. It can occupy different positions in the sentence.
It is usually placed before the word(s) it refers to.

– Non so più arrivare a casa di mia zia e non ricordo **neanche** il nome del paese dove vive.
(I don't know how to get to my aunt's home anymore and I don't remember the name of the village where she lives either)

Anche and **neanche** add something to what has already been said.
When **neanche** is placed before the verb the negation **non** is not used.

– **Neanche** quel passante **sa** come arrivare in centro.
(That passer-by doesn't know how to get to the centre either)

Dunque *(so)*.

It is used to introduce the consequence of what was previously said.

– Sono stanco, **dunque** mi prendo una settimana di ferie. *(I'm tired, so I'll have a week's holiday)*

(The consequence of my being tired is that I am taking a week's holiday).

Cioè *(that is)*.

It introduces the explanation of what was previously said.

– Non mi piace comprare molti vestiti, **cioè** mi compro solo i vestiti di cui ho realmente bisogno.
(I don't like buying a lot of clothes, that is/I mean I only buy the clothes I really need)

Sia...sia *(both... and)*.

They are used in *affirmative* sentences to join two parts of the sentence, more or less like **e**.
In modern Italian **sia...che** is often used.

– **Sia** Franco **sia** (**che**) Antonio giocano a calcio. *(Both Franco and Antonio play football)*

Né...né *(neither... nor)*.

They are used in *negative* sentences to join two parts of the sentence.

– Non ho visto **né** Paolo **né** sua moglie al cinema. *(I didn't see Paolo nor his wife at the cinema)*

They could be replaced by **e neanche**.

– Non ho visto Paolo **e neanche** sua moglie al cinema.

When **né...né** are placed before the verb the negation *non* is not used.

– **Né** Paolo **né** Luca parlano spagnolo. (*Neither Paolo nor Luca speaks Spanish)*

1. Complete the sentence using *e*, *o*, or *ma*, together with a sentence from the box below.

1. Ieri sera siamo andati al ristorante ...*e*...... *poi siamo andati al cinema*..........
2. Lo spettacolo teatrale è stato bello ....
3. La mia nuova macchina funziona bene ....
4. Di solito mi alzo alle 7 ....
5. Mia sorella ha un lavoro interessante ....
6. Stasera guarderemo un film ....
7. Vuoi una birra? ....
8. Ieri c'era lo sciopero dei treni ....

è costata una fortuna   vorrebbe avere più tempo per se stessa oggi ho dormito fino alle 9   ci metteremo a leggere   preferisci prima mangiare qualcosa poi siamo andati al cinema   non ho capito tutto   sull'autostrada ci sono stati molti incidenti

2. Complete the sentences using *anche* or *neanche*.

1. Lucy non sa lo spagnolo e *neanche*..... il portoghese.
2. Non mi piace il brandy e .... la tequila.
3. Mi piace vivere in paesi caldi e .... mia moglie lo preferisce.
4. Se tu sei contenta, lo sono ....io.
5. Non so suonare nessuno strumento e non so .... cantare.
6. Non vado spesso in palestra e .... correre non mi piace molto.

3. Complete the sentences using *dunque* or *cioè*.

1. Non c'è molto caldo in casa tua, ...*cioè*............... fa un freddo terribile.
2. L'aria delle città italiane è molto inquinata, ... si respirano sostanze velenose.
3. Fa molto caldo, ... gli anziani e i bambini dovrebbero rimanere in casa.
4. L'acqua del mare era fredda, ... non abbiamo fatto il bagno.
5. Anche se era già mezzanotte avevo molta fame, ... mi sono fatto un panino.
6. Il cartello dice: Vietato fumare, ... non si può fumare.

4. Complete the sentences using *sia...sia* or *né...né*.

1. ....*Sia*........ l'italiano ......*sia*......... il rumeno sono lingue neolatine.
2. Mi piacciono .... il blues .... il jazz.
3. .... l'Italia .... la Francia confinano con la Russia.
4. .... gli spaghetti, ... la pizza sono piatti tipici italiani.

5. Rewrite the sentences using *sia...sia* or *né...né*.

1. Tom non è australiano. Neanche Sarah.
   Né Tom né Sarah sono australiani..........
2. Sandro vuole andare a letto e anche Pietro.
   ....
3. Juan non voleva andare a ballare e neanche Sergio.
   ....
4. Ieri sera mia madre e mio fratello sono venuti a trovarci.
   ....

Oppure, altrimenti *(or otherwise)*.

They are used as synonyms of **o**.

- Regalale un libro **oppure** un cd.
  (Give her a book or a CD)

- Prestami qualcosa da leggere, **altrimenti** dammi un video.
  (Lend me something to read, or give me a video instead)

Però, tuttavia *(but, however)*.

They are used as synonyms of **ma**.

Tuttavia is more formal and is preferably used in written Italian.

- Credo che la capitale del Burundi sia Bujumbura, **però** non ne sono sicuro.
  (I think Bujumbura is the capital of Burundi, but I'm not sure)

- In Italia sono aumentate le esportazioni, **tuttavia** il mercato interno non si è ancora ripreso.
  (Italy has increased exports, however the home market still hasn't recovered)

Pure *(also, too)*.

It is used instead of **anche**, especially in the South of Italy.

- Recentemente sono stato a Sorrento e **pure** a Napoli.
  (I've been to Sorrento recently, and to Naples too)

Neppure, nemmeno *(neither)*.

They are synonyms of **neanche**.

- La strada statale per Cagliari è interrotta per il maltempo e **nemmeno** la provinciale è percorribile.
  (The main road to Cagliari is blocked due to the bad weather and the secondary road can't be used either)

Quando **neppure** e **nemmeno** sono prima del verbo non si mette la negazione **non**.

- Ho chiamato Sergio, ma non c'era e **neppure** sua sorella era in casa.
  (I called Sergio, but he wasn't in and neither was his sister)

Perciò, quindi *(therefore, so)*.

They are used as synonyms of **dunque**.

- Suo padre è inglese, **perciò** anche lei ha il passaporto di quel paese.
  (Her father is English, therefore she has a British passport)
- Occorre aumentare la produzione, **quindi** bisogna chiedere agli operai di lavorare al sabato.
  (Production needs to be increased, so we'll have to ask the workers to work on Saturdays too)

1. Join the sentences from the columns using *oppure/altrimenti* or *tuttavia/però.*

1. La ricetta che mi hai dato è complessa, tuttavia
2. Si può visitare il giardino botanico ....
3. Possiamo partire domani ....
4. La parte esterna della casa è rovinata ....
5. Ho bisogno di cambiare dei soldi ....
6. Silvano è stato ricoverato in ortopedia ....
7. Quel ristorante non ha una buona fama ....
8. Ho cantato una serenata alla mia amata ....

a l'interno è in ottimo stato.
b dovrò chiederti di prestarmene un po'.
c mi hanno detto che fra 10 giorni sarà guarito.
d se piove si può andare alla galleria d'arte moderna.
e vi si mangia benissimo e con pochi soldi.
f ho provato a farla.
g non si è nemmeno affacciata alla finestra. Cos'altro devo fare?
h possiamo aspettare fino a che il tempo migliori.

2. Correct the mistakes by putting *neppure/nemmeno, perciò/quindi, tuttavia/però, oppure/altrimenti* instead of the given conjunctions.

1. Mi piace molto il tuo cappotto *tuttavia* ho pensato di comprarmene uno uguale.
Mi piace molto il tuo cappotto perciò ho pensato di comprarmene uno uguale
2. Vieni da me *quindi* vengo io da te?
....
3. So guidare la macchina *nemmeno* non so andare in barca.
....
4. È importante mantenersi in forma, *però* bisogna fare un po' di ginnastica.
....
5. Vuoi leggere prima tu il giornale *nemmeno* te lo do quando l'ho finito?
....
6. Non ho ancora ascoltato l'ultimo cd di Zucchero e *altrimenti* quello di Pino Daniele.
....
7. Hai presentato la tua fidanzata ai tuoi genitori, *neppure* hai deciso di aspettare ancora?
....
8. Comunicare con Cuba è molto difficile, *quindi* si riesce a mandare e ricevere posta elettronica.
....

3. Make some sentences about yourself using the conjunctions in brackets.

1. (Anche) Conosco il francese e anche il tedesco
2. (Pure) ....
3. (Tuttavia) ....
4. (Altrimenti) ....
5. (Però) ....
6. (Oppure) ....
7. (Nemmeno) ....
8. (Quindi) ....

Subordinate conjunctions are used to join two main clauses in a single sentence.
The result is a main clause and a subordinate clause, which is introduced by the subordinate conjunction.
Some conjunctions are followed by the indicative form, others by the subjunctive, others by the infinitive.
For conjunctions followed by the subjunctive, see Unità 70.

Conjunctions of cause.
They introduce the *reason* behind what is stated in the main clause.
The verb is in the **indicative**.

Perché *(because).*

- Fabrizia è preoccupata **perché** non ha abbastanza tempo per finire la sua ricerca.
  (Fabrizia is worried because she hasn't got enough time to finish her reserarch)

Poiché *(as).*

- Non è possibile determinare con esattezza il numero degli stranieri in Italia, **poiché** molti sono immigrati illegalmente.
  (It's impossible to ascertain the exact number of foreigners in Italy as many of then are illegal immigrations)

Dato che/visto che/dal momento che *(since, as).*

- **Dato che/visto che/dal momento che** i membri dell'associazione sono tutti uomini, Lia non ha potuto aderirvi.
  (Since all the members of the association are men, Lia was not allowed to join)

Siccome *(since, as, because).*

- **Siccome** la vita in Italia è molto cara, molte famiglie devono fare attenzione a come spendono i soldi.
  (Because life in Italy is so expensive, many families must be careful how they spend their money)

Congiunzioni temporali.
The verb is in the **indicative**.

Quando *(when).*

- **Quando** si vive in un paese straniero bisogna cercare di capire le abitudini di vita degli abitanti.
  (When you live in a foreign country you must try and understand the inhabitants' way of life)

Mentre *(while).*

- **Mentre** mangio, mi piace ascoltare musica. *(I like listening to music while I eat)*

(Non) appena *(as soon as).*

- **Non appena** arriverò a casa mi farò una doccia. (*As soon as I get home I'll have a shower*)

The phrases *appena* and *non appena* are synonyms.

▶ **Non appena** does not have a negative meaning.

Da quando *(since).*

- **Da quando** vivo a Roma, esco tutte le sere. *(I have been out every evening since I came to lieve in Rome.)*

Da quando introduces an action which began in the past and continues in the present. Note: the verb is in the *present!*
Otherwise it can introduce an action which began in an earlier past and continued up to a more recent past.

- **Da quando** era cominciato a nevicare non si poteva uscire di casa.
  (We weren't able to get out of the house since the moment is started snowing)

Finché/fino a quando *(up to when).*

- **Finché** avrà soldi Juan girerà l'Europa. *(Juan will travel around Europe until his money runs out)*

Dopo che *(when, after).*

- **Dopo che** sarà passato il temporale, forse potremo andare in piscina.
  (When the thunderstorm is over, we might be able to go to the swimming pool)

Prima che *(before).*

▶ The verbs is in the *subjunctive.*
See Unità 70 and Unità 89.

With many subordinate conjunctions the sentence can begin either with the main clause or the subordinate clause.

- **Non appena** arriverò a casa mi farò una doccia. Oppure: – Mi farò una doccia **non appena** arriverò a casa.

1. Join the sentences using conjunctions of time or cause.

1. Alle tre sono arrivato alla stazione. Alle tre meno cinque il treno è partito.
   ......*Quando arrivai alla stazione il treno era già partito*......
2. Suonò il telefono e mi svegliai.
   ....
3. Mi ruppi una gamba perciò mi portarono all'ospedale.
   ....
4. Avevo bisogno di una traduzione dall'arabo all'italiano; mi rivolsi a un'agenzia.
   ....
5. Ugo compie gli anni, gli regalerò una scatola di cioccolatini.
   ....
6. Ricevetti il telegramma di mia madre e corsi a telefonarle.
   ....
7. Gli italiani quest'anno sono tutti un po' più poveri. C'è stata una forte svalutazione della lira.
   ....
8. La missione dell'O.N.U. è iniziata. La pace sembra poter affermarsi.
   ....
9. Mia madre è cubana e mio padre italiano. Io parlo sia l'italiano che lo spagnolo.
   ....
10. Tu mi restituisci il mio libro e io ti ridò le chiavi della tua bicicletta.
   ....

2. Complete the sentences.

1. Dato che ...*stasera sono molto stanco*...., ho deciso di restare a casa.
2. Poiché ...., mi porterò un suo libro in vacanza.
3. Perché ...., se non ha fatto niente.
4. Non appena ...., ti telefonerò.
5. Quando ...., andavo spesso al mare.
6. Dopo che ...., scoprì il furto.
7. Da quando ...., non l'ho più vista.
8. Finché ...., correrò dieci chilometri al giorno.
9. Prima che ...., devi scrivere una lettera ai tuoi.
10. Siccome ...., questa è l'ultima frase dell'esercizio.

Conjunctions of purpose.
They introduce the clause that expresses the *purpose*, the *aim* of the action in the main clause.

Affinché *(so that).*

- **Affinché** voi possiate superare l'esame, vi indico alcuni testi fondamentali.
  (I'll suggest some basic texts so that you can pass the exam.)

It is followed by the **subjunctive**. See Unità 70.

Conjunctions of result.
They introduce the *result* of what is stated in the main clause.

Così...che/cosicché *(so that).*

- Ieri sera ho lavorato fino a tardi **cosicché** oggi possiamo andare al mare.
  (I worked until late yesterday evening so that we could go to the seaside today)
- Ho preparato un risotto **così** salato **che** nessuno è riuscito a mangiarlo.
  (The risotto I prepared was so salty that nobody could eat it)

They are normally used with the **indicative**.

Conjunctions of concession/contrast.
Anche se, benché, malgrado, nonostante, sebbene *(even though, although).*

Anche se.

It is the only conjunction of connession followed by the **indicative**. All the others are followed by the **subjunctive**.
- Anche se la casa nuova era pronta, la famiglia Pacini preferì rimanere ancora nel vecchio appartamento.
  (Even though the new house was ready, the Pacini family preferred staying in the old flat)

Benché, malgrado, nonostante, sebbene are synonyms and are all used in the same way; they are followed by the **subjunctive**. See Unità 70.
- **Malgrado** faccia brutto, ho voglia di uscire in bicicletta.
  (Although the weather is bad, I feel like going for a bike ride)

Congiunzioni condizionall.
The introduce the *condition* for what is stated in the main clause.

Se *(if).* See Unità 74: the hypothetical clause.

- **Se** tu non sei d'accordo non ci possiamo sposare. *(If you don't agree we can't get married)*

Purché, a patto che, a condizione che (as long as, provided) are synonyms and are all used in the same way; the are followed by the **subjunctive**. See Unità 70.

- **A condizione che** tu me li restituisca presto, ti presterò i soldi che ti occorrono.
  (As long as you give it back to me soon, I'll lend you the money you need)

Conjunctions of similarity/comparison.
The express the way the action in the main clause takes place.

Come se *(as if).*

It is followed by the **subjunctive**.
- Mi parlò di sé **come se** fossimo amici da molti anni.
  (He told me all about himself as if we had been friends for ages)

Conjunctions of exception and exclusion.
The limit or exclude what is stated in the main clause.

Salvo che/tranne che *(except).*

They are followed by the **infinitive**.
- In casa Piero fa ogni cosa **tranne che** stirare. *(Piero does everything in the house except the ironing)*

A meno che non, senza che *(unless, without).*

They are followed by the **subjunctive**. See Unità 70.
- **A meno che non** si torni molto presto, non potrò venire a teatro con voi.
  (Unless we come back home very early, I won't be able to go to the theatre with you)

1. Complete the sentences with conjunctions.

1. *Nonostante*... sia piovuto molto, la terra è ancora molto secca.
2. Riuscirai a dimagrire, ... tu smetta di mangiare tanti dolci.
3. Adoro l'arte, ... non so tenere in mano un pennello.
4. Vediamoci stasera, ... ci facciate vedere le foto del vostro safari!
5. Mi è piaciuta la poesia che mi hai fotocopiato, ... non abbia capito molto.
6. Accetto il tuo invito al bar, ... tu non mi offra della coca cola.
7. .... non ricordo male, Anna compie gli anni il 17 di gennaio.
8. Mi guardò .... mi volesse mangiare con gli occhi.

2. Match the sentences from the columns using *affinché, cosicché, senza che, anche se, purché, a meno che non.*

1. ....*Affinché*....... l'inflazione possa abbassarsi,
2. .... tu non mi conosci,
3. .... non mi venga l'influenza,
4. .... tu non lo dica a Roberta,
5. Ho studiato tutto il giorno,............................
6. .... mia moglie lo sapesse,
7. .... i salari sono stabili,
8. Il governo taglierà le spese sociali ....,

a verrò al tuo matrimonio.
b andrò a sciare domattina.
c non sono potuto venire alla tua festa.
d ho portato a casa un gattino.
e l'inflazione aumenta sempre più.
f io so tutto di te.
g il debito pubblico possa ridursi.
h gli industriali hanno deciso di non aumentare i prezzi.

3. Finish the sentences.

1. Ho comprato un vecchio Pc, affinché ......*anche mio figlio impari a usarlo*......
2. Non ho tempo da dedicare alla lettura cosicché ....
3. Non andrò alla sua festa, anche se ....
4. I bambini non vogliono andare a letto, nonostante ....
5. Lo spettatore seduto davanti a me era così alto che ....
6. Le strinse forte il collo affinché ....
7. Mi regalerei un viaggio attorno al mondo se ....
8. Mi salutò come se ....
9. Finirò il corso d'italiano a meno che ....
10. Farò domanda per quel posto che mi hai indicato, purché ....

Study the pictures.

The suffix - **ino/a** modifies the meaning of the noun.
These nouns are called **diminutivi**.

Un gattino	=	un gatto piccolo	*(a little cat).*
Una casina	=	una casa piccola	*(a little house).*

The suffix - **one/a** modifies the meaning of the noun.
These nouns are called **accrescitivi**.

Un gattone	=	un gatto grande	*(a big cat).*
Una casona	=	una casa grande	*(a big house).*

The suffix - **accio/a** modifies the meaning of the noun.
These nouns are called **peggiorativi.**

Un gattaccio	=	un gatto brutto e cattivo *(a horrible nasty cat).*
Un ragazzaggio	=	un ragazzo cattivo *(a bad boy).*
Una serataccia	=	una brutta serata *(a bad evening).*

Study the examples.

Un bambino bellino	=	un bambino piuttosto bello	*(a pretty child).*
Ho dormito benino	=	ho dormito piuttosto bene	*(I slept quite well).*

Nouns, as well as adjectives and adverbs, can be modified in many other ways, by using different suffixes. Sometimes it is not easy to understand whether it is a "diminutivo" or an ordinary noun.

Some other examples.

Un quadr**etto**	=	un quadro piccolo	*(a small picture).*
Una finestr**ella**	=	una finestra piccola	*(a small window).*
Un ors**acchiotto**	=	un piccolo orso	*(a little bear).*
Un passer**otto**	=	un passero piccolo	*(a little sparrow).*

All these suffixes may have an endearing nuance, i.e. express fondness, affection.

Other diminutivi have a pejorative or derogatory nuance instead, i.e. they express something negative.

Un mostr**iciattolo** *(a little monster)*
Un vestit**uccio** *(a flimsy dress)*

In the following example, howerer, the suffix **-uccio** has an endearing meaning, not derogatory.
È una **casuccia** molto accogliente. *(It's a very cosy little house).*

Some nouns look like diminutivi, accrescitivi, etc., but they are not.

Il postino	il lavandino	il maglione
(the postman	*the sink*	*the pullover)*

Verbs can have modified forms too: *ridacchiare, giocherellare, saltellare, (giggle, play about, skip) etc.*

1. Write the adjective with the correct form of the suffix.

1. Una casa piccola e carina è una .... casetta ....
2. Un coniglio piccolo e carino è un ....
3. Un libro grande e complesso è un ....
4. Un ragazzo un po' monello è un ....
5. Un modello giocattolo di macchina è una ....
6. Un albergo brutto e sporco è un ....
7. Un posto brutto e malfamato è un ....
8. Un bambino alto e piuttosto grasso è un ....

2. Choose the correct suffix of the adjectives, adverbs and nouns.

1. Vedi una ragazza piuttosto carina, cosa dici al tuo amico?
Guarda come è *bellina/bellona/bellaccia* quella ragazza!

2. Vivi in un quartiere molto pericoloso e malfamato. Come lo descrivi?
È un *quartierino/quartieretto/quartieraccio*.

3. Stai passando un brutto momento, sei pieno di problemi. Cosa dici?
Sto passando un *momentino/momentone/momentaccio*.

4. Sei andato al mercato e hai trovato qualcosa che ti piace a un prezzo bassissimo. Cosa pensi?
Ho fatto un *affarino/affarone/affaraccio*.

5. Hai una stanza tutta per te che ti piace molto, ma è un po' piccola. Come la descrivi?
Ho una *stanzetta/stanzona/stanzaccia* tutta per me.

6. Devi fare un esame molto impegnativo e difficile. Cosa dici alla tua ragazza?
Questa settimana non ci vedremo molto perché devo preparare un *esamino/esamone/esamuccio*.

7. Hai comprato un regalo alla tua ragazza, ma non avevi molti soldi. Cosa le dici?
Ti ho comprato un *regalino/regalaccio/regalone*.

8. Ti senti in forma, ma c'è qualcosa che non va. Cosa rispondi a chi ti chiede come stai?
Sto *bene/benino/benone*.

Italian phonetic symbols

Vowels

/a/	/'mano/	**mano**
/e/	/'rete/	**rete**
/ɛ/	/'bɛllo/ /'bɛne/	**bello bene**
/i/	/i'dɛa/	**idea**
/o/	/'kome/	**come**
/ɔ/	/'ɔka/	**oca**
/u/	/'uno/	**uno**
/j/	/'pjatto/ /'pjeno/	**piatto pieno**
/w/	/'kwadro/	**quadro**

Consonants

/p/	/'krɛpa/	**crepa**
/b/	/'banka/	**banca**
/t/	/'trɛno/	**treno**
/d/	/ka'dere/	**cadere**
/k/	/'parko/	**parco**
/g/	/'gatto/	**gatto**
/tʃ/	/'mantʃa/	**mancia**
/dʒ/	/'adʒitare/	**agitare**
/f/	/'fresko/	**fresco**
/v/	/'vino/	**vino**
/s/	/'sempre/	**sempre**
/z/	/fanta'zja/	**fantasia**
/ʃ/	/'ʃarpa/	**sciarpa**
/ts/	/por'tsjone/	**porzione**
/dz/	/dzaba'jone/	**zabaione**
/l/	/'fatʃile/	**facile**
/ʎ/	/'darʎi/	**dargli**
/r/	/'radjo/	**radio**
/m/	/'mjo/	**mio**
/n/	/'sano/	**sano**
/ɲ/	/'ɲɔkko/	**gnocco**

The brackets contain the letter or word written in phonetic transcript.
The apostrophe is placed before the main stressed syllabe of the word, i.e. the stress is on the syllabe after the apostrophe.

Italian vowels and consonants

Italian vowels

			/i/
		/e/	
	/ɛ/		
/a/			
	/ɔ/		
		/o/	
			/u/

There are seven vowel sounds in Italian. Many words contain diphthongs (two vowels together: quadro */'kwadro/*, viene */'vjɛne/)* and there are also some with triphthongs (three vowels together: miei */'miɛi/).*

▶ In Italian the accent is not placed on the stressed syllable, except for when the stress is on the last vowel (e.g. virtù, realtà, più, già) and when it is necessary to distinguish between a few one syllable homonyms, for example:

da (preposition)	dà (verb dare)
li (pronoun)	lì (place adverb = là)
e (conjunction)	è (verb essere)

This feature of the Italian language can at times not only give rise to wrong pronunciation but can also cause misunderstanding, as some words have the same spelling but are pronounced differently in order to change meaning, for example:

principi [*'printʃipi*] (plural of principe/*princes*) principi [*prin'tʃipi*] (plural of principio/*principles*)

Italian consonants

Double consonants

In Italian a word can have a double consonant.
The double consonants can be placed

between two vowels	fatto	*/'fatto/*		
between a vowel and an **r** an **l**	attraente	*/attra'ɛnte/*	acclamare	*/akkla'mare/*

Here is a list of some words with double consonants.

p	cappello	/kap'pɛllo/
b	abbattere	/ab'battere/
t	gatto	/'gatto/
d	caddi	/'kaddi/
k	tacco	/'takko/
g	leggo	/'lɛggo/
tʃ	accendere	/at'tʃɛndere/
dʒ	legge	/'leddʒe/
f	affitto	/af'fitto/
v	avventura	/avven'tura/
s	assieme	/as'sjɛme/
ts	razza	/'rattsa/
dz	razzo	/'raddzo/
m	mamma	/'mamma/
n	canna	/'kanna/
l	bello	/'bɛllo/
r	carro	/'karro/

The sound */z/* cannot be doubled.

The following letters are always pronounced as if double consonants when placed between two vowels:

ɲ	ragno	/'raɲɲo/
ʎ	figlio	/'fiʎʎo/
ʃ	fascia	/'faʃʃa/

- In the North of Italy there is a tendency to give less emphasis to the double consonants when speaking, whereas in Southern Italy single consonants tend to be doubled when positioned between two vowels.

- Students need to pay special attention to the pronunciation of double consonants. Sometimes if the double consonant is not pronounced, then the word can take on a different meaning.

penna	/'penna/	pena	/'pena/
sette	/'sɛtte/	sete	/'sete/
rette	/'rɛtte/	rete	/'rete/
fatto	/'fatto/	fato	/'fato/
sanno	/'sanno/	sano	/'sano/

Rules for written Italian

In Italian some sounds are written in such a way that they can cause problems to the student as they do not correspond to the way the sounds are written in other languages.

/ka/	**ca**sa	/'kasa/	/ga/	**ga**tto	/'gatto/
/ko/	**co**ppa	/'koppa/	/go/	**go**la	/'gola/
/ku/	**cu**cina	/ku'tʃina/	/gu/	an**gu**stia	/an'gustia/
/ki/	**chi**amare	/kja'mare/	/gi/	a**ghi**	/'agi/
/ke/	ban**che**	/'banke/	/ge/	pa**ghe**	/'page/
/tʃa/	man**cia**	/'mantʃa/	/dʒa/	fa**gia**no	/fa'dʒano/
/tʃo/	mi**cio**	/'mitʃo/	/dʒo/	**gio**co	/'dʒɔko/
/tʃu/	**ciu**rma	/'tʃurma/	/dʒu/	**giu**sto	/'dʒusto/
/tʃe/	a**ce**to	/a'tʃeto/	/dʒe/	**ge**nte	/'dʒente/
/tʃi/	cu**ci**re	/ku'tʃire/	/dʒi/	**gi**glio	/'dʒiʎʎo/
/ʃ/	**sci**mmia	/'ʃimmja/			
	a**sci**ugare	/aʃʃu'gare/			
/sk/	**sche**rzo	/'skertso/			
	scala	/'skala/			
/kw/	ac**qua**	/'akkwa/	/gw/	**gue**rra	/'gwɛrra/
/ɲ/	i**gn**orante	/'iɲɲorante/			
/ʎ/	fi**gli**a	/'fiʎʎa/			
/ts/	**z**io	/'tsio/			
/dz/	**z**abaione	/dzaba'jone/			

Glossary

abbreviation = it is usually a word which has been shortened, abbreviated, often for a particular use.

abstract nouns = they are nouns indicating qualities which cannot be not perceived by the senses. E.g.: amicizia *(friendship)*, libertà *(freedom)*, etc.

accrescitivi = they are modified nouns or adjectives *(cf. alteration)* which express the idea of something bigger, e.g.: una casona (a big house).

action = it is expressed by a verb.

active = it is a form of the verb. The subject performs the action, e.g.: il cane ha morso il bimbo *(the dog bit the little boy)*. In the passive form instead the subject undergoes the action, e.g.: il bimbo è stato morso dal cane *(The little boy was bitten by the dog.)*.

adjective = bello, alto, mio, etc. They are words which are added to the noun *(cf.)* to describe it.

adjective adj. un poco un po' (a little, a bit).

adverbs = they are *invariable* words (cf.) which are used to modify and specify the meaning of a verb or an adjective. Example: parlare *lentamente (speak slowly)*. Un libro *molto* bello *(a very good book)*.

adverbs of frequency = sempre, spesso, a volte, mai, etc. (*always, often, sometimes, never,* etc.)

affirmation = opposite of negation. *Cf. affirmative form.*

affirmative = positive. Affirmative form *(cf.)*: for example in answers the affirmative form corresponds to "yes". It is the opposite of negative form *(cf.)*.

affirmative form = a sentence in the affirmative form expresses a statement (*yes*), it is the opposite of the negative form and it is different from the interrogative and interrogative-negative form.

affirmative sentence = cf. *affirmative form*.

agent = it is the phrase which indicates who/what performs the action in the passive. E.g.: la gazzella è stata uccisa *dal leone (The gazelle was killed by the lion.; The lion in the agent.)*

agreement = it is the sequence of the different parts of speech. For example article + noun *(cf.)* + adjective *(cf.)* are all in sequence according to the gender *(cf.)* and number *(cf.)*: le belle ragazze *(the pretty girls)*.

alteration = alteration of the noun *(cf.)* or adjective *(cf.)*: it is a change in the form of the adjective or noun to express a different idea from the original one. For example: un ragazzo piccolo = un ragazzino *(a young boy)*.

answer = what is said, done or written following a question.

auxiliary = auxiliary verbs are used to form compound tenses and the passive *(cf.)*.

auxiliary verb = *avere (to have)* and *essere (to be)*, in compound tenses. *Venire* and *andare* in the passive *(cf.)*.

cardinal numbers = one, two, three, etc.

clause = a basic unit which expresses a thought. Two or more clauses joined together form a sentence.

combined form of the preposition with the article = di, a, da, in, con, su, per, tra, fra plus the definite article; e.g.: del, al, dal, etc. *(of the, to the, from the,* etc.)

combined personal pronoun = double personal pronouns: glielo, te le, etc. *(it to him, them to you,* etc.)

comparatives = adjectives or adverbs which express a comparison *(cf.)* between two or more elements.

comparativo di maggioranza = it is expressed by *più* followed by an adjective or an adverb. Example: Flavio è *più vecchio* di me *(Fabio is older than me.)*. The comparison is in favour of the first element.

comparativo di minoranza = it is expressed by *meno* followed by an adjective or an adverb. Example: Flavio balla *meno elegantemente* di sua moglie *(Fabio doesn't dance as elegantly as his wife)*. The comparison is in favour of the second element.

comparativo di uguaglianza = it is expressed by *tanto/quanto* or *così/come* with an adjective or an adverb. Example: Flavio è *(tanto) simpatico quanto* te *(Flavio is as nice as you.)*. The comparison is in favour of neither of the two elements.

comparison = it can be between adjectives or adverbs, but also between nouns, pronouns and verbs.

comparison of adverbs = adverbs can have comparative forms too, example: Sara ora si comporta più intelligentemente di prima *(Sara behaves more intelligently now than she used to.)*.

compound tenses = tenses formed by an auxiliary *(cf.)* and a main verb; e.g.: passato prossimo.

concrete nouns = they are nouns which indicate tangible things. E.g.: cane *(dog)*, libro *(book)*, uomo *(man)*, etc.

conditional = finite form *(cf.)* of the verb.

conditional = io avrei *(I would have)*.

conjunction of cause = it introduces the *cause*. Poiché, dato che, etc. *(because, as)*

conjunction of concession = it introduces a clause of concession. It indicates a circumstance which takes place but does not modify what is stated in the main clause *(cf.)*. E.g.: *nonostante* faccia freddo, oggi pomeriggio esco in bicicletta *(I'm going to ride my bike this afternoon even though it's cold.)*.

conjunction of condition = it introduces the *condition* which is required by what is stated in the main clause. E.g.: *se* domani farà bello, andrò al mare *(If the weather is nice tomorrow, I'll go to the seaside)*.

conjunction of purpose = it introduces the clause which expresses the *purpose* of the action in the main clause. E.g.: Ti do £ 20000 *affinché* tu vada al cinema *(I'm giving you £ 20,000 so you can go to the cinema)*.

conjunction of result = it introduces the *consequence* of what is stated in the main clause. E.g.: ieri faceva brutto *cosicché* non sono andato al mare *(The weather wasn't good yesterday so I didn't go to the seaside).*

conjunction of time = it joins two clauses by taking time into consideration. E.g.: *quando, dopo che, mentre, etc. (when, after, while, etc.).* Es.: *quando* dormo non desidero essere disturbato *(I don't like being disturbed when I'm sleeping).*

consonant = in general, all the letters of the alphabet, except a, e, i, o, u.

coordinate conjunctions = they are used to join two main clauses. E.g.: *e, o, anche*, etc. *(and, or, also,* etc.) E.g.: c'è il sole *e* fa caldo *(The sun is shining and it's hot).*

definite article = il, lo, l', la, i, gli, le *(the).* Example: *il* cane *(the dog).*

demonstrative adjectives and pronouns = questo, quello, etc. *(this, that, etc.)*

demonstratives = demonstrative adjectives and pronouns; questo, quello, etc. They are used to indicate position in space and time.

diminutivi = they are modified adjectives or nouns (*cf. alteration)* which contain the idea of smallness and often express affection. E.g.: una ragazzina *(a young girl);* un giochino *(a little toy).*

diphthong = cf. *syllable*.

direct object = it answers the question : chi, che cosa? *(who, what?)* It undergoes the action of the subject. It has no preposition. E.g.: ho visto *Luca (I saw Luca).*

direct speech = when the exact words of a person are repeated without changing anything. It is introduced by " ".

E.g.: *Spero* che tu *stia* bene *(I hope you are well)*, but *speravo* che tu *stessi* bene *(I hoped you were well).*

ending = it is the variable part at the end of a noun, an adjective, a pronoun or a verb.

exception = something which does not follow the rule.

exclamations = words which are used to say something because of joy, admiration, etc. E.g.: *Che* bello! *(How nice!)*

expressions of place = words which define the place; they answer the question: dove? Da dove? etc. *(where, where from?,* etc.) There are different expressions of place: direction (it indicates movement), state (it does not indicate movement), origin, etc. E.g.: vivo *a Perugia*, ma vado spesso *a Roma* per lavoro. *(I live in Perugia, but I often go to Rome for work.)*

expressions of time = words which define the time; they answer the question: quando? Per quanto tempo? Da quanto tempo? *(When? For how long? How long?)* They express the time, duration, etc. E.g.: *Lunedì* sono stato a teatro *per cinque ore (I spent five hours in the theatre on Monday.)*

feminine = grammatical gender, opposite to masculine. There are only two grammatical genders in Italian: feminine and masculine.

finite forms = forms of the verb which express the person. Indicative, conditional, subjunctive, imperative. E.g.: io vado *(I'm going).*

first person = singular: io *(I)*, plural: noi *(we).*

formal = cf. *formal register*.

formal register = it refers to a way of using the language based on social context which usually expresses respect, it is typical of relationships between people who are neither friends nor relatives. In the formal register the structure with Lei is used. It is the opposite of informal.

frequency = this indicates how many times a certain word or something else is used.

function = some functions: introducing oneself, greeting, etc.

future = io avrò *(I'll have).*

future in the past = it indicates an action which happens in a future time in relation to the past, however still past in relation to the present. E.g.: mi disse che sarebbe tornato presto *(He told me he would come back soon).*

future indicative = avrò *(I will have).*

future perfect = io avrò avuto *(I will have had).*

future perfect indicative = avrò avuto *(I will have had).*

future time = future/tomorrow, present/today, past/ yesterday.

gender = it is the grammatical differentiation based on sex: feminine or masculine. It is important for the endings *(cf.)* of adjectives and nouns.

gerund = avendo *(having).*

gerund = indefinite form *(cf.)* of the verb.

hypothetical sentence = two or more clauses in which the subordinate *(cf.)* is introduced by *se (if).*

imperative = finite form *(cf.)* of the verb.

imperative with pronouns = compound form of the imperative with pronouns. E.g.: dagli *(give him)*, parlategliene *(speak to him about it).*

imperfect = io avevo *(I had, I used to have).*

imperfect indicative = avevo *(I had, I used to have).*

imperfect subjunctive = che io avessi.

impersonal form = when the subject is not defined. Impersonal subjects are: *si* and, in some cases, *tu*, *loro*, etc.

impersonal verb = a verb without a definite subject.

indefinite article = un, uno, una, un' *(a/an).* Example: *un* cane *(a dog).*

indefinite forms = forms of the verb which do not express the person. Gerund, infinitive, participle. E.g.: andando *(going).*

indefinite pronouns or adjectives = pronouns or adjectives which give indefinite information. E.g.: qualche *(some, any)*, qualcosa *(something, anything)*, etc.

indirect object = in general, any phrase containing a preposition.

infinitive = indefinite form *(cf.)* of the verb.

informal = cf. *informal register*.

informal register = it refers to a way of using the language based on social context which usually expresses friendship and friendliness, it is typical of relationships between people who are either friends or relatives. In the informal register the structure with tu is used. It is the opposite of formal.

interrogative form = a sentence in the interrogative form expresses a question, it is different from the negative and affirmative forms.

interrogative-negative form = a sentence in the interrogative-negative form expresses a negative question, it is different from the negative and affirmative forms.

intonation = they way the voice rises or falls when pronouncing a word or sentence.

intransitive verb = a verb which is not followed by the direct object *(cf.)*. It does not answer the question: chi/che cosa? *(Who/what?)* E.g.: io parlo con mia madre *(I'm speaking to my mother)*.

invariable = it does not change.

irregular forms = when they do not follow the rule.

letter = any element of the alphabet: a, b, c, etc.

main clause = clause which governs other clauses.

masculine = grammatical gender, different from the feminine. There are two grammatical genders in Italian: feminine and masculine.

modified forms = the modified forms of nouns, adjectives or adverbs are diminutivi, accrescitivi, etc. *(cf.)*.

monosyllables = words containing only one syllable *(cf.)*.

negative form = a sentence in the negative form expresses a negation *(no)*, it is the opposite of the affirmative form and different from the interrogative and interrogative-negative forms.

negative sentence = cf. *negative form*.

non = word used to deny, say no.

noun = words which indicate animals, people, things, etc.

number = it is the grammatical differentiation between singular and plural *(cf.)*. It is important for the endings *(cf.)* of verbs, adjectives and nouns.

object = *(cf.)* direct object; indirect object.

object personal pronoun = personal pronouns which act as object: mi, ti, ci, me, te, etc. *(me, you, us,* etc.)

opposite = antonym.

order = command.

ordinal numbers = first, second, third, etc.

participle = indefinite form *(cf.)* of the verb.

partitive = it expresses a part of a whole. *Partitive ne*, e.g.: "Quanto zucchero vuoi?" "*Ne* prendo due cucchiaini." *(How much sugar do you take? I'll have two teaspoonfuls.)*

passato prossimo = tense of the indicative. Io ho avuto *(I had, I have had)*.

passato remoto = tense of the indicative. Io ebbi *(I had)*.

passive = it is a form of the verb. The subject undergoes the action; e.g.: il bimbo è stato morso dal cane *(The little boy was bitten by the dog.)*. In the active form instead the subject performs the action; e.g.: il cane ha morso il bimbo *(The dog bit the little boy)*.

past and past perfect subjunctive = che io abbia avuto, che io avessi avuto.

past gerund = avendo avuto *(having had)*.

past participle = avuto.

past perfect = avevo avuto *(I had had)*.

past perfect indicative = avevo avuto *(I had had)*.

past time = past/yesterday, future/tomorrow, present/today.

peggiorativi = they are modified adjectives or nouns *(cf. alteration)* which contain a negative idea and express a negative opinion. E.g.: ragazzaccio *(a bad boy)*.

perfect conditional = io avrei avuto *(I would have had)*.

perfect infinitive = avere avuto *(to have had)*.

person = io, tu, lui/lei, noi, voi, loro *(I, you, he/she/it, we, you, they)*.

personal pronoun = pronoun which indicates the person or thing.

phonetic symbol = a special way of writing words which reproduces the way they are pronounced: cane = */'kane/*.

phrases = expressions or sentences; groups of two or more words which form a unit; e.g.: di solito, a proposito, andare giù *(usually, by the way, go down)*.

plural = it indicates a number of people or things above one.

polite form = when you address someone in a formal way, using the structure with Lei.

possessive adjectives and pronouns = mio, tuo, suo, etc.

prefix = particle added to the beginning of a word.

preposition = di, a, da, in, con, su, per, tra, fra *(of, to, from, in, with, on, for, between/among)*.

present indicative = io ho *(I have)*.

present infinitive = avere *(to have)*.

present participle = avente.

present subjunctive = che io abbia.

present time = present/today, past/yesterday, future/tomorrow.

pronoun = word which replaces the noun.

reflexive verbs = verbs in which the action falls back onto the subject; e.g.: io mi lavo *(I'm getting washed)*.

regular forms = when they follow the rule.

relative pronoun = it refers back to a previous noun or sentence. Che, cui, il quale, etc. *(who, which, that,* etc.)

reported speech = when what was said by someone is reported changing some elements. It is often introduced by the verb *dire (say, tell)* and *che (that)*. E.g.: Giovanni mi *ha detto che* domani...... *(Giovanni told me that tomorrow ...)*

rule = the dominant norm in a language.

second person = singular: tu *(you)*, plural: voi *(you)*.

sentence = two or more clauses joined together forming a meaningful unit.

sequence of tenses = it is the agreement of the tenses, for example between main clause and subordinate clause *(cf.)*.

singular = it indicates a number of people or things equivalent to one.

spregiativi = they are modified adjectives or nouns (*cf. alteration)* which contain a negative idea and express scorn. E.g.: ragazzaccio *(a very bad boy)*.

stem = part of the word which is left after the ending *(cf.)* has been taken away.

stress = it is a symbol (accent) or usually a certain intonation *(cf.)* of the voice which indicates the stressed vowel *(cf.)*.

stressed forms of the personal pronouns = e.g.: *a me, a te, a noi,* etc. They are stressed because they are strong, they emphasise the pronoun.

stressed pronouns = the stressed forms of personal pronouns *(cf.)* are for example: *a me, a te, a noi,* etc.

stressed vowel = vowel where the stress falls.

structure = the way the elements of a language are organized; or, sometimes: grammatical or syntactical rule.

subject = the person, thing, etc. which performs the action.

subject personal pronoun = io, tu, lui/lei, noi, voi, loro. They act as subject *(cf.)*.

subordinate clause = clause which depends on the main clause.

subordinate conjunction = it is used to join two clauses in a single sentence, one clause is the main clause, the other is the subordinate.

suffix = particle added at the end of a word.

superlatives = adjectives or adverbs which express a certain quality at its maximum.

superlativo assoluto = there is no comparison with other elements; it ends in -issimo. E.g.: un gatto bellissimo *(a very pretty cat)*.

superlativo relativo = there is a comparison with other elements. E.g.: il più bel film di Fellini *(Fellini's best film)*.

syllable = basic unit in a language, formed by a vowel or by a vowel preceded and followed by one or more consonants. Sometimes there are two or more vowels together (diphthong, triphthong).

synonym = a word which means the same thing as another.

term = word.

third person = singular: lui/lei *(he/she)*, plural: loro *(they)*.

transitive verb = verb followed by an object *(cf.)*. It answers the question chi/che cosa? *(who/what?)* E.g.: mangio una mela *(I'm eating an apple)*.

trapassato remoto = ebbi avuto *(I had had)*.

trapassato remoto indicative = ebbi avuto *(I had had)*.

unstressed forms of the personal pronouns = e.g.: *mi, ti, ci,* etc. They are unstressed because they are weak, they are supported by the verb.

unstressed pronouns = the unstressed forms of personal pronouns *(cf.)* are for example: *mi, ti, ci,* etc.

variable = something which changes. E.g.: masculine/feminine, singular/plural, etc.

verb = word which indicates an action or a way of being.

vezzeggiativi = they are modified adjectives and nouns (*cf. alteration)* which express affection. E.g.: la mia casetta *(my little house)*.

virtù *[vir'tu]* capitano *[kapi'tano]*.

vowel = the letters: a, e, i, o, u.

word stress = it is the intonation of the voice which stresses a particular syllable *(cf.) in*

▶ *The numbers refer to the units, not the pages.*

notes

notes

notes

Finito di stampare nel mese di Ottobre 2014
da Legatoria Umbra s.a.s. Bastia Umbra - Perugia
per conto di Guerra Edizioni Edel srl - Perugia